THEM AND US

BRITAIN, IRELAND
AND THE NORTHERN QUESTION
1969—82

Here is a perceptive study of the Northern Ireland problem in the period 1969-82. James Downey, deputy editor and a former London editor of *The Irish Times*, offers a new assessment of the turbulent events of the past decade. He traces the historical roots of the present troubles and analyses the far-reaching consequences of the policies of successive British and Irish governments regarding Northern Ireland. The book describes the real background to the most dramatic episodes of the Seventies, from the civil rights marches to the Provo campaign of violence, from the Sunningdale agreement to the Thatcher-Haughey liaison. There are illuminating insights into the operations of various factions and fascinating profiles of key political figures. In a thought-provoking final chapter, the author outlines the conditions on which a resolution of the conflict must be built.

Author photograph courtesy The Irish Times

James Downey

THEM & US

DUBLIN

WARD RIVER PRESS

First published 1983 by
Ward River Press Ltd.,
Knocksedan House,
Swords, Co. Dublin, Ireland.

© James Downey 1983

ISBN 0 907085 57 1

Cover design by Steven Hope
Typeset by Inset Ltd.,
171 Drimnagh Road, Dublin 12.
Printed by Cahill Printers Limited,
East Wall Road, Dublin 3.

CONTENTS

AUTHOR'S NOTE

In this book I have attempted to give as truthful and objective an account as possible of Anglo-Irish relations and the Northern crisis since the beginning of the present "troubles" in Northern Ireland. I have also set out purposely to dispel certain myths which surround the subject, including some which have become part of the "received wisdom".

Of course I claim no monopoly of truth or objectivity; and I make no attempt to conceal my own views of Irish history, and of how our problems might be brought to a resolution. Not everybody will agree with my interpretation of history, but as to the contemporaneous events and characters of the major part of the book, I can claim to have personally witnessed many of the first, and known most of the second, often intimately. Whatever the defects of the work, it is, in this regard, unique.

I apologise to readers for any inconsistencies of style, especially in the matter of that minefield, nomenclature. Here and there I have been driven to use the convenient term "Loyalist" both for extreme, though constitutional, Unionist parties and for violent Protestant organisations; but I have taken pains not to attach the term "Republican" to the Provisional IRA and Sinn Féin, for I believe that Irish republicanism is nothing unless non-sectarian. I have tried to avoid frequently used but misleading descriptions like "official" IRA and "official" Unionists (correctly, the Ulster Unionist party) but have sometimes found this impossible.

My thanks are owed to many who encouraged me to write this book, and helped me in numerous ways in the writing. Some would not wish to be named; some indeed — as in the case of officials still serving — cannot be named. Of those who can, I owe particular gratitude to the late Claud Cockburn and Donal Foley; to Dick Walsh and David McKittrick; for research, to Anthony Lennon and his colleagues on the staff of the *Irish Times* Library; and to Moira, Rachel and Vanessa, for their forbearance. Any mistakes are, like the opinions, my own.

James Downey
Dublin, June 1983

Nagasaki I

On 24 March 1972 the British Prime Minister, Edward Heath, announced in the House of Commons that the Stormont parliament was to be "prorogued" — in this case a euphemism for abolished — and that the Northern Ireland government, which had ruled the six north-eastern counties of Ireland for nearly half a century, with virtual autonomy from the sovereign British government and parliament at Westminster, would no longer exist.

The bill to give effect to the Heath government's decision was supported by the Labour opposition and had a quick and easy passage through the House of Commons and the House of Lords. While the bill went through parliament, I was drinking late one night in the Strangers' Bar with Ian Aitken, political correspondent (afterwards political editor) of the *Guardian,* Dr John Gilbert, later a Labour Defence Minister, and James Kilfedder, Unionist MP for North Down.

We had the place to ourselves until a prominent Conservative backbencher, a close friend of Heath, walked in. Someone invited him to have a drink but he declined, saying that he had only come in to buy some cigars. While the barmaid fetched his cigars, Aitken asked him his opinion of the situation in Northern Ireland. He gazed on the little group of us, then replied in a loud military voice: "The man who flew that plane to Nagasaki went in the wrong direction. He should have gone to Belfast." And he marched out of the room.

9

It was a while before anyone spoke. I watched Kilfedder, who was suffering from stomach trouble, turn several shades of green, white and orange. At last Aitken said in tones of awe: "There speaks the voice of the Prime Minister."

Gilbert said to me: "Can you use that in your paper? Or is everything said in here privileged?"

"That's right," I said, "I can't write a story about what anybody says in here. As the saying goes, I'll have to keep it for the book."

Chapter One

In 1972 the Provisional IRA claimed, and millions believed and still believe, that they brought down Stormont. They did not. Stormont brought itself down. It committed suicide in August 1969. It was only a long-dead corpse that Edward Heath buried in March 1972.

Stormont started life as a sickly child, and in half a century never grew into maturity. It was a bastard, the fruit of the failure of British Liberal and coalition governments over a period of more than three decades to settle the "Irish Question", itself already many centuries old, in a manner which would reconcile the aspirations of the Irish majority — which ranged from limited self-government under the overall authority of Westminster to total independence — with the desire of the great majority of Northern Irish Protestants to remain part of the United Kingdom.

In the 1920 Government of Ireland Act, Lloyd George, the Welsh wizard, tried to solve the question by setting up in Ireland two separate parliaments, one for the North and one for the South, each with very restricted authority, and a Council of Ireland was established as an instrument to bring them together in the fullness of time. A cartoonist of the day represented the Prime Minister as a conjuror putting the sundered bits of Ireland into a hat, telling his audience that he would take them out again in one piece, while thinking to himself: "At least I hope so. I've never done this trick before."

He never did, and neither did anybody else. By the time the first Northern Ireland parliament was opened, with great éclat, by King George V in 1921, the British government had been obliged to open negotiations with representatives of Dáil Éireann, the proscribed assembly, in which sat — when they were not in prison or "on the run" — the majority of the Irish members returned to the Westminster parliament in the general election of 1918.

They were obliged to do so by the effects of a sporadic but destructive guerrilla warfare which had raged for two and a half years; by a successful campaign of civil disobedience; and by the fact that the Irish, electorally and otherwise, had convinced British and world (especially American) opinion that they were in earnest in their struggle for self-determination.

In December 1921 Lloyd George and other representatives of the British government signed, with representatives of the Dáil, a treaty which accorded the twenty-six "southern" counties of Ireland (actually covering some five-sixths of the land area) what amounted to independence, designating the new territory the "Irish Free State". Lloyd George heavily pressurised the Irish delegates to concede a clause which allowed the Northern parliament to vote to exclude the six counties under its jurisdiction. They gave in.

When the Dáil debated the Treaty, it was forcefully attacked by the republican, or intransigent, deputies — not, for the most part, because it accepted the partition of the country, but because it did not distance the new Irish state sufficiently from the British Crown. Michael Collins, who had been the "organiser of victory" in the War of Independence, as well as leading figure among delegates who signed the Treaty, argued that the terms of the agreement, if accepted, would open the way to ultimate constitutional and legislative independence, with all the trappings of republican sovereignty. Most of the deputies agreed with him; besides, the Dáil and the country were war-weary. The Treaty was accepted.

Shortly afterwards a civil war broke out among the

former comrades who had sat together in the Dáil, languished together in prison camps, and lain in ambush together on the hillsides. The pro-Treaty side — the provisional government of the Free State and the new national army — won the war, but the bitterness common to civil wars was exceptionally strong in Ireland's then small and close-knit society. Collins himself was killed, aged only thirty-two, one of our most lamentable losses. His views were in a sense posthumously vindicated when the twenty-six counties, now the Republic of Ireland, did indeed at last achieve complete and formal independence; but the ill-effects which flowed from the division of the nationalist movement remained, and remain to some extent to the present time.

While the South adjusted to a settlement acceptable to perhaps two-thirds of the population, a settlement equally acceptable to two-thirds of the population took strong root in the North.

Hitherto, Northern Unionists had never wanted their own parliament: they had wanted all of Ireland to remain part of the United Kingdom; failing that, the nine counties of the province of Ulster, or, as a last resort, the six counties they eventually got, made up of a population of a million Protestants, overwhelmingly Unionist, and half a million Catholics, overwhelmingly Nationalist and separatist. A Protestant home-ruler mocked them: after all their opposition to Home Rule, he said, they had ended up with "a form of home rule that the devil himself could not have invented". But it worked very well — for some.

The Six Counties remained part of the United Kingdom, with powers over foreign policy, defence and finance reserved to the British government and parliament; and after the Second World War they benefited massively from British social welfare policy and aids to industry and agriculture. They had what they regarded as a special link with the Crown through a governor who represented the monarch. But they had great autonomy in local matters, to use or abuse much as they pleased. And they had a guarantee that they could not be forced to join a united Ireland without the consent of their parliament, with its built-in Protestant and Unionist majority.

As far as the British were concerned, the problem was solved North and South, the "Irish Question" settled. Not only in quiet times, but even after the air of the sixties began to fill with warnings, they found it easy to persuade themselves that nothing was wrong.

Norman St John-Stevas, Conservative MP for Chelmsford and later leader of the House of Commons, was regarded as an important spokesman for English Roman Catholics. He ignored the numerous reports that Catholics in Northern Ireland suffered discrimination in such matters as housing and employment.

Douglas Hurd was political adviser to Heath and afterwards a junior Foreign Office Minister under Margaret Thatcher. In a thriller, *Scotch on The Rocks*, written jointly with Andrew Osmond and published in 1969, he had a fictional Prime Minister say: "The Ulster system works well."

Until the sixties British consciousness of Northern Ireland — public, parliamentary or official — was astonishingly low. I have met journalists who did not know whether Dublin or Belfast was the capital of Northern Ireland. In so far as that territory was admitted to be a British responsibility at all, it formed one of an enormous rag-bag of concerns of the Home Office, where the few civil servants who actually knew anything about the question often had an excessively cosy relationship with their Stormont counterparts.

Up to the sixties communication between the Northern Irish and English parliaments was extremely limited. William Fitzsimmons, who held various ministries in a series of Unionist governments, told me after the abolition of Stormont: "Until Heath imposed direct rule, I hardly knew Westminster existed. Whenever I was appointed to a job, I would go over and meet the relevant minister in London. He would give me a glass of sherry and we would have a little chat for twenty minutes. Then I would go home and forget all about Westminster until the next time.

14

And the money kept flowing in."

The Unionists, themselves finding nothing wrong with the system, were hardly going to enlighten the British. The Nationalists, who tried, found it tough going.

Northern Ireland continued to be represented at Westminster, with twelve seats in the House of Commons. Three of the twelve constituencies — Mid-Ulster, Fermanagh and South Tyrone, and West Belfast — have Catholic majorities, and frequently returned Nationalist or socialist members. These, however, found it impossible to raise questions concerning discrimination, or ill-treatment of their constituents by the security forces, because a "convention" of the house, which remained unbroken until 1969, stipulated that such matters could not be discussed there. In theory this was because these were internal matters for the Northern Ireland parliament and government departments; less kindly, it could be said that the "convention" represented a quiet collusion between the authorities of the house and successive governments, none of which wished to be obliged to turn up the carpet.

In any case, the representatives of the Catholics in Northern Ireland, before the rise of the Civil Rights movement in the sixties, were very slow to concentrate on (and even slower to document, in any rigorous way) the grievances of their constituents. The reason for this non-assertiveness is not hard to find; it illustrates well the profound misunderstandings which characterise the different Irish and British perceptions of the relations between the two countries.

Whatever Lloyd George may have thought, not many in Ireland in 1921 expected his attempted settlement of the island to last very long. The great majority of Nationalists, and not a few Unionists, considered partition a temporary expedient. This consideration goes some way to explain the lack of interest in partition in the Dáil debates which followed the 1921 Treaty; it also helps to explain the subsequent thinking of Northern Catholics and their representatives.

These found themselves, in that period, a large minority

in a Protestant statelet. However, in a very important way, they did not regard themselves as a minority at all, but — along with an overwhelming preponderance of Southern Catholics, a substantial proportion of Southern Protestants, and even a small sprinkling of Northern Protestants — as part of the Irish *majority* which was heir to a tradition, stretching back by the shortest possible reckoning to the late eighteenth century, of nationalism, republicanism and separatism. This circumstance made their grievances all the more galling, but, in a curious way, less important.

It is most improbable (though speculation is fruitless now) that a majority of Northern Catholics could have been reconciled to the Northern settlement, however hard the new authorities might have tried. As it happened they did not try at all, thus allowing history to repeat itself: in the period after the legislative Union of Great Britain and Ireland in 1801, the British failed to take the measures necessary to reconcile the Irish to the Union.

The Unionist leader, Sir James Craig, later Lord Craigavon, declared that they had "a Protestant government and a Protestant people." One of his successors as Northern Ireland Prime Minister, Sir Basil Brooke, later Lord Brooke-borough, advised his supporters in County Fermanagh to follow his example and employ no Catholics as servants or farm workers, boasting in 1933, "I have not a Roman Catholic about my own place".

No Catholic, even among those of proved loyalty to the state, could hope for government office or expect to reach the top levels of the administration. The few Catholics of Unionist sympathies were ostracised along with their Nationalist brethren, being denied, for example, nomination as Unionist election candidates. At the other end of the scale, areas with Catholic majorities were gerrymandered in such a way as to produce Protestant majorities on the local councils.

These councils ensured that the jobs in their gift, down to road workers and drivers of school buses, went to Protestants. In some areas, Catholics were refused council houses, regardless of need, until all the Protestants on the list had been accommodated. It was possible for a council house to be tenanted by a young, unmarried Protestant woman while a large Catholic family lived in a nearby slum.

Catholic areas had much the highest unemployment rates, and while there was a large Catholic middle class, very few Catholics had skilled manual jobs. It is true that there were complex geographical and social reasons for this, but certainly some companies made a practice of employing only Protestants, and there were instances (most notably in the Harland and Wolff shipyard in Belfast) in which Catholics were driven out of their employment by violence.

Catholics were subjected to petty and absurd provocations. In one small town where everyone's religion was known, they were made to wait in the post office and social welfare office while Protestants took precedence. In the city of Derry, which had a large Catholic majority but a Unionist council, a new bridge was named after Craigavon. A more serious, and recurring, provocation came from the Orange bands which paraded annually through Catholic as well as Protestant areas, proclaiming the Protestant ascendancy.

For Catholics, freedom of assembly was more restricted. If they wanted to march or demonstrate, they were frequently refused permission by the authorities, or allowed to congregate only in confined areas. If they defied restrictions, they found themselves up against a battery of "emergency" (actually permanent) legislation which was enforced both by the ordinary police, the Royal Ulster Constabulary (about 90 per cent Protestant) and also by a wholly Protestant militia, the B Specials. These latter delighted, especially in rural areas and at times of tension, in harassment of their Catholic neighbours, including many whom they knew to be perfectly law-abiding. Their favourite form of harassment was time-consuming and thorough searching of persons and vehicles at roadblocks, but they had other and more vicious methods too.

Why did they, why should they, behave like this — aside from the fact that abuse of power, including petty power, is a constant in human behaviour? And why, by the same token, did the campaign of violence by the Provisional IRA in the seventies and eighties assume such savage forms? After all, the grievances listed above must seem small indeed by comparison with the atrocities since committed by violent gangs on both the Catholic and Protestant side, as well as by the British Army.

The easy answer, for the British, is that the Irish go in for this sort of thing. The easy answer, for an increasing number of people in the Irish Republic, is that Northerners have a natural tendency to both religious bigotry and violence — they are "imbued with violence", in the words of Liam Cosgrave, Taoiseach from 1973 to 1977. In the case of the Northern Protestants, any misconduct on their part is liable in particular to be attributed to the fact that they regrettably suffer from a "siege mentality".

The humdrum reality is that the Irish, including Northern Catholics and Northern Protestants, are no worse and no better than anybody else, but are merely somewhat less fortunate in their history and circumstances.

To an outsider, the "siege mentality" may seem unreal; but it is very real to a Protestant farmer on the border who has seen a neighbour, or a member of his family, murdered by the Provisional IRA. To the same outsider, the claim of a Provo supporter that the Provos are fighting the last campaign to end eight hundred years of British oppression may seem equally unreal; but there has been enough real oppression over the centuries to give force to that belief.

But although it helps an understanding of the present current Irish predicament if one has an insight into the feelings and motivations of ordinary Catholics and ordinary Protestants in Northern Ireland, such an insight explains neither the nature of the Northern state nor the tangle of confusion and misconceptions that has wound itself round Anglo-Irish relations for centuries.

In *The Sins of Our Fathers,* a colourful and perceptive account of the early stages of the present troubles, Owen Dudley Edwards divided Northern Protestants and Unionists into the "fearful" (mostly workers and small farmers) and the "confident" (essentially the Protestant upper classes). A look at these "confident" Unionists, and their origins, will explain a good deal. This involves going some distance back into the earlier history of Ireland — and England. You cannot really know where you are unless you know where you have already been.

Chapter Two

Bernard Shaw said that no two nations were more foreign to each other than the Irish and the English. He thought our mission was to civilise the English. (Oscar Wilde said that only we could prevent them from dying of respectability).

At once contradicting and emphasising our real and apparent similarities, this foreignness, as well as the intensely close connection of the islands, antedates history. Ever since the Iron Age the pattern of settlement, ethnic and cultural, of both islands has been immensely complex (and the complexity of settlement in Ulster in the modern period confounds those who put forward crude ethnic reasons for the Northern troubles), but ethnic differences are relatively slight. The political and cultural differences, however, have been enormous ever since the Roman conquest of Britain.

Neither the Romans nor the Saxons came to Ireland, except as traders. Their systems of law and government, and their flair for urbanisation, passed Ireland by. No towns in the modern sense — and no mint — existed in Ireland until close to the end of the first millennium AD. Not the Celtic Irish, but the Vikings who established themselves here in petty coastal kingdoms, built our first towns and minted our first coins.

For more than a thousand years Irish society remained essentially tribal. From the time of St Patrick in the fifth century, a native form of Christianity was practised, often with fervour. There was literacy; the arts flourished as in few places in Western Europe in the Dark Ages. There was a universally accepted, and remarkably liberal and humane, code of laws: in particular, women of the upper classes enjoyed large property rights and a degree of freedom which later shocked the English (as they also professed to be shocked by the amazing licentiousness of the clergy). Primogeniture was unknown: kings and chiefs did not inherit as of right but were elected by the male members of their *derbh-fhine*, or extended family. In theory, the tribal chiefs, scores or hundreds of them, owed allegiance to five (sometimes seven) provincial kings, who in turn owed allegiance to a high king, but it was rare for any high king to succeed in imposing his authority for any great length of time outside the boundaries of his own province.

In the eleventh and twelfth centuries various attempts were made to establish a stronger central authority, and to impose Church reform. None succeeded, though tribalism was tempered — or corrupted — by Frankish and Norman feudal ideas, and the Irish Church affected by English and French notions of Church organisation.

Hopelessly outdated in military methods and arms, as in political organisation, the Irish seemed easy prey for the Anglo-Norman (or, more properly, Welsh-Norman) invasion of 1169, despatched with the blessing of King Henry II. But feudal England simply did not have the resources to conquer the sister island. For hundreds of years the English writ ran only in the "Pale", an elastic area often consisting of no more than a few hundred square miles around Dublin. The Norman lords and English settlers intermarried with the Irish, adopted their dress, language and customs, and a brilliant new literature developed from the fusion of the *amour courtois* tradition with Irish verse forms.

The crucial change in Anglo-Irish relations came in the Tudor period, which saw the completion of the conquest of Ireland, along with the first clear appreciation, on the part of English rulers, of Ireland's strategic significance. That consideration has remained of the first importance ever since. Historians date the modern period in England from the accession to power of Henry VII in 1485, and the modern period in Ireland from 1603, when Hugh O'Neill, Earl of Tyrone, made his submission after a lengthy and destructive war of rebellion to the deputy of Henry's granddaughter, Elizabeth (she was already dead, but the news of her death had not reached Ireland).

The Tudors smashed feudalism in England, transforming her from a fairly backward country of the second rank into a world power in just over a century. Freed of continental territorial entanglement by the loss of Calais, the last residue of the long-lost Hundred Years' War, they set England on a course to maritime imperial glory. At the same time, they completed the unification of the archipelago with the reduction of Ireland and the union of the Crowns of England and Scotland under the Stuart James I, immediately following Elizabeth's death.

James and his ministers, like the Tudors before them and like many statesmen in times to come, were acutely conscious of the danger from Britain's western flank. England had lately had two narrow escapes, one from the Spanish Armada in 1588 and another, a decade later, when O'Neill had appeared close to succeeding in setting up either himself or another magnate as king of all Ireland, in alliance with Spain. So far from entertaining dreams of imperial splendour, England would then have been hard put to defend her own independence.

It is worth recalling at this point that the population of Ireland, now only about one-tenth of Britain's, normally measured about one-third of that of Britain in the pre-industrial period. In 1603 it is thought to have fallen as low as half a million, after many years of wars, devastations and partial famines; but peasant societies recover quickly and arms and money could come, and would indeed come soon again, from England's continental enemies; and British material resources, greatly dissipated in Elizabeth's wars in Ireland and elsewhere, were far from lavish. The threat was real.

· To counter it — and to save British resources — James

resorted to a time-honoured device: colonisation. This had been tried many times before in Ireland, and had failed on every occasion because of the relative paucity and feebleness of the colonists and the rapidity of their assimilation with the natives. The difference this time was that while the Irish — the native Gaelic race and the subsequent waves of "old English" — had remained Catholic, almost untouched by the Reformation, those who took part in James's Plantation of Ulster were uniformly Protestant, either Anglican or Presbyterian. Thus were sown the seeds of the sectarian bitterness which persists in Northern Ireland to this day; thus, too, England finally succeeded in planting a community in Ireland who would not readily intermingle with the native population. And very soon the occasion would arise for the formation of myths and traditions which would emphasise the differences and stand in the way of assimilation.

In 1641, coinciding with the civil wars in England and Scotland, the "Great Rebellion" broke out in Ulster and elsewhere in Ireland. In Ulster farms and townships were overrun and numbers of Protestants, including innocent non-combatants, were slaughtered. The extent of these massacres is unknown, but the victims were probably numbered in thousands. Preposterously exaggerated accounts were published in London, alleging the slaughter of scores or even hundreds of thousands — more than the Protestant population of the country. The massacres provided a potent source of Protestant myth, a confirmation of the supposed treachery and bloodlust of the natives, and a justification for the "siege mentality".

A decade of confused warfare ensued, involving at least four armies: one of Scottish Covenanters, one Parliamentary, one Royalist and one of Irish Catholics in alliance with Spain and the papacy which set up a parliament or "confederation" at Kilkenny. There were numerous shifting alliances and switches of allegiance. The decisive battle of the war, for the possession of Dublin, was fought at Rathmines between Royalists and Parliamentarians. The Parliamentarian victory enabled Oliver Cromwell to proceed to Dublin and carry out the pacification of Ireland. His methods of pacification, including wholesale massacre of Catholics, were such that three hundred years later, "the curse of Cromwell" still ranked first among Irish maledictions.

Massive land confiscations followed, but the Catholic aristocracy had one remaining throw of the dice. They rallied to James II when he arrived in Ireland in 1689 to try, half-heartedly, to win back his kingdom from William of Orange. James and an army mainly composed of Irish Catholics laid siege to Derry, one of the plantation towns. The siege was raised by an English fleet after a stout resistance and great hardship on the part of the besieged Protestants. On 12 July 1690 William's army forced the crossing of the Boyne at Oldbridge, thirty miles from Dublin, defeating an army of Irish and French led by James, and cleared the way to Dublin. These two Protestant victories are still celebrated annually in Northern Ireland, with as much triumphalism as the authorities of the day will permit.

Deserted by James, the Irish withdrew, first to Athlone, then to Aughrim, where they suffered a defeat much heavier than that at the Boyne, and finally to Limerick, to withstand a siege which equalled in heroism and severity that of Derry. At last their commander, Patrick Sarsfield, Earl of Lucan, surrendered on good terms; the Catholic peasantry were left to lament as most of their remaining leaders, along with the best of their surviving fighting men, sailed away to France. There, and elsewhere on the Continent, they and their descendants distinguished themselves in many capacities, especially as soldiers; no such opportunities would arise for those left behind.

Sarsfield had signed the Treaty of Limerick with William's representative, guaranteeing religious liberty and peaceful enjoyment of such land — by now very little, perhaps one-sixth of the total — as remained in the possession of Catholics. The English parliament, however, and the subordinate parliament in Dublin, composed of Protestant colonists, had no intention of honouring its

24

terms. On the contrary, the infamous penal laws were passed with the aim of extirpating the remnants of the Catholic gentry along with the priesthood. They forbade Catholics to enter into the professions or to hold commissions in the army, and proscribed Catholic education.

And there was more: priests, for example, were hunted down for reward. Numerous refinements were applied in the twisting of the screws: the son of a Catholic landowner, if he turned Protestant, inherited all the land; if there were several sons, all Catholics, the land had to be divided among them. The law, said one of England's ministers in Ireland, did not recognise such a person as an Irish Catholic.

In the middle and late eighteenth centuries the laws were greatly relaxed, until by the end of the century, Catholics suffered only a few prohibitions, the most outstanding being the inability to sit in parliament. Active persecution dwindled; long before their formal relaxation, the laws ceased to be enforced with any great rigour, and frequently the more generous Protestants helped Catholics to evade them.

Nevertheless, the oppressed Catholics — or such as had energy and leisure to do more than make a miserable living — burned with anger and resentment. English and Protestant hypocrisy, it appeared, knew no bounds. A war had been fought, and won, by those who proclaimed their object to be religious and civil liberty; these same people took away, most brutally, the liberties of the vanquished.

The same thought occurred to not a few liberal-minded Protestants; and many of these had their own grievances. The great Jonathan Swift was among the first of them to protest at the abominable misgovernment of the country. Those who administered Ireland for Britain were corrupt and idle; the parliament in Dublin was weak and powerless; the assembly itself was totally subordinate to the British government and parliament, which imposed intolerable restrictions on Irish trade, from which even the privileged Anglicans suffered. In the north, the Presbyterians had their own grievances. They laboured under forms of discrimination milder than those imposed on Catholics, but galling enough; great numbers were evicted by their landlords when their leases fell in. This was one of the causes of a mass emigration to America, and thereby an invaluable source of recruits for Washington's army.

Slowly the Enlightenment penetrated, if not into the draughty mansions of all the wine-swilling, hard-riding, heiress-abducting Sir Condy Rackrents of Maria Edgeworth's novel, at least into some great houses, and into rectories, manses and schools. And slowly the Catholics recovered a little ground. The vast majority lived wretched lives as rack-rented tenant farmers or landless labourers and paupers, but by the middle of the eighteenth century, a growing middle class had emerged. Its members had either made their way up the social scale by way of crafts and petty trade, or (as was frequently the case with descendants of the old gentry) made money from land. Some engaged in smuggling (a large industry because of the trade restrictions) and maintained a close connection with the French wine trade, in which many Irishmen flourished.

But the first great catalyst of massive change in Ireland — and the first inspiration of one of the most important modern Irish political movements — was the American Revolution of 1776. Partly inspired by the successes of the American colonists, partly using a supposed French threat to Irish shores as an excuse to raise a citizen army, an organisation called the Irish Volunteers sprang into being. They paraded in Dublin in 1782, firing off cannon outside the parliament building while loudly proclaiming their loyalty to King George III, and rapidly frightened the British into lifting the trade restrictions and granting the Irish parliament legislative independence.

The Volunteers were very far from being a *Jacquerie*. They were almost exclusively Protestant — preponderantly Anglican — and middle class, with an aristocratic leadership. But they had grasped one great idea: that the English colony, or "nation", in Ireland, must become an *Irish* nation; and that in order to do so it must join with its Catholic fellow subjects. They rejoiced, they said, in the easing of Catholic disabilities; they looked forward to the abolition of the remainder.

But to accomplish this — and to ensure that the easy triumphs of the Volunteers would not soon be dissipated — would require not merely parliamentary independence, but parliamentary reform. And the parliament itself remained obdurately corrupt and ignorant, full of the British government's placemen, heedless of the warnings of the radical members. The executive itself, of course, remained not Irish but English, so that the country was still largely at the mercy of whoever held the chief offices of state in Ireland under the British government.

The French Revolution of 1789 brought to birth in Ireland a far more radical organisation, the United Irishmen, composed of members of all classes and including Catholics, Anglicans and Presbyterians. Though the United Irishmen were drawn chiefly from the middle and artisan classes, their most indomitable hero was Lord Edward Fitzgerald, brother of the Duke of Leinster; while their activists included Presbyterian ministers, several of them were Jacobins, Deists and freethinkers. Their chief thinker — in so far as his writings influenced later generations — was Theobald Wolfe Tone, "the father of Irish republicanism", whose ideas profoundly influenced the subsequent course of Irish history.

Tone, in his writings, unforgettably linked republicanism, separatism and non-sectarianism, which he took several stages farther than the Volunteers. A thoroughgoing Jacobin and revolutionary, he regarded mere reform as insufficient. Ireland, he declared, must rid itself of its "execrable government" and "break the connection with England, that never failing source of all our political evils". The means he proposed for achieving this was to "abolish the memory of past dissensions" and unite Catholic, Protestant and Dissenter under "the common name of Irishman".

Tone may thus be said to have invented one of the three great strands, and in the present writer's view, the most important strand, in modern Irish nationalism: revolution;

27

the other two, pre-existent, elements being the constitutional movement and the agrarian movement, which frequently took, then and later, violent and Catholic-sectarian forms.

Appointed a brigadier-general in the French Army, Tone took part in an abortive French invasion of Ireland in 1796, was captured and cut his throat in his cell to cheat the hangman. Two years later United Irish risings took place in several parts of the country. These were largely unconnected with one another. They received only a little belated French help; they were only partly organised, being provoked in some areas by brutalities committed by government troops in arms searches. All were suppressed with great ferocity, and followed by tortures and executions.

The authorities took fright. Ireland — and England — must be saved from Jacobinism and Bonapartism. To achieve this, the two countries must be bound much more closely together, in a legislative union. This was effected with great speed. Sufficient members of the Irish parliament were bribed with money and titles to ensure that a majority would vote for their own dissolution. The best of the Protestant ascendancy argued for independence to the last, but most of them sold out.

It would of course be naive to suppose that all this happened simply as a reaction to the events of 1798. The British leaders, notably Pitt and Castlereagh, had plotted it for a long time, convinced as they were, that the measure was vital to the safety of the empire. They played the game, including the sectarian game, very dirtily, using not one but two sectarian cards.

The Catholic middle class, and the Catholic bishops, were as conservative as might be expected for men in their position. They could not sit in parliament, but they had influence none the less. As early as 1795 the government had funded a Catholic college at Maynooth. Now they tempted the Catholics with a promise of full emancipation as soon as the Union took place.

On the Protestant side, they exploited, and partly encouraged, a form of violent sectarianism already in existence. Government forces fighting Protestant United Irishmen near Belfast in 1798 had been helped by members of a new organisation, the Orange Order, which had as its genesis sporadic fighting incidents between Catholic and Protestant gangs over agrarian issues (usually complaints that Catholics were willing to pay higher rents than Protestants).

From its small beginnings as not much more than a band of rural brawlers, the Orange Order grew rapidly but unevenly. Its relations with the authorities for most of the next century were frequently ambiguous. Some of its members supported the government forces in suppressing the 1798 rising in the north, but two years later the Orangemen opposed the Union. During the nineteenth century the authorities often found themselves obliged to take action against the Orange Order when its members provoked or encouraged anti-Catholic rioting.

Ostensibly a religious and "brotherly" organisation, dedicated to religious tolerance, the principles of the English Revolution of 1688, and the Protestant succession, the Orange Order with its offshoots, the Royal Black Preceptory and the Apprentice Boys of Derry (named for the apprentices who shut the gates of the city in the face of James II's Irish Army), constituted in fact, and still constitutes, a powerful force for the maintenance of the Protestant ascendancy and discrimination against Catholics in the North. A greater contradiction in its principles and make-up lay in its class composition and the relations between the different interests within it. The Orange Order is unquestionably a populist movement, in the sense that it has a large membership and support among all classes of Northern Protestants, including the working classes. But from a very early stage in its development, it was used by the ruling classes, especially those of the landed interests, in support of the rule of the oligarchy, which saw very clearly the danger of the threat posed by the popular and non-sectarian movements.

Although Catholics and nationalists are quite wrong in

regarding the Protestant workers as merely the dupes of their landed and moneyed masters, and although the Orange tail has often wagged the Conservative/Unionist dog — in the sense of obtaining policies and actions more extreme than the cautious upper classes would have liked — the Orange Order certainly became, and remained, an instrument for the maintenance of British rule (in turn based on the perception by the British ruling class of the movement's political importance) in alliance with the Protestant ascendancy in Ireland.

Terrified by the French Revolution and the Irish events of 1798, the Protestant aristocracy, along with the great bulk of the middle classes both Protestant and Catholic, supported the Union, which produced a form of government that turned out to be oppressive, highly corrupt and inefficient. Many Protestants actually transferred their residences to England after the fall of the Irish parliament, thus abandoning all interest in spearheading an independence movement, as well as exposing Ireland to the evils of absentee landlordism.

The British, preoccupied with a series of continental wars and the European settlement after 1815, plainly had no idea that they had made a calamitous mistake in their Irish policy. Long afterwards, Arthur Griffith, one of the founders of the modern Irish state, wrote a book called *The Resurrection of Hungary,* published in 1904. Its main argument, in favour of an Anglo-Irish dual monarchy on the Austro-Hungarian model, has only curiosity value nowadays; the book is much more interesting for its powerful polemic against Pitt and Castlereagh. Griffith argued that these statesmen were mistaken in believing that a legislative union was necessary for the survival of the empire, and that the interests of the empire would have been better served by allowing Ireland to keep an independent parliament, along with independence in trade and finance.

This "might-have-been" is appealing, and so is the possibility that the Union might have worked. But the Union could only work on two conditions: one, the early granting of Catholic emancipation (which might have bound the conservative Catholic élite to the state); two, good government.

Neither of these conditions was fulfilled. Full emancipation was delayed for a whole generation, until 1829, thus to some extent radicalising some elements of the Catholic middle class. As to good government, Ireland for most of the first half of the nineteenth century was arguably the most misgoverned country in Europe. From time to time benign holders of the three chief offices of state (Viceroy, Chief Secretary and Under-Secretary) struggled with some success to ameliorate the system, but the general picture of Ireland given by foreign observers, and by such luminaries as Peel and Wellington, was one of nearly general, and from a political viewpoint unforgivable, misery.

During that half-century the country underwent a population explosion, not based on prosperity and industrialisation, but on their opposites. The vast bulk of the people were at best tenants-at-will — subject to eviction at the whim of the landlord or agent, without compensation for any improvements they might have made in their holdings — or, worse, sub-tenants or sub-tenants of sub-tenants; worst of all, they were landless people who might be allowed to cultivate a little patch of ground in exchange for their labour, and who migrated in search of seasonal work throughout Ireland and to England and Scotland. At the very best, distress and pauperism were common every year before harvest time; at worst, the poor were subject to serious malnutrition and even famine.

The circumstances which fostered a massive increase in population while these conditions prevailed was of course the notorious reliance on the cultivation of the potato. For most of the peasantry, the money earned from the raising of animals and of all other crops went in the payment of rent, and a majority of the population relied exclusively on the enormously prolific and easy-to-cultivate potato for sustenance. Accordingly, when blight struck the potato crop, totally or partially destroying it, for several years in the 1840s, the mass of the people in the poorest areas were deprived entirely of their staple food; and instead of endemic hardship and seasonal distress, Ireland was subjected to the horrors of the Great Famine.

The history of the famine, and the sufferings it inflicted on the people, are too well known to need rehearsal here. Briefly, the number of deaths from starvation and disease may have exceeded a million, and in a few years another million were lost to the country through emigration. Many of those who fled the country joined earlier emigrants in America, where they taught their descendants a bitter hatred of England which has survived to the present day. The population of the country, which was eight and a half million in 1841, continued to fall catastrophically until the middle of the twentieth century, when it stood at four and a half million. (The recent baby boom in the Republic has raised the population there to three and a half million, as against one and a half million in the North).

What provoked the greatest horror, as well as the greatest hatred of the system, was the knowledge that the suffering was avoidable: that the rigid and inhuman *laissez-faire* attitudes of the British government allowed people to perish while great quantities of agricultural produce were actually being exported from the country. The famine was the culmination of British maladministration in Ireland, and a powerful argument for independence. It is impossible to imagine that any native government, be it ever so conservative, corrupt and inefficient, would not have taken the most vigorous steps to feed the starving people.

In fact, for some time afterwards, all strands of the nationalist movement languished. A beaten and despairing people was in no mood for politics. In addition to the catastrophe of the famine, it had suffered two other grave blows: the death of the great constitutional leader Daniel O'Connell, the man who had finally achieved Catholic Emancipation in 1829; and the collapse in 1848 of a feeble and ill-planned armed rising organised by the Young Irelanders. These latter, more memorable for their writings than for their pathetic attempt at insurrection, had revived the ideas of Tone and the United Irishmen, under the impetus of the concurrent revolutionary events in France and elsewhere in Europe.

Throughout most of the half-century, the constitutional movement had played a significant part under the sway of the powerful personality of O'Connell: first, in the abolition of the remaining Catholic disabilities; and secondly, in the unsuccessful struggle for limited independence, called the Repeal of the Union. O'Connell, universally regarded throughout Europe as one of the greatest leaders of the liberal-nationalist movement, has a claim to be regarded as the inventor of mass democracy. Working closely with the Catholic lower clergy, and with the support of the Catholic middle class, he organised the people on a vast scale, held "monster" meetings attended by hundreds of thousands, and hoped by the sheer weight of his popular support to persuade or frighten the authorities into granting repeal. But he completely rejected violence, and when his bluff was called by the proscription of one of his meetings, he climbed down rather than risk conflict.

The exasperation of the young radicals with O'Connell's moderation is easy to understand, but it is important to remember that he, no less than they, identified the Irish nationalist movement with the great contemporary European movements of thought. The charge, often laid against him in turbulent times, of responsibility for the obscurantist and sectarian elements of the nationalist movement, is entirely unjust. On the contrary, the movement in Ireland, as elsewhere in Europe, was identified with religious tolerance and the enlargement of civil liberties.

After his death in 1847, the constitutional struggle languished for decades, while the other two strands, the agrarian and the revolutionary, revived. The first took the form of an agitation for fair treatment for tenant farmers, later translated into a demand for the transfer of ownership of the land to the tenants. Like previous agrarian struggles it frequently adopted violent means, from the maiming of cattle to the shooting of landlords. It was finally settled at the beginning of the twentieth century with the transfer of all but a tiny proportion of the land to the tenants.

The revolutionary tradition temporarily went into exile, first in France, later in the United States. It continued to be influenced by events in those countries, notably the Paris Commune, and to draw sustenance from the United States, mostly in the form of money. It took on several forms and names. The republicans of the late nineteenth century are best remembered as the Fenians, under which name they attempted another abortive insurrection in Ireland in 1867 and carried out several bomb attacks in England. These had much the same consequences as those of our own times: the deaths of a number of innocent people and the alienation of liberal English opinion. Karl Marx, as great a sympathiser with the Irish cause as his tragic daughter Eleanor and his friend Frederick Engels, denounced them in savage terms.

But the Fenians were only the tip of the republican iceberg. Under the surface lay the backward and still (though less than previously) poverty-stricken Irish masses, ready to be radicalised; and under it also operated the real revolutionary directorate, powerfully motivated, intellectually formidable, and ruthlessly conspiratorial. The members of the directorate called themselves the Irish Republican Brotherhood (IRB); they were the direct heirs of the Young Irelanders — and through them of the United Irishmen — and the ancestors of the later Irish revolution.

When Ireland experienced a cultural renaissance in the late nineteenth and early twentieth century, the IRB did not concern themselves with attempts to revive the Irish language — English has always been the language of revolution in Ireland — or hark back (save in reviving the name of a legendary band of warriors for the Fenians) to past golden ages. Rather, they set out cold-bloodedly to take over and turn to their use the various organisations thrown up by the revival, most notably the Gaelic Athletic Association, which they rightly saw as an invaluable source of foot-soldiers. At the same time they raised money in the

United States for a revolution in Ireland. They planned the 1916 Rising in Dublin, and one of their leading members, Michael Collins, led the armed struggle against Britain, ending with the 1921 Treaty — which the IRB in Ireland and America, being highly practical men, supported. Intensely conscious of the betrayal by informers of several attempted insurrections, they kept themselves a secret, oath-bound society. So secretive were they that although their significance was publicly acknowledged in the Proclamation of the Irish Republic during the 1916 Rising, the rank and file of the 1919-21 period were barely aware of their existence, much less of their role.

I have heard doughty veterans of the War of Independence and of the Civil War claim, half a century later, that the IRB's only function was to provide American money; but historians nowadays know better. The modern Irish state grew from an armed struggle, plotted, initiated and heavily supported by an organisation which legitimately and closely traced its descent to 1798 and beyond, and thus to the American and French revolutions. Such sectarian and backward characteristics as exist in the Irish state today, alike with the activities of the Provisional Irish Republican Army and the Irish National Liberation Army, make a mockery of those origins, which explicitly rejected sectarianism, much as the Orangemen unknowingly mock the principles of the English Revolution of 1688, to which they proclaim adherence. But to discuss that is to get a little ahead of our story.

Chapter Three

In the 1880s Charles Stewart Parnell, a half-American Wicklow landowner, took into his hands all three strands of the Irish nationalist movement, agrarian, revolutionary and constitutional. He controlled the agrarian struggle by placing himself at the head of the Land League, founded in 1879 by a former Fenian, Michael Davitt, which used among its weapons the withholding of rents and ostracism of collaborators with landowners (thus giving the language the word "boycott", from Captain Boycott, a land agent against whom the policy was first practised). He flirted, and more than flirted, with the IRB; he went so far with them in their desire for a republic as to declare that "no man has the right to set a boundary to the march of a nation"; and he hinted, to pressure the British government, that he might not stop at violence, that he might bring, as he put it, "the hillside men" into play. But his chief contribution was to challenge O'Connell for the title of the greatest Irish constitutional leader of the century by seizing an opportunity presented to him by an accident of British (and Irish) parliamentary politics.

In 1886 the great Liberal Prime Minister, William Ewart Gladstone, introduced in the House of Commons the first Home Rule bill. By this time, a certain amount had been done to alleviate Irish grievances. The shape of ultimate settlements of the land and religious questions — which meant, in the latter case, that the Catholic bishops would have their way in the matter of education — could be discerned; already the Anglican Church of Ireland (to which the Catholic majority had once, scandalously, been obliged to pay tithes) had been disestablished; British governments had shown some enlightenment in subsidising the study of Irish antiquities and folklore.

Gladstone appears to have reached an intellectual and moral conviction that the time was right to take an incomparably larger step and concede the Irish claim to self-determination. But Irish nationalism did not rely on him or the Liberal party: it relied on Parnell. A recent enlargement of the franchise had ensured that the great majority of the Irish seats in the House of Commons had gone to home-rulers; and the Home Rule party, intensely disciplined (and thus setting a model for modern political parties) and tightly controlled by the aloof and autocratic Parnell, held the balance of power in the House. Parnell cared nothing for Liberals or Conservatives; Home Rule was the price of his support for either party and Gladstone was prepared to pay that price, and he did so with the introduction of the Home Rule bill.

Three main political groups opposed the Home Rule bill. The first was the conservative and aristocratic interest, including, very vocally, the Irish landowners in the House of Lords. Many of these were not Irish at all and had little connection with the country beyond owning large estates there; a minority of the great landowners did in fact live part of the year in Ireland and kept some touch with local affairs, but were mostly oblivious to the main movements of popular opinion. A little lower down the social scale, the Sir Condy Rackrents were dying out, their bankrupt estates taken over by the sons of their old retainers (as Maria Edgeworth would have had it) or, more likely, by Catholic families of some substance. The opposition of the minor gentry to land purchase was feeble at most, and they had little political influence. The great Anglo-Irish magnates had plenty of influence, and were prepared to use it.

The second group comprised the liberal and radical imperialists, whose chief figure was Joseph Chamberlain.

At this apparent zenith of empire (only a very few of the most perceptive could see that the empire was already in decline) these believed that Britain had a duty to civilise and evangelise the world, and that this mission would be vitiated by a weakening of the core, the Union. Their opposition to Home Rule caused an almost fatal split in the Liberal Party.

The third group were the northern unionists, whose detestation of the prospect of a Home Rule parliament and executive in Dublin, even one with very limited powers, was based on three main objections: religious, economic, and a conglomeration of issues centred on questions of ethnicity, culture and loyalty.

For most of a century the Protestant majority areas, essentially the eastern half of Ulster, had grown steadily apart from the rest of Ireland. This was most strikingly the case in the matter of prosperity and industrialisation. The Union had killed off infant Irish industries, and the industrial revolution had not reached most of the country; subsistence farming remained the chief economic activity of the majority. But by a series of historical accidents, east Ulster had prospered, with flourishing textile, shipbuilding and engineering industries. Those who depended on these industries feared a loss of the British connection and British markets. Their fears may have been exaggerated, because the 1886 and subsequent Home Rule proposals envisaged that Westminster would retain control not only of defence and foreign affairs but also of trade, finance and navigation, but they were real.

Industrialisation further complicated the already complex pattern of settlement, with all its ethnic and cultural implications. It brought into Ulster, particularly to East Belfast, a further influx of immigrants from northern England and southern Scotland, who saw themselves as even more emphatically British than had earlier settlers. At the same time it brought into west Belfast and other areas Catholics of native stock from the hinterland. A good many of these embraced Protestantism — religious conversions in Ireland are not, as is often supposed, all one way —

but most remained Catholic, and competition for jobs replaced competition for land as a source of grievance and an occasion for riot, eagerly seized upon by the Orange Order in its more militant phases.

The greatest difference remained religion, and religious differences continued to grow in bitterness and formality throughout the century. Only a small minority of Protestants maintained the non-sectarian tradition of their United Irish ancestors (though this tradition has never entirely died out among them) and the new Catholic migrants, usually poor and ill-educated, had never shared it. Developments in all the main Churches made matters worse. The granting of Catholic Emancipation in 1829 coincided with the settlement of a long-standing controversy between Presbyterian liberals and conservatives in favour of the conservatives and fundamentalists. In the middle of the century, a powerful evangelical revival imbued Protestants with the kind of hysterical fundamentalism characterised in our own time in Ireland by the Reverend Ian Paisley and in the United States by the outpourings of the Moral Majority. This in turn coincided with remarkable, even revolutionary, developments in the Catholic Church.

Up to the early nineteenth century the Catholic Church in Ireland was still characterised by the licentiousness and negligence among the clergy and laxity of practice among the laity which had caused such scandal in medieval times. In the more remote, less accessible parts of the country, great numbers of nominal Catholics had only the most tenuous grasp of the principles of the Christian religion; superstition flourished, and there prevailed practices, only lightly Christianised, which were manifestly survivals of the prehistoric Druidical religion.

All this changed in the most radical way after the famine. From Rome came the new transmontanism and triumphalism, tempered and sweetened for the masses by an associated outburst of sentimental piety, and spread in Ireland by dedicated bishops and priests — often men of formidable intellect and great political astuteness — with a fanatical devotion to Rome hitherto almost unknown in Ireland. In politics they were of course extreme conservatives; they substituted for the earlier Church support of Britain a strong identification with — and frequently considerable influence in — the constitutional movement, but denounced in the most ferocious terms revolutionary activities and agrarian violence (civil disobedience gave them some problems; they trimmed, but usually opposed it). With great energy, they built churches, convents and schools, and recruited great numbers of young men both for the Irish priesthood and to serve as missionaries abroad. But the goal which they were most determined to achieve was control of education at every level — a controversy over university education, which went on for decades, was finally settled in their favour; they could thus imbue the minds of their people, especially during the opinion-forming years, with Catholic triumphalist ideas. In this they succeeded all too well.

Together with the religious changes, and partly attributable to them, went enormous social and psychological changes. Rural Ireland became a country of late marriages, often of lifelong celibacy: these, along with emigration, were the post-famine methods of population control. The decline of the native language, spoken in perhaps half the geographical area of the country before the famine, accelerated, along with a decline in traditional folk culture. For a great many Irish people, Catholicism, rather than any individual culture, became a badge of nationality. By a stroke of bad luck, the cultural revival at the end of the century, which formed a fourth strand in the national movement, accentuated the differences between Catholics and Protestants, especially northern Protestants — although members of the Protestant intelligentsia were among its leading spirits — instead of providing common ground, because most Protestants did not regard themselves as sharing the history and traditions to which the cultural renaissance appealed.

Politically, the Protestant-Unionist sense of separate identity and allegiance was strong enough in 1886 to swell the ranks of the Orangemen and Unionists, and to cement the alliance between these and the British Conservative and Unionist party — characterised in the notorious statement by Lord Randolph Churchill that he proposed to play "the Orange card" — a crucial factor in the subsequent separation of most of Ulster from the main Irish settlement.

Looking back, it seems most improbable that a local agitation in Ulster, even helped by powerful allies in Britain, could have prevented the application at that time of a measure of Home Rule to the whole of Ireland — if, that is, Gladstone's bill had succeeded in passing through parliament. But the defection of the Liberal Unionists from Gladstone ensured its defeat in the House of Commons.

Soon afterwards the Home Rule party split in the scandal which erupted over the divorce of Mrs Kitty O'Shea, who had long been Parnell's mistress; although it eventually reunited under John Redmond, the bitterness provoked by the split, which was quickly followed by Parnell's untimely death, fatally weakened the party and the constitutional movement. Nevertheless the indomitable Gladstone, at the age of eighty-two, introduced a second Home Rule bill in 1892. This was accepted in the Commons, but heavily defeated in the House of Lords.

In 1912, after the power of the Lords had been so severely curbed that they could no longer prevent, but only delay, the passage of a major bill, another Liberal Prime Minister, H.H. Asquith, brought in yet a third Home Rule bill. There followed a conspiracy to reject it, involving the Unionists led by Craigavon and a Dublin lawyer, Sir Edward (afterwards Lord) Carson, the Tories under Bonar Law, other important sections of the British ruling class and significant elements of the army.

The events that followed are among the best documented of modern Irish history; they are all set out in Professor A.T.Q. Stewart's celebrated book *The Ulster Crisis.* Plans were laid for the establishment of a Unionist provisional government in Ulster; guns were run in from Germany; British officers serving in Ireland, led by a general, threatened to resign their commissions rather than serve against the Unionist citizen army, the Ulster Volunteers.

The Unionists' original aim — and this is particularly true of Carson — was to reject Home Rule for any part of Ireland; but they and their British allies quickly recognised that they could not prevent the majority from achieving self-determination, and so they urged the exclusion of six Ulster counties. The Home Rule bill passed through parliament, but was suspended for the duration of the war against Germany which broke out in August 1914; after the war Redmond was bullied (as were the Treaty negotiators later) into accepting the exclusion of Northern Ireland.

Irish nationalists during this decade turned away from the seemingly fruitless struggle in the British parliament to support the radical Sinn Féin Party (which demanded that an Irish parliament should control finance, trade and industry). The 1916 Rising in Dublin was suppressed with much loss of life and followed by the execution of its leaders. The Rising had little popular support, but a massive change of public opinion in favour of the revolutionaries rapidly occurred. Nationalists had plenty of justification for the view that their aspirations had been frustrated by an unholy alliance between the Irish Unionists and the British ruling class.

Where they were mistaken was in regarding the Protestant foot-soldiers as merely the dupes or tools of their rulers and in underestimating the strength of their Unionist convictions. The mistake is all the more understandable when one considers that the leadership of the threatened Ulster revolt was drawn exclusively from the upper classes, whereas men and women of all classes were among the leaders of the radical nationalist movement — and one of those who led the insurgents of 1916 was the noted trade unionist and Marxist writer, James Connolly. But nationalists of all views, all classes and all religions shared the comprehensive ideal of the Irish nation as embracing the entire population of the island. Redmond, a Catholic landowner whose brother was killed in France (along with nearly fifty thousand other Irishmen) in the war, declared:

"We cannot give up a single Irishman." Nationalists still find it exceptionally hard to bring themselves to believe that the Protestant workers and small farmers of the North should genuinely reject common membership of the Irish nation. This is in effect the circle which will have to be squared in any ultimate settlement.

As to the strategic question, it simply did not arise at the time. Not only the Treaty itself, but also the curious Document Number Two which de Valera proposed for discussion as an alternative, provided for the maintenance by Britain of naval bases in the Irish Free State; Ireland thus to all intents and purposes remained part of the British defence system. The more radical nationalists would not long remain content with that.

The infant left-wing movement regarded neutrality as a moral question; Connolly was disgusted at the way in which the labour and trade union movement in most of Europe had abandoned pacifism in 1914 and supported a war among the imperialist powers. The mainstream nationalists regarded it, more pragmatically, as a sign of sovereignty. It did not become a practical proposition until 1938, when de Valera negotiated the return of the naval bases and thus made it possible for the state to remain formally neutral after the Second World War broke out the following year. Even then neutrality had more shadow than substance, and was heavily biased in favour of the British, who supplied the Free State with weapons and ammunition in exchange for food and labour. In the event of a German invasion, the Irish Army would have co-operated with the British in opposing it; in the event of a British and/or American invasion, they would have offered only a token resistance. The government closely watched and severely curbed the activities of German spies and of the faction of the IRA who gave these some very inadequate assistance; a number of IRA men were executed, and others allowed to die on hunger strike in prison.

But Irish neutrality in the war, and de Valera's new Constitution which closely preceded it, helped the two parts of Ireland to grow even farther apart. The latter, as well as including sectarian or "confessional" clauses (such as a prohibition on divorce which still stands), offended and seemingly threatened Unionists by claiming sovereignty — though not jurisdiction — over the whole island. Wartime events had a deeper effect in Britain.

The British, deprived of the use of the Free State ports, found Northern Ireland strategically essential to them, both as a base for the protection of the North Atlantic convoys and as a staging post for their American allies in advance of the invasion of France. The spectacle of Northern loyalty, coupled with apparent Southern indifference and hostility, affected British opinion, Labour as well as Conservative; and the Unionists made the most of it.

A general election in 1948 unseated de Valera after sixteen years in office, and brought to power a coalition government led by John A. Costello of Fine Gael, the successors of the pro-Treaty party, but whose External Affairs Minister was Seán MacBride, son of the executed 1916 leader Major John MacBride and the revolutionary heroine Maud Gonne, and himself a former IRA leader. This government brought in and steered through parliament a bill declaring the state a republic, taking it out of the British Commonwealth, and removing from the British monarch the functions he had formerly performed in Irish external relations. De Valera, with one eye on the North, had always shrunk from leaving the Commonwealth and breaking the last tenuous link with the Crown. The move was untimely. Although Britain now had a Labour government, including members highly sympathetic to Irish independence and unity, the contrast with "loyal Ulster", so closely following the wartime experience, was too much: a bill was passed at Westminster declaring that in no event could Northern Ireland cease to be a part of the United Kingdom without the consent of the Stormont parliament.

At this point the strategic question raised its head again, in an extreme form. The Irish government refused to join the new North Atlantic Treaty Organisation while the country was partitioned; as an alternative, MacBride suggested a bilateral defence pact to the Americans, who showed no interest. Simultaneously, a British cabinet memorandum was drafted, which offered the opinion that, so important was Northern Ireland's role in British defence, it should not be allowed to leave the United Kingdom even if that was the desire of a majority of the population there.

These events did not materially affect Anglo-Irish relations, still less relations between ordinary Irish and British people. The Labour government's bill did not give the Republic, in Britain, the status of a foreign country, and Irish citizens living in Britain retained the right to vote in elections. During the fifties the stagnation of the Irish economy under a succession of Fianna Fáil and coalition governments resulted in an increase in the number of Irish living in Britain; in one five-year period emigration to Britain reached a quarter of a million. There was a different kind of stagnation in the North, where the Unionists appeared more entrenched than ever.

Chapter Four

At some quite imperceptible point early in the War of Independence the guerrillas ceased to be known as the Irish Volunteers and became popularly known as the Irish Republican Army; the anti-Treaty forces in the Civil War still called themselves the IRA. The successor parties of the pro-Treaty and anti-Treaty factions are the present Fine Gael and Fianna Fáil. After de Valera founded Fianna Fáil in 1926, the once-powerful Sinn Féin Party dwindled into a remnant, allied with the small hard core of intransigents who still called themselves the IRA. It can be misleading to describe them as the political wing of the IRA; the army council of the IRA, who regarded themselves as the legitimate heirs of the first Dáil of 1919, made the political as well as the military decisions, and that remains the case with the Provisional IRA of our own time.

The hard core regrouped sufficiently to carry out sporadic attacks against the security forces and in some cases against civilians, in both the Northern and Southern states in the thirties and forties; and to carry out bomb attacks in Britain, which claimed a number of civilian lives, at the beginning of the Second World War. But they suffered the usual disadvantages, chiefly internal wrangling and lack of supplies, common to small, conspiratorial and unpopular underground movements; in particular they were weakened by a split between pro-German and anti-German factions during the war. In both parts of the country they were suppressed quite easily, in the South with some severity by de Valera, in the North by the Royal Ulster Constabulary and the B Specials, without any need to call on the help of the British Army.

In the Republic, where they could see that they had negligible public support, they ceased all violent activities after the war; but in the North they made what then seemed to be one last throw, between 1956 and 1962, in a campaign of attacks against military and police barracks, mostly in border areas and mostly mounted from across the border. It caused little loss of life and no massive inconvenience, and received little support from Northern Catholics. Its humiliating failure caused the army council and the Sinn Féin leaders to reappraise their strategy. They put their guns away and went, like so many of their predecessors, into constitutional politics — but with a difference.

In the South the beginnings of a new prosperity under a new Taoiseach, Seán Lemass, who succeeded de Valera in 1959, had not cured the already existing social ills — had, indeed, exacerbated some of them as disparities of wealth grew more visible. Sinn Féin went into street politics, agitating on issues ranging from bad housing to civil liberties. At the same time they assumed a strong left-wing tinge, of the kind which would be called a decade later "Euro-communist", invoking the name of Connolly as well as that of Wolfe Tone. Thus they began a real if modest progress which would eventually bring them into the Dáil as yet another constititutional party. In the North, matters were more complicated.

By the mid-sixties both Britain and Northern Ireland also had new leaders. The 1964 general election in Britain made Harold Wilson, who had opposed the pro-Stormont Ireland bill of 1949, Prime Minister. This election and the election of 1966 also brought into parliament large numbers of young or youngish Labour MPs, many with substantial blocs of Irish voters in their constituencies, some whose reading of history had convinced them of the justice of Ireland's claim to independence and unity, many more concerned with discrimination against Catholics in

Northern Ireland. Many of them were persons of great courage and principle, willing to compromise or even destroy their political careers. Among those who defied warnings about the "Irish graveyard" and suffered in consequence may be mentioned in particular Paul Rose, Jock Stallard, and Kevin McNamara. People like these formed an important parliamentary pressure group, the Campaign for Democracy in Ulster, and made common cause with existing Labour "Friends of Ireland" and with Gerry Fitt (then Republican Socialist, later leader of the Social Democratic and Labour Party, later Independent Socialist) who was first elected Westminster MP for West Belfast in 1966. With this kind of pressure, and Wilson's known instincts, British demands for reform in Northern Ireland were certain to become insistent.

These demands found a ready listener in the new Northern Premier, Terence O'Neill (later Lord O'Neill of the Maine), who had succeeded the fainéant bigot Brookeborough in 1963. Although himself an aristocrat — he traced his descent both to plantation magnates and ancient Gaelic kings — he was by Unionist standards a liberal, who tried to achieve better relations between Northern Catholics and Protestants, and between North and South. O'Neill argued for an extension of the local government franchise; he visited convent schools and he held meetings in Belfast and Dublin with Lemass and with Jack Lynch, who succeeded Lemass as Taoiseach in 1966.

But the task of reconciling Catholics to the Northern Ireland state was already impossible — impossible, at any rate, without rapid and sweeping reforms — and whatever about his own wishes or the pressure to which Wilson constantly subjected him, O'Neill knew that he could not bring his Cabinet very fast or very far in this direction. While he tried to proceed with excessive slowness and caution, events overtook and overwhelmed him.

The Nationalist party at Stormont, the representatives of the traditional Catholic middle and farming classes, had long been a derisory force in Northern politics. If they stayed away, they were forgotten; if they attended, their attempts to raise the grievances of their community were ignored. Most of the know-nothing Unionists thought they could continue to ignore them. O'Neill knew better.

In the sixties a whole new breed of Catholic representative sprang up. This was no accident of generation or *Zeitgeist;* the new leaders represented and indeed belonged to a new class, a greatly expanded Catholic middle class produced by a generation of free education, including university education — a class whose counterparts were coming into power elsewhere in Europe, but whose members in Northern Ireland were denied any share in power on sectarian grounds.

These Catholic representatives, and a number of like-minded Protestants, drew a good deal of their inspiration and some of their tactics and slogans from the black Civil Rights movement in the southern United States, and later from the "French events" of 1968. They used their education and training to document, far more accurately and tellingly than ever in the past, instances of discrimination against Catholics; this was a feature of the activities of the Campaign for Social Justice, from whose foundation in Dungannon, County Tyrone, in 1963 the Northern Civil Rights Movement can be dated. But their most visible activities consisted of marches and demonstrations, at which they sang, not Irish rebel songs but the black American anthem "We Shall Overcome".

The great majority of the Civil Rights agitators of the middle sixties not only genuinely eschewed violence, but did not then question the constitutional position of Northern Ireland, seeking only reforms within that framework: the ending of gerrymandering, police bias, and discrimination in housing, employment and the local government franchise ("one man one vote"). Even had they wished to challenge the constitution, this would have been tactically unsound since it might have threatened their axis with the British Labour Party. But in addition to the moderate majority led by John Hume (later leader of the SDLP and a member of the European Parliament) the Civil Rights movement contained two other important elements.

One was the extreme left, represented chiefly by the People's Democracy, an organisation centred on Queen's University, Belfast. Their leaders included Michael Farrell, Eamonn McCann and Bernadette Devlin (later Mrs Bernadette McAliskey), who was elected Westminster MP for Fermanagh and South Tyrone in 1969. The extreme left saw the struggle for reform as merely the prelude to revolution. Their considerable intellectual fire-power (Farrell is the author of a standard work, *Northern Ireland: The Orange State)* was not matched by any great popular support, but they had the ability to force the pace.

The other was the membership of the new-style, non-violent, republican movement. Former IRA men and recent Sinn Féin recruits flung themselves enthusiastically into the Civil Rights agitation, using their discipline and talent for organisation, for example, to provide much of the stewarding for marches. Meanwhile the irreconcilable elements of the IRA, who deplored any resort to constitutional means, sat at home and bided their time; they would re-emerge soon enough.

All these subtleties escaped most members of the Unionist government, who should have known better, and *a fortiori,* the generality of "fearful" (and ill-informed) Protestants, who saw nothing wrong with the system under which they lived and who viewed the Civil Rights movement simply as the IRA in another form.

The prejudices of the "fearful" Protestants were strengthened by an event which at the same time reinforced the new-look republicans: the celebrations in 1966 of the golden jubilee of the 1916 Easter Rising in Dublin. One effect of the commemorations was to draw attention to the role of the Marxist leader Connolly, and to the possibility, as the republican movement of the time saw it, of a synthesis between nationalism and socialism. Most Protestants, however, were entirely unaware of the very possibility of such a development, and viewed the celebrations — as they viewed the Civil Rights movement — as yet another manifestation of the threat posed to their own position by what they supposed to be a conglomeration of the IRA, the Catholic Church and the Southern state.

In the Unionist party the cry was raised, not for the reforms desired by O'Neill and Wilson but for harsh measures of law and order. In the back streets of the Protestant Shankill district, bordering the Catholic areas of West Belfast, the Ulster Volunteer Force (UVF) of the 1912 period was revived in a new form, as a gang of Protestant assassins. The first sectarian murders, of Catholics by the UVF, occurred in the summer of 1966. The same period also brought to birth, or strengthened existing Protestant demagogues. Of these by far the most significant was the Reverend Ian Paisley, a small-town fundamentalist preacher and associate of extreme fundamentalist groups in Scotland and the United States, who seized the opportunity provided by the crisis to achieve membership first of the Stormont, then of the Westminster and finally of the European parliament, and to challenge the "official" Unionists for the political leadership of the Protestants.

Paisley, a large man who looks even bigger than he is, has tremendous physical presence, a crude but forceful wit, and considerable talent for organisation. Originally ordained a minister in a small breakaway Presbyterian sect, he founded his own Free Presbyterian Church, which eventually grew to displace the Methodists as the third Protestant religious denomination in the country, after the Church of Ireland and Presbyterians. He also established his own Protestant Unionist Party, which he later renamed the Democratic Unionist Party.

Most of his political successes still lay in the future, but already in the sixties his Church was making rapid progress. Thousands of ordinary Presbyterians intensely disliked the ecumenical movement, which they regarded as a cunning plot by Rome to take over the Protestant Churches; they wanted to hear their ministers preach hell-fire and damnation, the whore of Babylon and the pope as Antichrist. Similarly, many of the Unionist rank and file regarded the feeblest efforts at reform as a sell-out to the IRA. While many deserted their previous places of worship for

Paisley's, traditional Unionists began to desert O'Neill, and one of the most prominent — Desmond Boal, QC, MP, one of the leading lawyers in Northern Ireland — gave Paisley political advice. The fatal Northern combination of politics and religion was hard at work.

One of the commonest forms of Protestant opposition to the Civil Rights movement became counter-demonstrations, organised by Paisley's and other groups. On one occasion Paisley and a crowd of his supporters occupied part of the small cathedral city of Armagh to prevent the passage of a Civil Rights march.

The response of the security forces was crucial. It was also completely predictable, given the sectarian composition and backgrounds of the police and B Specials and their political direction by a hardline Home Affairs Minister, William Craig — eventually, but too late, dismissed by O'Neill. Their conduct became a major factor in alienating the Catholics from the security forces and from the very concept of "law and order", an alienation which would endure through more than a decade of reform and of strenuous efforts to make the RUC at once more efficient and more even-handed.

In October 1968 the RUC broke up a demonstration in Derry, batoning and gassing Gerry Fitt and British Labour MPS who accompanied him. British television viewers saw policemen, including officers, using batons on the demonstrators. The RUC "invaded" the Catholic Bogside area, breaking into numerous homes and killing an unquestionably innocent man, Samuel Devenney. In January 1969, a People's Democracy march was attacked at Burntollet Bridge, near Derry, by a mob which included off-duty B Specials. Several people were seriously injured.

O'Neill now found himself under intolerable pressure from two sides: on the one side, from the Civil Rights movement and the British government, on the other, from within his own party. The Unionist dissidents — led by Craig, John Taylor and the man who had long been regarded as the natural successor to the premiership, Brian Faulkner — caballed against him. Plainly he must act firmly in one way or another, or go. After the Burntollet incident he decided to risk everything on one throw. He called an election in which he tried to rally to himself as much moderate opinion as could be rallied under the banner of reform.

This election not only brought about O'Neill's downfall, but saw the beginnings of the break-up of the formerly monolithic Unionist Party. It also showed in a new light the importance of the class issue in Northern politics. The leadership of the various Catholic, nationalist and Civil Rights groups was overwhelmingly middle class — often the new middle class so significant in the Civil Rights movement. On the Protestant and Unionist side, O'Neill retained the support of the squirearchy which had continued, so archaically, to rule the area. The sons of great lords came out of their castles, former British senior officers from their country mansions; but not enough support or leadership came, then or later, from the suburban villas, for the comfortable and affluent Protestant upper middle class had too long remained content to abdicate leadership and leave power to the gentry and to middle-class hacks.

The election was essentially a struggle for the Protestant vote, and the candidates on the Unionist side divided into those for and against O'Neill, who endorsed both "official" and "unofficial" Unionist candidates. And when the votes were counted, the calculations were made less on the basis of parties than on the numbers of members of the new Stormont parliament who supported or opposed O'Neill. On the latter basis, he lost — though very narrowly; another couple of thousand votes, cast in the right places, would have given him a majority.

O'Neill resigned, with solemn and all too accurate warnings, delivered in episcopal tones on television, about what was now likely to follow. He was succeeded by another member of the squirearchy, a distant cousin, James Chichester-Clark, who was elected Unionist leader by a small majority over Faulkner. Chichester-Clark, a large, decent, bumbling man whose clothes never quite seemed to fit him (they improved considerably later, when he became Lord Moyola and joined his distant relation, by then Lord O'Neill of the Maine, in the House of Lords) greatly preferred his country estate and his salmon fishing to politics. (The last four Northern premiers all lived in considerable style in various parts of the country, a fair distance from the unpleasantnesses of Belfast).

Chichester-Clark had never wanted the premiership; he inherited a party and government in crisis; he had few advisers of any quality, and little or no idea what to do. He had a "line" to the Tory Party through his brother Robin, a friend of Edward Heath; but he had little knowledge of or interest in British politics at large, and virtually no personal relationship with Wilson. Cabinet meetings were at first agonising, then futile, finally ridiculous. What would the British insist on? What would the party accept? The answers never came out right.

As the crisis grew, the meetings went on later and later, the discussions went round and round. As often as not, the Prime Minister would tire of the pointless talk, get up, call for his car and go home. Some of the other ministers would remain, drinking copiously from a store provided at their chief's own expense; the more generous would some-times bring in their own bottles. At last the Premier's private secretary took to locking up the drinks cabinet and putting away the key.

While the ministers drank, the North began to burn. Every year on 12 August the Apprentice Boys of Derry hold a demonstration in that city to commemorate the lift-ing of the Jacobite siege. Although their title recalls the shutting of the gates by the city apprentices in the face of James II's army, "they are not apprentices, they are not boys, and for the most part they do not come from Derry" (as a Stormont official would later explain to William Whitelaw). They are in fact a particular kind of Orangemen whose most important activity for generations was the annual assertion of Protestant supremacy in a city inhabited mostly by Catholics. With the growth of Catholic con-sciousness in the sixties, their marching and drumming had

54

become more and more a source of resentment; for some weeks before the 1969 march, the authorities and Civil Rights leaders alike knew that a concerted effort to break up the demonstration was being organised. The moderate Civil Rights leaders begged the government to avert violence by proscribing the march, but the government, fearful of alienating Protestant opinion, dared not do so.

The march proceeded, as planned; it was attacked, as planned, initially by gangs of stone-throwing youths; the RUC and Specials intervened; the Catholics threw up barricades and the "Battle of the Bogside" ensued. The battle lasted for two days and nights, with one side using petrol bombs and the other CS gas.

Rioting on the borderlines between the Catholic and Protestant areas of West and North Belfast followed, and took a far more serious form. In Belfast, Catholic streets were attacked by Protestant mobs, sometimes including RUC men with armoured vehicles and Specials. Several people were killed, and hundreds of Catholics driven from their homes, which were then burnt down.

The events of August 1969 are usually, and rightly, taken as the starting date of the present "troubles". Their origins, as has been seen, have to be traced back a long way; but the crisis in Northern affairs came with the August riots. This crisis brought the despatch of British troops to Derry and Belfast; it brought about (though not at once) the end of the Stormont government and parliament; it created a new and far more formidable IRA. Of that IRA we shall hear much more, but first it is necessary to look at the British response.

Chapter Five

The appearance of British soldiers in the streets of Derry and Belfast had an immediate calming effect. Initially most Catholics in the Bogside and West Belfast were greatly relieved at the arrival of a protective force, apparently impartial and certainly far stronger than the Stormont security forces whom they regarded as their enemies. Women carried cups of tea and platefuls of cake to the puzzled soldiers.

Their view — widely shared in the Republic at the time — of the British as deliverers was reinforced by the arrival in the Bogside, promising all the reforms so long delayed, of the responsible British minister, the Home Secretary, James Callaghan. Nor did the British fail to deliver on their promises. Chichester-Clark was summoned to London and made to sign the "Downing Street declaration", which committed him and his government to implementing the reforms. The police were disarmed and the Specials disbanded, to be replaced by the Ulster Defence Regiment, a unit of the British Army. To encourage good relations with the Republic, and to counteract the influence of the Home Office and the Stormont civil service, a senior official of the Foreign Office was posted to Belfast. The Foreign Office had no concern with the internal affairs of Northern Ireland, but was deeply concerned with the greatest issue, then and since, of British foreign policy: Europe. It was also greatly concerned with opinion in the Republic, in Western Europe and more widely afield, especially in the United States.

But the British intervention was, in important respects, flawed; and the manner in which it took place gave rise to its own quota of myths and misunderstandings.

The chief myth — which Callaghan's flair for public relations helped to foster, and which Wilson himself, with his frequently professed fondness for Irish Catholics, probably at least half-believed — was that the troops were sent in "to protect the Catholics". They were not. They were sent in, as is usual in such circumstances, in aid of the civil power. Chichester-Clark had in fact, on the advice of the RUC, sought their despatch two weeks earlier. And the civil power was still, nominally at least, Stormont. The "Protestant parliament" still sat in its gleaming building on the hill outside Belfast, while the Unionists still argued about reform and the troops, more and more warily as time went by, patrolled the mean streets.

It was far from obvious to the mass of Belfast Catholics that Stormont had become, in almost a literal sense, a whited sepulchre — that when Chichester-Clark asked for troops, he was admitting something incomparably more serious than any failure to achieve equality or justice: he was admitting that he and his local forces could not control the tiny territory and population entrusted to his government. He was admitting that half a century of Unionist hegemony had come to nothing.

To commit troops in Northern Ireland, where the civil power was a subordinate government, was a very different matter from committing troops on any part of the island of Britain, where the civil power was the British government itself. It challenged — undermined — the whole constitutional settlement under which Britain ruled the North at arm's length, and Stormont retained responsibility for internal law and order.

Wilson knew, as Chichester-Clark clearly did not, that, paradoxically, this new and closer British involvement in the North would weaken, not strengthen, the Union and force a constitutional review — than which, as Machiavelli pointed out in one of the most famous passages in *The Prince*, there is nothing more difficult or dangerous. That is why Wilson and Callaghan hesitated when they received the first request for troops from Chichester-Clark. But having sent in the troops, why did they not go the rest of the way and impose direct rule on Northern Ireland?

Later Wilson was blamed by many people — most notably and publicly by O'Neill — for not immediately, in that ominous August week, recalling parliament and rushing through a bill to suspend Stormont, as Heath was obliged to do two and a half years later. He did, as is known, contemplate such a move then and on future occasions. It is hardly fair to accuse him, as some have done, of cowardice or taking easy options. He knew that once the troops had gone in there were no easy options; indeed, to allow a local administration to carry on in any form was to run the risk that Britain would be blamed for its errors, as would in fact happen soon enough.

He had several reasons for shrinking from the ultimate step. One of the most important was fear of the Protestant reaction — a factor which in different forms still governs a great deal of British thinking. In August 1969 there was in Whitehall a grave lack of detailed knowledge of the psychology, arms and organisation of the Protestant militants, coupled with a fear that the local security forces might actually resist the British in arms if their government and parliament were abolished.

Wilson disliked the idea of having to recall parliament to bring in a suspension bill. Just a year earlier he had recalled the House of Commons from the summer recess to discuss, fatuously, the Soviet invasion of Czechoslovakia — an event about which nobody in Britain could do anything beyond making outraged noises. The move was mistimed because Britain at the time happened to be deeply involved in the Nigerian civil war, one of the great moral and emotional issues of the day. Many Labour as well as Conservative backbenchers were furious because they had been deceived about the extent and nature of British intervention in that conflict. They took advantage of the recall to force a debate on the question, a debate which greatly embarrassed the government.

In 1969, on the Irish question, Wilson had little to fear from parliamentary opinion. Although some anti-Irish and anti-Catholic feeling does exist in the British Labour Party, most Labour backbenchers historically and emotionally had little love for the Unionists or their regime; their sympathies lay with the harassed Catholics whose grievances filled many pages of the newspapers and many hours of television time. But he had to tread cautiously with the Conservatives.

Bipartisanship on "national" issues is almost a fetish with British governments and parliaments, and actions like the abolition of Stormont are rarely if ever undertaken without consultation between the government and opposition. An exceptionally close form of bipartisanship on Northern Ireland lasted for at least a decade after 1969. At the very beginning of the crisis, the Labour government consulted the Tory opposition on the despatch of troops and on the reform programme; when a Tory government abolished Stormont two and a half years later, they consulted their Labour opposite numbers at every step. Bipartisanship often involved not merely information, but the giving and taking of advice.

In the crisis of 1969 the Tory front bench fully supported the government. They might have accepted even more drastic measures, measures like those they themselves had to introduce later. But it is more than probable that if Stormont had been suspended in 1969, dissent — nothing insurmountable, but nevertheless uncomfortably open and inconvenient — would have arisen among their backbenchers.

Historical and personal links between the Tories and Unionists still had some force. Traditionally, as we have seen, these links were between the hereditary ruling classes in Britain and the North. Great magnates as well as backwoodsmen, some of the latter sunk as deep in reaction as the Jacobite but anti-Roman Catholic ("high and dry church") squires found in the pages of Fielding or Trollope, had conspired with the Unionists against Home Rule.

By 1969 the House of Lords had long been emasculated,

and the country squires in the House of Commons no longer counted for very much. Those members of the aristocracy who engage in active politics — they are still numerous, though under the Thatcher government their influence has been much reduced — tend to be rich, clever, rather cynical men of the world, practitioners of "the art of the possible", both moderate and unsentimental.

But there were still a good few of the archaic type around, who did not share the knowledge of the world or capacity for compromise of the richer, harder-headed members of the "old gang"; and in the decade that followed they found themselves large numbers of new allies on the Tory back benches, and eventually on the front bench. These were men — and at least one formidable woman — of a different stamp and different social origins, with their roots in the middle and lower middle classes. They shared the prejudices, the tendency to jingoism and reaction, once so much the prerogative of the squires. Though the Tory extreme right were then less numerous and noisy than they later became, they were sufficiently a threat for neither Wilson nor Heath to wish to disturb them too greatly.

Wilson had another reason for delay, even for complacency. He thought he had time on his side — at least in terms of British domestic politics. He planned to hold a general election in the early summer of 1970. He had absolutely no doubt that he would win. By that time he would have a draft bill ready for the imposition of direct rule on Northern Ireland. He expected to have plenty of time to implement any policies that would follow that move, for he intended to remain Prime Minister longer than Gladstone.

Chapter Six

When the Belfast Catholics were attacked, the IRA in the Falls Road area possessed six guns. Some thought and still think the number much higher; plenty of people suppose, quite wrongly, that the IRA receive quantities of weapons and money from the Soviet Union, and plot red revolution in Ireland in alliance with groups of terrorists and anarchists all over the world. A markedly different computation was given to me by the highest possible source at Stormont. He put the number of guns at three — three, that is to say, that could be fired with any degree of safety to the firer or any hope of hitting a target. But six is a nice round figure, which has become part of the popular mythology. Six let it be.

Not everybody can understand *haute politique,* but almost everybody can count up to six. Anyone can see that with six guns one cannot defend scores of thousands of people, including old men, women and children, who are under attack from an enemy numerically much stronger and in possession of machine guns, armoured cars and the like.

Those six guns were one of the things that created the Provisional IRA. A great many other factors helped to bring them into being, and to swell their power and support to such an extent that they would become at last a real threat to democracy, stability and civilised life itself throughout all of Ireland; but none was so powerful as the predicament of the Northern Catholics in 1969, which gave them the opportunity to present themselves as their defenders and champions.

The Provos' most enduring roots lie in that trauma, that defencelessness. What, after all, were people to do when they came under armed attack and could not turn to the forces of law and order — when, indeed, elements of those very forces were among the attackers? They could put their trust in the new forces of law and order, the British Army; but history suggested that any such trust could not last very long, subsequent events would convince them that the army also were their enemies, and in any case, troops are notoriously ineffective and inadequate in providing protection in civil disturbances. (Wilson and Callaghan understood this very well, and neither their government nor that of Heath which succeeded it could bring itself to believe that the troops would remain, not for years but for decades). They could seek outside intervention, which meant United Nations or Irish troops, or both. But the objection to the use of British troops to do work more properly the province of the police applied with at least equal force to the use of UN or Irish troops; and in the case of the first option, the British were certain to claim, as they did, that Northern Ireland was an internal United Kingdom matter, and to veto UN intervention. As to an intervention by Irish troops, many Northern Catholics hoped for and expected it, many Protestants feared it, and some members of the Dublin government sought it; but to move troops into the North was not only out of the question politically, but militarily it would have been a hopeless exercise. At the time the army was exceedingly small and weak, having been neglected for many years by penny-pinching governments. Had units crossed the border, they could at most have held down only a negligible amount of territory.

So a great many Catholics, in Belfast and elsewhere, convinced themselves that their only choices were flight or self-defence. Quite a number took the first option. Some hundreds of refugees, mostly women and children, fled south but soon went home again when things appeared a little quieter. Not hundreds but thousands supported the second option. They sympathised with the frantic search, into which the IRA now entered, to obtain arms from any source; they encouraged even more strongly the formation of "citizens' defence committees", which oversaw the erection of barricades and the organisation of vigilante groups to patrol Catholic areas and guard against assault from outside. These activities, in Belfast and Derry, were the genesis of the "no-go areas" which would soon become notorious as centres of Provo recruitment, organisation and arms concealment. But at this time the Provos did not yet exist, and the defence committees were for the most part organised by prominent and respected citizens, and frequently manned by former members of the British armed forces.

It is important to remember — what is often forgotten, even in the Republic, at this distance in time — that the Catholics were seen, in Britain and abroad as well as in Ireland, as the innocent victims of a persecution which, when they protested, escalated into genocidal onslaughts. It is even more important to remember that that view was not too far from the truth.

The attacks on the Catholics naturally inflamed opinion in the Republic. Solid citizens loaded the boots of their cars with guns and drove North. Southern politicians and businessmen appeared in the streets of Derry, handing large-denomination banknotes to revolutionary leaders, one of whom later described to me gleefully his astonishment as he felt the money pressed into his hand. Others invited noted Northerners of a militant hue to their comfortable Dublin houses, where they discussed earnestly how best to organise armed resistance. (Many people have a knack of forgetting awkward incidents in their past, so it is worth recalling that members of the Fine Gael and Labour parties, as well as of Fianna Fáil, backed militancy those days with words and occasionally with deeds. A few of them later joined the ranks of those loud in denouncing the Provos, in supporting repressive legislation and in libelling as crypto-Provos those who resisted the dilution of civil liberties). In border areas of the Republic timid and naive young men knocked at the doors of people who possessed or were believed to possess firearms, asking for "a lend of a gun". In later years the knocks would become louder, the mild requests replaced by threats and force, but at this time they received sympathy, if rarely co-operation.

Crisis cabinet meetings at Stormont were followed by crisis cabinet meetings in Dublin, some of them going on for days on end. The Taoiseach, Jack Lynch, declared that the Irish government could not stand by — the phrase has gone into history and folklore as "stand idly by" — but what, in all conscience and all practicality, was the alternative?

A large body of opinion in his Fianna Fáil Party, and one or two members of his cabinet, wanted to send in the army. Since at the time no more than a couple of thousand properly armed, equipped, trained and led men could have been mustered, they could obviously have achieved very little. They might have managed to occupy the Catholic part of Derry, on the left bank of the Foyle; they almost certainly could not have reached Belfast, and even if they had done so, they could not have given much help to the beleaguered Catholics there. The argument in favour of military intervention, so far as it had validity, was not really a military one at all, but a call for an "international-isation" of the question, forcing some kind of UN intervention. Others argued for the despatch of arms and support for the citizens' defence committees; this was the genesis of the arms crisis of the following year.

Lynch, of course, had not the smallest intention of invading the North. He contented himself with sending some army units to the border, and setting up field hospitals. Apparently with the consent of one minister, a small number of young men from the North were allowed to receive training in arms at an army camp in the Republic. Unionists, who seemed to have an exaggerated idea of the strength of the Irish Army, chose to interpret the despatch of troops to the border as a threat.

Lynch tried whatever diplomatic initiatives he could see open to him. He sent his Foreign Minister, Dr P.J. Hillery (afterwards an EEC Commissioner, later President of Ireland) to the United Nations, where he made a speech in which he blamed the recent disturbances on the partition of the country — accurately enough, at two or three removes. But like the poor young men knocking on the doors, he received sympathy instead of help. Lynch also mounted an "information" campaign through Irish embassies in Europe and farther afield, and employed an international public relations agency to promote the Irish government's case, with derisory results.

These moves did little to placate the more militant elements in the government and Fianna Fáil Party. More than one minister held informal talks with members of the IRA and Sinn Féin in Dublin, and one claimed afterwards that he had helped to provoke the split in the IRA which followed a few months later, and led to the formation of the Provisionals. The following year two ministers, Michael Moran and Kevin Boland, resigned from the government, the latter claiming that ministers were being spied upon by the Special Branch of the police. Two others, Charles Haughey and Neil Blaney, were arrested on charges of smuggling arms. A district court in Dublin found that Blaney had no case to answer and discharged him; Haughey and three other persons were sent for trial to a higher court but were all acquitted by a jury.

Haughey and Blaney were dismissed from the government. Blaney afterwards had the party whip removed from him when he refused to vote confidence in another minister, James Gibbons, who had given evidence against Haughey in the arms trial; he continued to sit as an "independent" Fianna Fáil deputy. Haughey clung on in the party, in the face of many humiliations inflicted on him by Lynch — including being forced to vote confidence in Gibbons — and eventually became Taoiseach himself.

These events lay some distance in the future, but they illustrate the atmosphere of the time and the background against which the IRA and Sinn Féin split, as they did at the turn of the year.

That split was carefully prepared by those who became the Provisionals, and they made no bones about the grounds on which they engineered it. Curiously enough, the "defenders of Catholics" argument, although their trump card and the basis of their future support, was by no means the one that loomed largest in the minds of their leaders. There were two reasons for the split which they considered far more important, and on which their attitude must be understood in order to obtain an insight into Provo psychology — and Provo power.

First, the Provos, like the various manifestations of the post-1923 IRA which preceded them, consider all partitionist institutions illegitimate. They do not accept the Republic's constitution, government, parliament or courts, any more than they accept the legitimacy of any Northern Ireland institution.

Their opponents in the movement, who at this time began to be known as the "Officials" or more colloquially as the "Stickies", were prepared to accept both. (Consideration of future developments in that quarter, through a bewilderment of changes of name, will appear in its proper place. To avoid over-use of the slang term "Stickies", it may be necessary sometimes to refer to the "Official" IRA or "Official" Sinn Féin, misleading because the word "official" may wrongly suggest some kind of government sanction. A similar difficulty arises with the "Official" Unionists, commonly used to refer to the mainstream Unionist Party as distinct from other Unionist and Loyalist groups; their proper name is the Ulster Unionist Party).

A second cause of the split was the vehement objection of those who became the founders of the Provisionals in 1969-70 to the Marxism of the Stickies. To understand this attitude is important, in view of the miasma of misconception which surrounds Provo politics. They are constantly taken for communists of one sort or another, in alliance with like-minded groups all over the world. This notion is completely false, except in so far as they do have some tenuous connection with revolutionary groups abroad and are supported in Ireland by some small and un-important Trotskyist groups, who are interested in revolution, or rather in chaos, for its own sake. They have from time to time published policy documents which speak of "democratic socialism", but they have never defined that phrase and it has no real meaning for them. On the other hand they have been frequently condemned, especially in Ireland, as fascists; but this accusation is equally inaccurate. Certainly some of their activities remind one of those of fascists, and a Provo regime, if one can conceive of such a thing North or South, would be completely anti-democratic; but where the danger of fascism arises it comes not directly from themselves, but from the possibility that the response to their activities, and to the concurrent social and economic crisis, could take authoritarian forms.

No: the reality of the politics of the Provos is that they have no politics — that they are, indeed, anti-political. They believe that the armed struggle is everything, and that anything resembling a normal political process must be delayed until Ireland has been united by force of arms. This absurd idea, like so much else in their philosophy, runs directly counter to the great strands of true Irish republicanism and nationalism, which were closely tied to the main progressive movements of their times. But it has, like many powerful simplistic ideas, a hideous force of its own, a force which has seduced many young men and women — often idealistic, intelligent and, in the contro-versial but accurate words of Bishop Cahal Daly, "even noble" — and has wasted many valuable lives. It is all the more powerful because it is closely linked with a kind of masochism.

There is an old, terrible but seductive Irish tradition that what matters is not success, but carrying on the torch. "All their wars were merry," G.K. Chesterton wrote of us, "and all their songs were sad." We are often accused of glorifying violence; our real sin is glorifying violent failure. This attitude is well illustrated in Ernie O'Malley's *On Another Man's Wound*, one of the best books to come out of the

War of Independence. O'Malley, tough, highly educated and élitist, was a kind of inspector-general of the IRA. Like Michael Collins, he was interested in success, and to a very considerable extent they and their colleagues did succeed. It infuriated him when aged rebels told him that "the lads" of 1918-21 did not equal those of 1867, or 1848, or 1798, or the date of whatever abortive revolt one cared to mention. The old men thought success unimportant: what mattered was simply that the struggle should be renewed from generation to generation.

This tradition greatly influences the Provos, and it is no coincidence that their support tends to run in families. It militates enormously against their chances of becoming a serious political force. It helped to bring about the split between them and the Officials; and if the move recently seen among their ranks towards a form of participation in constitutional politics gains momentum, it could produce a further split in their own organisation. As the seventies wore destructively on, leadership moved inexorably from the old, often Southerners, to the young, almost all Northerners and almost without exception much better educated, more capable in both organisational and military matters, and incomparably more politically conscious.

By the end of the seventies, the Provos, particularly in Belfast, had produced, on the military side, a distinct "officer class", and on the political side a leadership, exemplified by Gerry Adams and Danny Morrison, with decided, somewhat left-wing, political views and a willingness at least to contest elections. It was one of the latter group who asked during a Provisional Sinn Féin ard-fheis (annual conference) if anyone present would object if they took power with a ballot paper in one hand and an Armalite rifle in the other. But in the view of the old guard, which carried much more weight, the Armalite mattered far more than the ballot box, which they saw as something for use only as propaganda and as an adjunct to the terrorist campaign.

To cover its political nakedness, Provisional Sinn Féin, soon after its foundation, produced an idiotic policy document called "Eire Nua" (New Ireland) which proposed, *inter alia,* that Ireland should become a federal state with four provincial parliaments, including one for a nine-county Ulster which would have within its borders more or less equal numbers of Catholics and Protestants. The document contained a good many other proposals of a like kind, founded on geographical and economic false conceptions and ideas of devolutionism run riot. It was never taken very seriously, and in 1981 it was at last effectively abandoned as party policy, leaving in its place little but a general commitment to the proposition of British withdrawal from Ireland — and, more sinister, to a general anti-Protestant stance.

It is easy to mock the Provos' political illiteracy, but the simplicity of their approach contains its own power and danger. Recruitment is made easier, and motivation higher, when appreciation of complex historical realities is not required, and when every failure can be plausibly interpreted as yet another success. While the memory of past injustice and knowledge of present repression — and repression is reality, not myth — press on the nerve, at the same time the pronouncements of the "political" leadership (often merely ignorant and self-righteous) can appear lofty and inspiring: Provo publications, in plainer language, tend to extol the glories of the resistance. There is, moreover, the endless spur to emulate their comrades, and there is, from their viewpoint, much to emulate. The Provos stand rightly condemned for a multitude of crimes, but the accusation of cowardice frequently levelled against them is absurd. Many of them are, on the contrary, extremely brave. They run terrible risks, suffer numerous casualties in dead and injured, and are even prepared to die, in a grisly fashion, on hunger strike in a mistaken cause.

The hunger strikes of 1980 and 1981 illustrated at once their courage and their political naivety. It was not by accident that the Provos in the Republic exploited them so well for propaganda, or that the Belfast leadership found itself taking contradictory attitudes.

Because the Provos are not the only people who misunderstand history and political ethics, it was easy to represent the hunger strikers as having suffered non-violently in the face of persecution. Their confusion, ignorance and bad faith are shown by the fact that, while the hunger strikes went on, the organisation continued a campaign of murders of Protestants, thus weakening their moral position.

The hunger strikers drew much of their inspiration from the example of Terence MacSwiney, who died in Brixton Prison, London, after a lengthy hunger strike during the War of Independence. MacSwiney was the author of a celebrated dictum of the Irish struggle: that victory would go, not to those who could inflict the most, but to those who could endure the most. The Provos, and their supporters, missed the point of the association of "endurance" with non-violence.

But simple ideas can have political force too, even when they are those of the politically illiterate. From the beginning of the crisis in August 1969 the Provos grasped the simple fact that Stormont was dead — unlike the more sophisticated but misguided Stickies, who foolishly called for its maintenance, restoration and "democratisation". When it fell, the Provos claimed a victory. Again, they could see from their early days that their greatest enemy was not the Unionists or the British Army, but the Social Democratic and Labour Party (of whom more later), whose foundation followed closely on that of the Provos themselves, and who for the ensuing decade retained a grip on the votes and minds of the Catholic population. Much later, when the SDLP and other potential candidates were tricked and bullied out of contesting the two by-elections in the Fermanagh-South Tyrone constituency in 1981, the Provos grasped another simple idea: that they could use their successes in this constituency as a springboard to replace the SDLP as the political representatives of the Catholics. Their successes in the by-elections and in the Northern Ireland assembly (October 1982) election have proved that they have popular support, which can be translated in favourable circumstances into electoral support.

They have weakened the SDLP and caused them to lose face; and they now hope to challenge the SDLP as the political voice of Northern Catholics. But if they ever become real politicians, they will cease to be the Provisional IRA and become something quite different.

The question still remains to be answered, how have they succeeded in maintaining an organisation, in carrying out so many acts of violence, and in retaining a substantial measure of popular support in spite of the cruelty with which they wage war against civilians?

In part the answer lies in the plausibility of their "defenders of Catholics" claim. Most Northern Catholics, like most people anywhere, abhor violence; but they do not, for the most part, trust British governments or any Northern authorities, still less British and Northern security forces. The attacks on their ghettos by Protestant mobs, led by the RUC and Specials, are part of their folk memory; more recently, they have suffered severely from the activities of British soldiers, whom they regard as an occupying force. Any outsider who visits a Catholic area of Belfast will find people eager to detail for him incidents, well-documented to the point of tedium, little known in the outside world. For every act of violence committed on "their" side they can cite at least one by "the other side" (which includes, impartially, the British Army, the local security forces, and the Protestant terrorist organisations). Large numbers of people in those areas regard the Provos, while disliking them and sometimes suffering under them, as having no more and no less legitimacy than the forces of law and order.

Secondly, one must always bear in mind the depth and viciousness of Northern sectarianism, and the long history of repression of Catholics. The Catholics know very well — as the Secretary of State and the chief constable of the RUC know equally well, but helplessly — that certain Protestant spokesmen, on the surface respectable and law-abiding, are in fact guilty of urging on others to violence, and probably even of collusion in violent acts. What is the difference, they argue, between such people and the

71

Provos? And are we not in danger of a repetition of their genocidal attacks? And in such a case, who shall defend us? The Provos respond in a manner characteristically Northern and sectarian, by becoming a mirror image of their enemies and by justifying their actions in precisely the same self-righteous and hypocritical terms in which Unionists deny that they ever did anything wrong in their long and squalid tenure of power.

Thirdly, there has been the moral and practical support which the Provos have received from outside: mainly from the Republic and the United States, but also from Britain and elsewhere. The effects of the 1969-70 crisis in the Republic were enormous, but on the whole unfavourable to the Provos; however, moral and financial support from the Republic helped to create them, and it has been renewed, in varying degrees and in varying ways, from time to time ever since. The United States has been their most important source of arms and one of their most important sources of finance: at a very conservative estimate, the amount of money they have received from contributions by persons of Irish birth or descent there has exceeded ten million dollars. They have also enjoyed a small but not negligible degree of support from Irish immigrants in Britain, chiefly by way of contributions and propaganda, and in a smaller but still significant way in recruitment and in the provision of "safe houses" and escape routes when they have attacked targets in Britain.

The fourth, and perhaps most important, part of the answer is — Britain itself. British folly, British dishonesty, British sweeping under carpets, British vacillation and policy changes, British "muddling through", British mistiming, British failure to understand Irish issues and how they can affect, always for the worse, the sister island.

If the British had been just a little more clever, those six guns could not have wreaked nearly so much destruction.

Chapter Seven

At the end of the nineteenth and the beginning of the twentieth century British politics was preoccupied, often to the exclusion of almost all other considerations, with the Irish question. Ireland became known as a "graveyard" of British political reputations. Intense weariness with Ireland was one of the reasons why the Northern question was neglected for so long; and in 1969-70 nobody wanted Ireland to become again the dominant issue in British politics. Thus, even after the intervention of August 1969, the British still tried to rule the North at arm's length.

The trouble was that they were obliged to do this through the medium of the Chichester-Clark government at Stormont, which their own actions had fatally undermined, and which came increasingly under two kinds of internal pressure. One was from the intransigent Unionists: Chichester-Clark had Brian Faulkner breathing down his neck within the party, and Paisley attacking him from without. The second was a new and much more formidable opposition, the Social Democratic and Labour Party (SDLP), formed from elements of the Civil Rights movement, the constitutional left wing in Belfast, and younger and more radical elements of the old, ineffectual Nationalist Party.

The SDLP would tire soon enough of the role of a constitutional opposition and demand a new constitution with a guaranteed share in power for themselves. But Chichester-Clark at this time was little concerned with any opposition other than that from within his own party. Under unceasing Westminster pressure, he had to go ahead with the reform programme; under the pressure of his own right wing, he had to proceed as slowly as possible; to save face, he and his ministers had to pretend that the programme was their own, not — as everybody knew — something imposed from outside. His position was, in short, untenable.

He also suffered from the fact that, although Britain had taken over from him responsibility for security, he continued to be blamed by his Unionist enemies for the deterioration in law and order. In the early months of the crisis, before the Provos succeeded in building up their arms and popular strength, this largely took the form of sectarian rioting, with the British Army and the RUC in the middle. These riots were sometimes fomented by a variety of Loyalist (Protestant) militant organisations, some of which had existed before the crisis, some brought into being by it. The oldest was the Ulster Volunteer Force (UVF) which, in addition to murdering Catholics in 1966, had carried out a number of acts of sabotage in early 1969, with the object of helping to bring down O'Neill; of the new ones, three in particular deserve mention.

One of the smallest, but also one of the most violent, the Red Hand Commando, specialised in sectarian assassinations. The strangest was called Tara: its membership was largely homosexual, and it was engaged in some altogether amazing activities, which would not become public knowledge for another decade; its policies included the proscription of the Roman Catholic Church, and the teaching of fundamentalist Protestant doctrine to all children. By far the most important militant organisation was the Ulster Defence Association (UDA), which at one time claimed a membership of 50,000. This figure was of course grossly inflated. Its highest nominal membership at any one time was 26,000, and the number of activists perhaps one-fifth of that figure; but that still made it by far the biggest of the Protestant paramilitaries. It had strong contacts with militant Protestant workers in industry — a matter of some importance a few years later — and it was never short of manpower when it wanted to throw up barricades and man roadblocks. As time went by, it engaged in a variety of somewhat contradictory activities. It ran clubs and protection rackets in Belfast (much as the Provos would soon do) and it was suspected, but never proved, that assassinations and attempted assassinations of some of its leading figures had some connection with the control of funds. It threw up a political offshoot, the Ulster Loyalist Democratic Party (ULDP), which proposed that Northern Ireland should become an independent state; the ULDP has fared badly at the polls. So far as the mass of Catholics were concerned, however, by far its most significant and sinister manifestation was another offshoot, the Ulster Freedom Fighters, which specialised, like the UVF and the Red Hand, in sectarian assassinations.

Unionists for the most part ignored or excused — and in some cases connived at — militancy on the Protestant side, while they loudly denounced the existence of "no go" Catholic areas. In this last respect they were right (or would have been right had they opposed Protestant "no go" areas too) for the barricades made it easier for the gangs on both sides to establish protection rackets, to patrol streets and to present themselves as the effective rulers of their districts and their defenders against outside attack. Clearly rapid and effective action was needed, and since the British hoped not to have to rely for too long on the army, this meant reform of the local security forces to make them at once more competent and more acceptable to Catholics.

Reform of the police, under a new English commissioner, Sir Arthur Young, began at once — and it began with two mistakes, of different orders of magnitude.

The first demonstrated admirably the way the comic mingles with the tragic in Northern Ireland. The RUC had always worn uniforms of a shade of bottle green so dark as almost to be indistinguishable from black. Now, with English *sancta simplicitas,* it was decreed that they should wear the blue uniform of the friendly English bobby. With

English simplicity went English insensitivity: the RUC were offered *second-hand* uniforms, discarded by the London metropolitan police. They revolted, and to this day they wear green uniforms — uniforms, just to rub in the point, of a much lighter shade of green than previously.

The second false move was disarming the police. When the scale of violence, which remained low throughout most of 1970, began to grow again, the authorities were obliged to rearm them. (Armed police have since become a more common feature in Britain and the Republic also).

Over the next decade, the RUC made considerable progress in both competence and acceptability, though in the absence of a satisfactory political settlement they have never achieved unchallenged legitimacy. The same could not be said of the Ulster Defence Regiment, which was constituted as a regiment of the British Army to replace the Specials; they were locally recruited and contained both full-time and part-time members. This was planned as a non-sectarian force, with a high proportion of Catholic officers and other ranks, and initially some nationalist politicians urged Catholics to join. But few Catholics responded, and those who did join mostly left very soon — partly because they found themselves unwelcome, mainly because of fierce intimidation, including the abduction and murder of one of the few Catholic officers. Soon the UDR had become, in the minds of most Catholics, indistinguishable from the Specials. Indeed, a good many of its members were former Specials; and over the years not a few, along with other former Specials, became involved in the activities of Protestant terrorist organisations. Further to swell the numbers of Protestants in the local security forces — by 1982 probably not less than 25,000 — large numbers also joined the RUC Reserve, which like the UDR admits full-time as well as part-time members.

Misconduct by members of local forces, especially the UDR, gave colour to claims of continuing Protestant persecution of Catholics; their possession of arms was an added cause of fear; off duty, they made easy targets for the Provos and other assassins, while the general Protestant fondness for uniforms helped, to the Provos' great advantage, to confuse Catholic minds as to the distinction between civilians and security force members. But in the long term, the worst effect of the failure of the UDR, following that of the Specials, may be to prejudice the future successful formation of a non-sectarian and acceptable militia, without whose presence it is hard to envisage the withdrawal of the British Army or the policing, in the wider sense, of an agreed settlement.

But by the time of the Westminster general election of June 1970, some of these problems had not yet clearly emerged, and those that had appeared soluble. Wilson, Callaghan and the other members of the Labour Government concerned with Northern Ireland took for granted that they would have another four or five years in office, plenty of time to find answers to the political and security questions alike.

The election result — a solid victory for Edward Heath and the Conservative Party — shocked them, and almost everybody else. It disturbed opinion in Dublin, and among Northern Catholics. It pleased the Unionists, with their long-standing links with the Tories; and it also pleased the more extreme Loyalists, for Ian Paisley was returned as MP for North Antrim.

In fact, the Tories came into office pledged to carry on Labour policy in Northern Ireland, which meant pressing ahead with the reform programme and repressing violence from both Catholics and Protestants; their assurances that there would be no change of policy were sincerely meant. But within a month of their assumption of office, an event occurred which seemed to bear out the worst fears of the Catholics. It was the first of three major disasters involving the British Army.

In July 1970 the British Army imposed a three-day weekend curfew on the Lower Falls area of Belfast, where the Official IRA had its greatest strength. Passage in and out of the area was held up, while soldiers searched, mostly unsuccessfully, for arms. Supplies of bread, milk and other goods were cut off. Thousands of people were confined to their homes, shot at if they ventured out; three were killed. Hundreds of people, not all Catholics, who were innocently making their way through the streets on the first night of the curfew, were arrested and detained for short periods. And Unionist ministers from Stormont rode triumphantly on British Army vehicles through the Falls, as through a conquered territory.

To many in the Republic, and most Northern Catholics, it appeared that the Tories were showing themselves in their true, Orange colours. And as to the Army, the "defenders of Catholics" argument would never have the same plausibility again. It seemed that the sinister old alliance of British government, British Army and Unionists had been revived; and this perception was not far from the truth. Although the Downing Street Declaration of the previous year had removed control of security from the Stormont Government, there existed at Stormont a joint security committee comprising representatives of all these three; and it looked as though, under the new regime, the Army and the Unionists were to have a free rein.

Heath increased the sense of alienation in the Republic and among the Catholics by brusquely rejecting protests about the Army's disruptive action. He could not yet see that those most likely to exploit for their own ends his political inaction would be the militant and ruthless groups on the Catholic side.

The Provisional IRA were still very weak. Like their Protestant counterparts, they had begun to steal or smuggle in explosives and bomb places of public resort; they were bringing in arms, and building up funds by a variety of illicit means in both parts of Ireland, as well as starting fund-raising in America. But they were still feeble in all three areas of organisation, supply and public support — so feeble that it was another six months, more than a year after their formation, before they first succeeded in killing a British soldier. They needed the spur of more overt acts of repression like this — and the spur would be applied again.

On the other side of the equation, the Army action did

nothing to help Chichester-Clark. His right wing, as well as disliking the reforms, wanted the police rearmed, the Specials brought back, and an all-out return of security powers to Stormont. The disintegration of the Unionist Party, which had begun under O'Neill, continued; there were outright splits, like the foundation of the Vanguard movement under William Craig (who inspected substantial parades, albeit of unarmed men) and the Premier was the victim of internal cabinet and parliamentary party splits and cabals like those which had plagued O'Neill.

As the autumn of 1970 wore into winter, meetings of the Stormont cabinet grew longer, Chichester-Clark's visits to London more frequent — and British impatience more pronounced. Ministers wondered whether it was necessary to keep Chichester-Clark in office, or take a chance on Brian Faulkner, still eagerly awaiting his chance. Chichester-Clark did not help his case by an extraordinary proposal now put forward, either by himself or by someone on his behalf. This was that full control of all the security forces should return to Stormont. Coming from a harmless country squire it was unexpected, and from a former British officer astonishing: for no British government could hand over control of its own armed forces to a subordinate authority. After the request was denied, Chichester-Clark quietly resigned, and Faulkner, inevitably, succeeded him.

Westminster took the departure of Chichester-Clark and Faulkner's accession to power with great fortitude — or complacency. As to the first, it was as if a not very close relation, affectionately enough regarded, had passed to a better sphere after a lingering illness; as to the second, there were rumblings about him in the Labour Party, descriptions of him ranging from "untrustworthy" to "bigoted"; but the government, far removed from the feverish quarrels of the Unionist Party, recalled his undeniable competence as Minister of Commerce, and friends of Heath put it about that he greatly impressed the Prime Minister.

In reality, those in a position to know the truth of

Faulkner's position realised that he had taken office under the worst of auspices. Whatever he himself may have thought, he had no real hope of placating the extremists inside and outside the Unionist Party: Paisley, indeed, proclaimed that he and his supporters had brought down O'Neill, had brought down Chichester-Clark, "and now we're going for the hat-trick". Nor were Catholics disposed to trust him: he had a record of taking part in Orange marches through Catholic areas, and opening Orange halls in Catholic towns. Rumours abounded that Heath had given him one year to prove himself or be removed in favour of direct rule, and these, in spite of their inherent improbability, were widely believed.

A better estimate of Faulkner's tenacity and resilience came from Gerald Barry, a reporter for Radio Telefís Éireann, who offered a colleague, Kevin Healy, a small bet that in three years from the date of his accession to power — March 1971 — Faulkner would hold the job of Prime Minister of Northern Ireland, or the equivalent position. Barry won his bet, but at the time it seemed clear that Faulkner faced several enormous and irreconcilable tasks: to unite his party, promote material prosperity, placate the Catholics and suppress the Provos. Not many would have taken on such a job at all, but Faulkner had, besides intense ambition, a burning belief in himself and his capacities — a belief, besides, reinforced by class and personal resentment. He was a Presbyterian and — although very rich, with a handsome country estate of his own — of middle-class origins. He despised what he regarded as an effete and fumbling squirearchy, which had kept him too long out of the top job.

In one respect at least, he was entitled to believe that he could count on all the support he needed from the British. The latter, although they continued to talk rhetorically about suppressing "violence from all sides" and meting out even-handed justice, had decided that they could not fight a war on two fronts, and that they must concentrate their fire on the Provos.

About this time selected journalists, including myself,

were invited to the Defence Ministry in Whitehall and briefed by the Defence Secretary, Lord Carrington. He spoke to us in Delphic terms. The briefing, as is usual in Whitehall and at Westminster, was "non-attributable", that is to say, the content of his utterances could be reported but not ascribed to him. But on this occasion Carrington, one of the smartest and ablest of British ministers, said nothing that could be built into a coherent newspaper story. We walked away from the Ministry shaking our heads and asking one another, "what was he trying to tell us?"

What he was trying to convey would emerge soon enough out of all the smokescreens about impartiality. The military advice was that the Army could not, and would not, try to fight the Provisional IRA and the Loyalists at the same time: they must suppress the Provos by any means available, and hope that the Loyalists, encouraged by the appearance of stern action, would remain quiet.

There were two flaws in this British political and military thinking. In the first place the IRA could not be defeated by military means alone; secondly, there was only one way in which a one-sided attitude by British security forces would be interpreted in Ireland: namely that, as in the past (and as would happen in the near future), British governments and armies would shrink from confronting Loyalist violence or threats of violence, that in the "crunch" they would always take the Unionist side.

It was one of those legendary long hot summers, meteorologically and politically. Bombings and attacks on the security forces continued. The Unionist splits failed to heal. Calls by the Unionists and their allies on the Conservative right wing for various extreme measures increased: they demanded martial law, curfews, the sealing off of the border between Northern Ireland and the Republic, a task literally impossible unless one were to undertake the most ruthless — and expensive — measures on the East German model. The border meanders for nearly three hundred miles from Lough Foyle in the north-west to Carlingford Lough in the east; it ambles along the beds of streams, leaps bridges, divides village streets and in some cases even houses; in many places it twists and turns so bewilderingly that, since it is mainly unmarked, it is impossible to tell whether one is in, for example, County Fermanagh in the North or County Monaghan in the Republic. It has since been "sealed" to the extent that most crossing roads have been cratered and blocked with armour by the British Army, leaving traffic to flow on only a handful of "approved" roads; but armed men and explosives still cross it with some ease.

But in 1971 the demand most often heard was for the introduction of internment. It had helped in putting down the last IRA campaign, when IRA men, North and South, were locked up without being charged or tried. Faulkner firmly believed in it as a tactic. But what did the Army advise? And where did Heath stand? One thing at least was fairly clear. If Faulkner had asked permission to introduce internment, and Heath had agreed, it would not take place before the parliamentary recess. It would not be made a subject of embarrassing debate.

In the first week of August the House of Commons adjourned. Very early on the morning of Monday, 9 August, internment began. Before dawn all over Northern Ireland soldiers were kicking in doors and taking away the first batches of hundreds of men to be detained in various locations, the names of which would become household words wherever English is spoken: the Maidstone hulk, anchored in Belfast docks, Girdwood Barracks, Holywood Barracks, Magilligan Camp. And Long Kesh.

Almost at once it became obvious that the operation had been both misconceived and bungled. Hundreds of Catholics were arrested, along with three innocent Protestants who had associations with the Civil Rights movement. *Not one* organiser or member of the Loyalist gangs was detained, and of those detained on the Catholic or Republican side, probably as many as 50 per cent were innocent. The inadequacy of the intelligence provided by the RUC was glaringly exposed. Some of those detained were former IRA men from the forties and fifties; in other cases quite simply the wrong people — fathers, sons, brothers or persons with the same name — were taken instead of those on the list. Meanwhile, the backroom boys of the Provisional and Official IRA, along with the Loyalist leaders, remained at liberty.

As if to prove the ineffectiveness of internment, violence on an unprecedented scale broke out on the streets of Belfast. Both the Provos and the Officials attacked the British Army, with young men (and some girls) in black uniforms fighting what amounted to pitched battles with the soldiers. The Provo leadership mocked the authorities by holding a press conference in one of the no-go areas. Catholics felt a particular sense of shock when a priest was killed while tending the wounded: nobody knew who fired the bullet that killed him, but the Catholics had no doubt whom to blame.

Mostly, they blamed Faulkner, and they continued to blame him in spite of his many subsequent good deeds. And regardless of who might share the blame, to a great extent they were right. In the first place, his motive could be considered base, a last desperate throw in the game to retain power. Secondly, he caused the most damaging repercussions in the Republic, in two ways: he further alienated Southern opinion, and he made the option of internment almost impossible for any Dublin government. (Lynch had in fact some time earlier threatened to introduce internment because of an alleged plot to kidnap ministers; now he condemned, not the thing in itself, but "one-sided" internment; but it had become a dirty word). Thirdly, Faulkner's manner of overseeing the operation was amazing. He claimed, untruthfully, that he personally and closely scrutinised the circumstances and background of every person proposed for detention. In fact (as highly placed eye-witnesses have informed me) an official would carry in to him a batch of detention orders, which he signed without reading them.

Nevertheless, there were other guilty persons. The Army's precise view on internment has never been made clear, and it is fairly certain that most of the military leaders as well as their political chief, Carrington, opposed the tactic; but they very quickly took advantage of it for their own horrible purposes.

Before long, newspaper reports began to appear describing the manner in which the operation had taken place, and the ill-treatment of internees. The *Irish Times* published accounts, smuggled off the Maidstone, written by a Dublin journalist, Seamus Ó Tuathail, who had been detained presumably because of his connection with an Official Sinn Féin newspaper. A Sinn Féin leader, the journalist and propagandist Des O'Hagan, was interned in Long Kesh; his reports also appeared in the *Irish Times*. It was alleged in other quarters that internees had been beaten, starved, made to run barefoot on broken glass, threatened with being pushed out of helicopters, and had had guns, which they believed to be loaded, put to their heads and the triggers pulled.

The first reports of ill-treatment appeared as early as September 1971. But much the most serious allegations and much the best documented — again in the *Irish Times*, but more thoroughly in various articles in the *Sunday Times* and later in British official reports — concerned a method of torture euphemistically known as the "Five Techniques": hooding, wall-standing, deprivation of food, deprivation of sleep, and subjection to an intolerable, mechanical "white noise". Wall-standing means being obliged to stand, legs wide apart, leaning forward with one's fingertips against a wall, for periods which can exceed forty-eight hours. The object is to produce disorientation; it can also produce lasting mental and physical ill-effects. It emerged that these techniques were quite commonly used in the armies of the North Atlantic Treaty Organisation, allegedly with a view to training certain soldiers in how to withstand them if practised by an enemy. It required no great feat of imagination to conclude that the experiments were designed for use *against* an enemy; that experimentation in the British or any other army must be limited by a desire not to hurt one's own soldiers too severely; and that the British Army now eagerly seized its chance to practise them, almost to the limit, on English-speaking Europeans.

After the official inquiries confirmed the allegations, the British Government banned the use of the "Five Techniques", at any rate within the United Kingdom. However, in December 1971, the Irish Government brought proceedings against Britain before the European Commission and Court of Human Rights. The case dragged on for six years, poisoning Anglo-Irish relations; the court eventually found Britain guilty of "inhuman and degrading treatment" but not of torture. Compensation had already been paid to the victims.

The activities of the British Army proved, then and later, a major obstacle in the way of political progress. Internment stood in the way of a variety of political initiatives which were pressed, in some cases pretty half-heartedly, in the autumn of 1971. On the other hand it is at least arguable that the new and greatly worse security situation helped to bring about more radical initiatives, once British minds had grasped the full gravity of the position.

This was certainly true of Harold Wilson, who within two months proposed first a twelve-point and then a fifteen-point plan for an Irish settlement. In both cases the plan envisaged a united Ireland with the consent of a majority in Northern Ireland; in neither case did he make it entirely clear whether the Unionists still retained a veto. The SDLP and their friends in the British Labour Party welcomed his proposals, but believed they did not go far enough.

At Stormont Faulkner offered the SDLP a share in government, not as members of an executive, but as chairmen of parliamentary committees which he maintained would dispose of significant power. A similar offer was implicit in a proposal made by the Home Secretary in Whitehall, Reginald Maudling, for a series of talks with all the Northern Ireland parties, in which everything would be "on the table".

But so far from considering either offer, the SDLP refused even to sit at Stormont while internment lasted. It is one of the minor Northern myths that they boycotted Stormont because of internment: they had in fact already withdrawn after an unrelated incident, the shooting of two young men by British soldiers in Derry.

Now, however, they demanded a complete end to internment and the release of all the detainees as a condition of dropping the boycott or entering into talks with Maudling. Their position was difficult, and they knew they were offering hostages to fortune; some of their most important members opposed the boycott, but the majority believed it politically impossible for them to take a conciliatory line at a time of such tension and alienation. They had further reasons — a mixture of policy and personal — for maintaining their stand. At the policy level, Hume believed that by abstention they were manifestly declaring the unwillingness of the minority to be governed, and thereby removing part of Faulkner's faltering legitimacy; at the personal level, they disliked and distrusted Maudling, whom they rightly regarded as a dilettante. (To this day he is remembered in Northern Ireland for his remark to an official as he thankfully settled into a seat on a plane taking him away from Belfast: "What a bloody awful country. Get me a large whiskey.").

Very secretly, John Hume and Paddy Devlin put out feelers to see if an IRA ceasefire could be arranged, in exchange for an end to internment. Meanwhile, despite the urgings of some of their close friends (including Dr Garret FitzGerald) they maintained their intransigence, believing that the end of Stormont was now in sight. And for all but the blindest, it was indeed.

In October 1971 I reported in the *Irish Times* that the British Government was considering the imposition of direct rule or, as a half-way measure, the abolition of the Stormont joint security committee and the taking into its own hands of all responsibility for security and the administration of justice in Northern Ireland.

The publication of the story caused a considerable rumpus, possibly more than it deserved, which was certainly surprising, since newspapers had been speculating along these lines for years. The attention it attracted was due partly to the fact that it was obviously "sourced" and checked, not mere speculation, and partly to the timing. It appeared at a highly sensitive time for the British, who for public consumption had to continue to proclaim their faith in Faulkner, and who, in order that Northern Ireland might be governed at all, had to do whatever they could to prop him up while considering whether and when they would have to bring him down.

It was of course officially denied. Donald Maitland, Heath's press secretary (later Sir Donald Maitland, Ambassador to the United Nations) called it "bunkum". If the denial reassured Faulkner, he cannot have been comforted by the statements of one of his greatest enemies, Ian Paisley. Paisley (who at the time was making a meal out of denouncing internment and blaming Faulkner for it) has frequently claimed to have excellent sources of information in the British Government, the RUC and other interesting quarters, and it is unwise to take his claims too lightly. This time he said his highly placed contacts had told him the direct rule story was nonsense.

He soon found out his mistake, but in a curious manner. It appears that a week or two after his premature denial, he attended a luncheon party given by the London *Times*, where he met journalists who confirmed the story. On his return to Belfast he denounced the proposal to take away the Protestant parliament as a violation of Protestant liberties.

By the end of the year almost everybody except Brian Faulkner knew that the curtain must fall on Stormont soon. But before it did, one terrible last scene of the drama was played.

On "Bloody Sunday", 30 January 1972, paratroopers fired on a crowd of Civil Rights demonstrators in Derry, killing thirteen young men. A fourteenth died later of wounds. The bullets of that cold afternoon completed the work of the six guns of 1969. They also probably did more damage to British prestige in the world since the Suez invasion in 1956.

People everywhere watching television saw on their screens, with horror or with anger, men running, bodies falling, blood flowing in the gutters. They saw a priest, Father Edward Daly (afterwards Bishop of Derry) crouching, holding up a bloodstained white handkerchief as a sign of truce, as he helped to take a wounded man out of the line of fire.

To a great many Irish people, including large numbers who feared and hated terrorism, it was like a declaration of war.

John Hume declared that after this catastrophe, "for the people of the Bogside it's a united Ireland or nothing".

Poems and songs were composed about the massacre. One, by the noted poet Thomas Kinsella, was called "Butcher's Dozen".

In the House of Commons Bernadette Devlin left her place, ran across the floor and struck Maudling, who had refused to make any expression of regret, several blows in the face.

Dr Conor Cruise O'Brien called for the withdrawal of British troops from Northern Ireland.

Lynch recalled his ambassador, Dr Donal O'Sullivan, from London, for "consultations".

The British Embassy in Dublin was destroyed by petrol bombers while the police stood by, making little or no attempt to intervene. It was almost universally believed that they had orders not to provoke the hotheads, for fear that they might turn their anger against the parliament building nearby. Grotesquely, while the Embassy burned, thousands of peaceful demonstrators watched calmly, many of them holding up umbrellas to protect themselves from the pouring rain.

Bloody Sunday did not bring down Stormont any more than the Provos did, but it accelerated its fall. Had Faulkner succeeded in bringing about any kind of stability — the sort of stability implicit in another notorious phrase of Maudling's, "an acceptable level of violence" — Heath would very likely have been willing to leave him at his post at least a little while longer. But after Bloody Sunday, it was plain in Whitehall, as everywhere else, that the earth had moved.

Faulkner and members of his cabinet were summoned to London for a series of meetings which possessed a far higher degree of gravity and tension than all the "crisis" meetings which had been commonplace since the mid-sixties. At last they were presented with an ultimatum they could not possibly accept, and which it was not intended that they should accept: they could remain in office only on the conditions of a total transfer of powers over law and order to Whitehall, negotiations to bring the SDLP into government, and new arrangements to "institutionalise" the interest of the Republic in the affairs of the North. When the expected refusal came, Stormont was prorogued and William Whitelaw, leader of the House of Commons, appointed Secretary of State for Northern Ireland with something approaching dictatorial powers.

Heath, in a state of exhaustion, grey in the face and fumbling his words, gave a briefing to journalists. He told us that Bloody Sunday had been the last straw.

Heath, of course, had other, and for him, far more important, preoccupations. But Faulkner seems to have understood neither these preoccupations nor the implications of the events in Derry. He reacted to his dismissal not just with understandable resentment, but in a foolish and intemperate way. He joined right-wing Unionist leaders in addressing a mass protest rally at Stormont. When it was proposed that a council of worthies should be set up to advise the new Secretary of State, he said angrily that he would see "who would crawl out from under their stones". His numerous enemies, from Paisley to the Provos, gloated, believing he would never rise again. In fact he would do so in time, but in March 1972, British exasperation with everything Irish — the exasperation which burst out in that reference to Nagasaki — was at its height, and it was directed, very specifically, against Faulkner.

Faulkner's relations with Heath were never repaired, a circumstance which would produce unfortunate effects for years to come. Liam Cosgrave, who would soon assume power in the Republic, had already commented that the British always betrayed their friends and comforted their enemies. This was emphatically true in Faulkner's case; it was also true among Unionists more widely, because they so deeply resented the abolition of their parliament. In later years Unionist distrust of Britain waxed and waned; but when it waned it was not accompanied by any increase of trust in the Republic or the Catholics, or in mutual understanding between the two parts of Ireland.

Afterwards the British wrote a sequel to Bloody Sunday, a most unsatisfactory sequel, which left more loose ends dangling than it tied up. An inquiry under the Lord Chief Justice, Lord Widgery, produced a report which purported to show that the paratroopers had been fired on first. No convincing evidence to this effect had been given to the tribunal, and the report was generally regarded, not only in Ireland but in Britain, as whitewash. A new phrase, "widgery pokery", was coined. There was no evidence that any of those killed had handled arms, and compensation was paid to their families.

The inquiry altogether failed to answer the question: why had the paras run riot? Paras are not raw, frightened "squaddies" apt to fire on imaginary terrorists without orders: they are tough experienced men, highly trained and disciplined. The evidence to the Widgery tribunal tended to show that they had acted on orders issued at general officer level. But — terrifyingly — it was fairly clear that such orders had been issued without the approval, indeed without the knowledge, of the Government in London. The question was not so much "what were the soldiers up to?" as "what were the generals up to?" It would be asked again, and again and again.

Chapter Eight

That magic decade, the sixties, enthralled no country more firmly than Ireland. We seemed to have all the best of it; and until the North erupted, we were spared the worst.

Student protests, the struggle by younger and livelier people for influence in the trade union movement, pickets outside the American Embassy complaining about atrocities in Vietnam: in these we echoed other countries, but a more profound effect was produced on the Irish (twenty-six county) psyche by the papacy of John XXIII and the Second Vatican Council. Bishops and archbishops came back from Rome and assured us that nothing had changed, but we knew better: in a very important respect, everything had changed. The theology might be incomprehensible, but the questions were unanswerable: Did such places exist as hell and purgatory? Did such a thing exist as mortal sin? The concepts of sin and guilt would never again, in this generation, hold the same deadly grip on the Irish Catholic mind.

The island, like the enchanted isle of *The Tempest,* was full of music, for this was the time of the great revival of Irish traditional music, which happily has continued through all our subsequent travails. But another song filled all the air, the song of individual freedom, the song of the sleeper awakened.

All of us had learned at school about warriors, poets and queens, some historical, some legendary: Oisin, Maeve, Grace O'Malley, Brian Merriman. But the Gaelic revivalists who had brought the Irish cultural tradition to the world's attention at the turn of the century had pulled over it a heavy, stifling blanket of Victorian respectability. Now the heroes were rediscovered, and more accurately reinterpreted; and a country where divorce and contraception were forbidden and a wry saying prevailed that sin consisted only in enjoyment, rediscovered at the same time the sexual freedom for which Ireland had once been notorious.

In 1963 I took my English bride to the fleadh cheoil (traditional music festival) in Mullingar, where she saw with amazement and incredulity scenes she had never thought to witness in (her own words) "holy Ireland". The same Dionysiac events moved a Northern poet, John Montague, who saw them, to write, perhaps with more optimism than foresight: "Puritan Ireland's dead and gone."

Censorship was relaxed, so that the works of great — and some inferior — Irish writers, hitherto banned, could be legally sold. Books and pamphlets, usually taking a revisionist view of Irish history, instead of the crude and confused nationalistic line previously taught in schools, poured off the presses (the objectivity of the history texts now used in Irish schools puts more imposing countries to shame). In 1966 a scheme of free secondary education and free school transport was introduced, which in time was bound to give birth to a new middle class.

In the same year, the emphasis which the commemoration of the 1916 Easter Rising gave to the role of the Marxist thinker, James Connolly, encouraged not only the left-wing republican movement, but the left wing in the Labour Party and the trade unions. And the Fine Gael party, which contained and still contains some of the most conservative forces in Irish society, took a swing to the left with the publication of a policy document called "The Just Society".

This document, which committed the party to economic planning and the welfare state, was the work chiefly of Declan Costello, later Attorney-General, later a High Court judge. The son of a former Taoiseach, he was admired almost as much by the traditionalists in the party as by the moderates. Fine Gael are not only the descendants of the pro-Treaty wing of Sinn Féin of the 1921-23 period, but also of the older middle classes and propertied classes, "people with a stake in the country", former home rulers and even former Unionists; the phenomenon of "deference", well known in Britain, is much more firmly established in Fine Gael than in other Irish parties. Costello's backers saw him as a future Taoiseach, but the smart money went on Garret FitzGerald, who did not enter the Dáil until 1969.

But it was a member of the Fine Gael right wing, Gerard Sweetman, who had much earlier become the prime mover of a process which, along with the *aggiornamento* set in motion by John XXIII, transformed Ireland. It was Sweetman who, as Finance Minister in the Fine Gael-Labour Coalition Government of 1954-57, marked out for promotion a bright, youngish official, a step or two from the top of the Department of Finance ladder, and commissioned him to draw up an economic and social plan or "programme" for the following decade. That official was T.K. Whitaker, who became Secretary of the Department, later Governor of the Central Bank, still later a two-term senator, appointed by both a Fianna Fáil and a Fine Gael Taoiseach. The implementation of an economic new departure had to wait for some time, for when Fianna Fáil returned to office in 1957, the ageing Eamon de Valera became Taoiseach again and did not resign until 1959 (he then served a further fourteen years as President). His successor, Sean Lemass, put Whitaker's ideas into operation, and their names have since been inextricably linked in the public mind.

The paradoxical elements of this relationship will be considered in a moment, along with developments in the Fianna Fáil Party, but first it is worthwhile to look at the effects on Irish society of the policies they jointly promoted, at a time when so many other influences for radical change were being brought to bear on the society.

The first visible effect of the adoption of more enlightened and innovatory economic and social policies was a considerable alleviation of the poverty hitherto endemic in Ireland — though the poverty itself also became more visible and *less tolerable* during the sixties, when a huge fall in emigration (which had drained the state of an estimated 400,000 people in the fifties) raised in a more acute form questions like unemployment.

But a much more profound effect on our society was produced by the sudden and capricious affluence which development and modernisation thrust upon us. We had been poor far too long; now we got rich far too quickly. And the subsequent twenty years have proved all too starkly how ill-equipped we were to handle either our new wealth and lifestyles, or the set-backs which would follow.

At first it seemed as if we were destined to have the best of all possible worlds. Irish society had not yet lost its charm, its intimacy, its informality, its spaciousness and courtesy — and its indomitable capacity for ingenious improvisation. If we had a class system (and what society has not?), it was far less rigid and structured than anything that existed elsewhere in western Europe.

Our new affluence manifested itself most dramatically in the matter of enjoyment, now so much less guilt-ridden. Many years later a witty academic friend of mine ascribed the Irish sexual revolution to Joe Walsh Tours, a travel agency which grew fat on the pilgrimage trade to such destinations as Rome and Lourdes, but which also carries people to purely secular locations such as the Canary Islands. My friend argued that this and other travel agencies had provided young Irish people with the opportunity to discover the delights of sex in warm climates, which they translated to the Irish sphere in the days of cheap central heating.

Possibly more lasting effects came from the springing up of a new breed of bright, young entrepreneurs. That this should have happened was, on the whole, good; for there is no life without change, and the older business classes (those predating independence, and those who derived from protectionism in the thirties) were almost moribund.

If the new men lacked the relative charm and cultivation of their predecessors, they were, at least in the beginning, better businessmen, and their activities helped to generate sorely wanted wealth and employment.

Nevertheless, it would be necessary to civilise them, and to take a very radical look at the whole society. If we wanted to preserve the best of the past and use the new developments in the interests of social justice and civil liberty, in order to achieve a coherent and civilised society, we would have to curb the scramble for power and money. We would have to do this by using both cultural and political instruments. The cultural instruments still exist, though often feebly; the political instruments, when put to the test, were found wanting. But it would be unfair to blame the political system or the politicians for faults which can be more properly attributed to ourselves as individuals and to the whole nature of our society. For the events of the last twenty years have, above all, exposed the extreme moral backwardness of Irish society.

We had abandoned most of our indigenous popular culture; the aristocratic and élitist elements, though the foundation of one of the great literatures of the world, are common to only a tiny minority; efforts, preposterously misdirected, to make Irish the spoken and written language of a majority, had already failed hopelessly, and more recently it has become clear that reforms in the teaching of the Irish language and culture may meet with a similar fate. We derived many of our moral attitudes — along with an all too important part of our concept of nationality — from the teaching of a predominant triumphalist Church, propped up by popular pietism; too much of our political culture is based on the concept of the hero-leader: O'Connell, Parnell, de Valera.

The interpretation placed on ecumenism by some Irish bishops was laughable: they said it meant being on neighbourly terms with Protestants, but such Catholics in the Republic as knew any of the 5 per cent Protestant minority were usually on excellent terms with them anyway. Some fervent Catholic ecumenists took a radically different view: they saw the ecumenical movement as requiring them, in effect, to *be* Protestants, with a Protestant emphasis on conscience and free will. But in taking this view they ran the danger of letting individualism get out of control. For modern urban society, in order to operate effectively and without too much friction and violence, needs neither a received nor an individualistic ethic: it needs a *community* ethic. And in the sixties, the Irish sense of community began to collapse.

The newly affluent and "permissive" young embraced, in a large degree, mere hedonism. The most vigorous and ruthless set about the pursuit, in the classical order, of wealth, power and social status. The political parties suffered a series of traumas. The Catholic right wing, clerical and lay, were least upset. They knew there would be other popes, and other political leaders.

Since the British in the nineteenth century bit by bit handed over control of Irish education to the Churches — mainly to the Roman Catholic Church — the bishops, before and after independence, occasionally interfered more or less overtly in political affairs. For the most part they contented themselves with influencing politics indirectly through their control of the education system, and especially through their hold on the minds of those in positions of influence, above all in the professions. In no case in the Republic does sectarianism so manifestly influence events as in the North, but at all times the power is there — more or less profound, more or less sinister — stemming less from the Catholic Church itself than from its lay agents. In the sixties, while moulds were broken and revolutions proclaimed, under the surface lay the semi-secret organisations like the Knights of St Columbanus and Opus Dei, and along with them an amorphous but significant middle-class mass, obscurantist and authoritarian, trained in school and university to think of itself as an élite, reminiscent slightly of Iberian fascism, but above all deeply sectarian, ignorant and unthinking, fed on confused and barbarous distortions of the teachings of Aristotle and Aquinas.

Not very long ago, I heard a leading Unionist, who thinks himself a liberal, describe Southern society as "pre-Renaissance". That seems ridiculous to someone like myself, who regards our polity, with all its flaws, as deriving from the American and French revolutions; but it describes accurately enough the obscurantist element of the Catholic middle class.

A better comparison might be with that "liberal" Unionist's own kind of people, the Northern upper-middle class Protestants who made no effort to help either O'Neill, or Chichester-Clark, or Faulkner, to avert catastrophe, and who exert themselves all too little still. Too many of the Catholic middle and upper middle class in the South cared nothing for the North and the repercussions of the crisis in the Republic; and the worst actually tried with some success to use North-South alienation as a means of creating a more sectarian and more authoritarian society in the South.

But it is time to return to developments in the Fianna Fáil Party after Lemass took it over — bearing in mind that somewhat different kinds of sectarianism and confusion from those outlined above always prevailed in that party, and that its members were even more susceptible than the rest of us to the worship of the hero-leader.

Members of the Fianna Fáil Party claim, usually in perfectly good faith, that they are true republican-separatists, the heirs of Wolfe Tone who wanted a union of "Catholic, Protestant and Dissenter". In fact, their dishonesty and double-think exceed those of other Southern parties (though the competition is fierce) in two ways: first, they are very ready to play the "Catholic card" for Southern political advantage, as lately in the case of the abortion issue; secondly, though they claim they want a united Ireland, they conceive of this united Ireland, if at all, merely as a swollen version of the existing, sectarian Republic.

Fianna Fáil have always laboured under a unique combination of problems of personality and misunderstanding — misunderstanding not merely of Irish history generally, but of themselves. By the time de Valera founded the party in 1926, most of the great men of the War of Independence and Civil War period were either dead, or on the other side, or both. There were, however, several truly outstanding men in his early cabinets. One was Gerald Boland, an anti-clerical left-winger who played a major part in the suppression of the IRA at the time of the Second World War. (His son Kevin resigned from Lynch's Government in the crisis of 1969-70). Another was Sean Lemass.

De Valera, for all his nationalist rhetoric and all his genuine political achievements — claiming sovereignty over the North and abolishing the oath of allegiance to the British monarch on the one hand, regaining the naval bases and maintaining neutrality during the war on the other — saw the whole question of nationality as primarily cultural. To this child of the Gaelic renaissance, the Irish language mattered more than any number of ports or counties. Lemass — the first important Irish leader born in the twentieth century, with which he was almost exactly coeval — had nationalist qualifications almost the equal of de Valera's, for as a boy he had taken part in the Easter Rising. However, culturally de Valera's passions meant nothing to him, since he could scarcely speak a word of the Irish language and it is not recorded that he ever read one line of poetry in any tongue; politically he allowed people to praise him as a pragmatist (he could not prevent other people from denouncing him as an opportunist). His policies, whether one calls them pragmatic or opportunistic, were very largely forced upon him; what is undeniable is that in every case he administered them superbly. Lemass was completely urban, and completely modern. No role pleased de Valera more than those of Chancellor of the National University and founder of the Dublin Institute for Advanced Studies. Lemass, by contrast, found himself more at home on the racecourse and at the card table.

In the thirties he embarked on a policy of building up native industry behind a shield of protection; though Irish industry was inefficient, the effect on employment was stunning. During the Second World War he became Minister for Supply and totally reversed his policy, but he was enormously successful in ensuring that Ireland did not go in want of raw materials. In the sixties he initiated a third and even more dramatic change of policy, but not before a long, dreary and damaging wait to attain the supreme office.

Unembarrassed by dogma, unashamed of what are now called U-turns, Lemass negotiated a free-trade agreement with the United Kingdom, and applied to join the European Economic Community. (The EEC application lapsed when General de Gaulle vetoed British membership, and the two countries did not become members of the EEC until 1 January 1973).

At home Lemass pursued equally innovatory policies. He set up a committee of the Oireachtas to examine the 1937 Constitution, whose most contentious provisions included the claim to Dublin sovereignty over Northern Ireland, a ban on divorce, and a reference to the "special position" of the Roman Catholic Church (this last is the only provision to have been dropped, so far, from the Constitution); and he initiated a series of meetings with the then Northern Premier, Terence O'Neill, which were continued by Jack Lynch when he succeeded him in 1966.

The inspiration for those meetings came from neither Lemass nor O'Neill but from T.K. Whitaker. The Lemass-Whitaker axis was a curious one, since the two men were very dissimilar. Whitaker was born in Northern Ireland but brought up across the border in County Louth. The conception of him, once popular, as the promoter of unbridled economic growth, is false; on the contrary, he is interested in financial probity and wage restraint — as well as in the Irish language, the theatre, and the possibility of reconciliation between the two parts of Ireland.

Lemass was conscious that much of his party, especially its rural wing, thought of him as a pretty ordinary chap, so unlike the almost superhuman de Valera, and he felt keenly the dangers involved in tampering with de Valera's sacred Constitution, and establishing friendly relations with the Northern Unionist leader. When he first met O'Neill he told him he was running a risk; O'Neill replied, all too prophetically, that he himself ran a far greater risk.

It took more sensational events than these to produce open splits in Fianna Fáil, but Lemass was right to fear the effects of his modernising drive on the party. Throughout the sixties, under his leadership and for a time under that of Lynch, it gave the appearance of becoming just another European-style party, Christian Democrat but with a populist tinge. Under the gloss of modernisation, however, lay the traditional irredentist Fianna Fáil, and many of the rising generation were greatly the inferiors of the old guard, who possessed some of the idealism of the "troubled times" and in not a few cases mildly left-wing and anticlerical attitudes. By contrast, many of the new men were more truly the descendants of the sectarian agrarian agitators of the nineteenth and even the eighteenth centuries than of the Wolfe Tone republicanism on which they prided themselves. Their brand of republicanism was above all tribal and Catholic, and many of them reacted emotionally when the Northern Catholics came under direct attack in 1969.

Lynch responded to the challenge in the government and party with considerable skill and it is a tribute to his political acumen that he managed to retain the party leadership, in and out of office, for another decade. He fought off his internal enemies largely by keeping control of the party organisation and by appealing, within the parliamentary party, to the tradition of ferocious discipline and loyalty. In the early part of the crisis the policies pursued at Westminster and Stormont dealt him several blows, particularly after Heath's accession to office in Britain in June 1970. He had to contend not only with the passions aroused by the Falls curfew, Bloody Sunday (his recall of his ambassador in London was the minimum response he could make) and internment, but also with a brusque statement by Heath that Northern Ireland was an internal United Kingdom matter and no concern of Dublin.

Helped by some outstanding officials in his own office and in the Department of Foreign Affairs, and by John Hume, he set about devising a new policy, which postulated that Dublin was the "second guarantor", after Britain, of the rights and safety of the Northern Catholics. Heath — with the help of some pressure from Wilson and the British Labour Party, and from the Foreign Office — reconsidered fairly rapidly his attitude to Ireland, and by the time direct rule had been imposed, had come round to an acceptance of Dublin's "legitimate interest" in Northern affairs. Heath was partly moved by the consideration that EEC entry, in which Ireland was a partner of Britain, was now imminent, but nevertheless the concession marked a considerable advance for Lynch.

Lynch also benefited initially from the fact that both major opposition parties in the Republic were internally divided, as well as split on the issue of whether to coalesce against him. Fine Gael had their own atavistic problem: a strong tendency to revert in any crisis to authoritarianism. The left, dubbed "mongrel foxes" by the party leader Liam Cosgrave, wanted to push him out of the leadership; they also wanted to reverse the party's traditional extreme approach to the question of law and order. Their chance seemed to come in December 1972 when Lynch's Justice Minister, Desmond O'Malley, was putting through the Dáil a measure — the first of many from both Fianna Fáil and coalition governments — for new emergency legislation. Although the Fine Gael parliamentary party had decided to oppose the bill, Cosgrave was determined to vote for it. The Fine Gael left assumed that he would then have to resign the leadership. Lynch, for his part, had made up his mind to call a snap general election and fight it on two gold-plated issues: law and order and a divided opposition. Shortly before the Dáil vote was due, two people were killed in bomb explosions in Dublin. (The bombs were the work of the UVF, not, as was widely suspected, of some element of the British Army or intelligence services). Fine Gael panicked and fell into line behind Cosgrave.

Of the minor parties, the problems of the Official IRA,

the "Stickies" were, literally, the deadliest. After the split of 1969-70 it took them several years to settle down to constitutional politics. At first they regrouped, took part in the feverish search for arms, and fought four distinct campaigns.

The first was directed at political and military targets, and included bombings in Britain and an unsuccessful attempt on the life of a leading Unionist, John Taylor; the second against the Loyalists (though they also held secret meetings with the UDA, trying to find common ground on the left). After the imposition of direct rule they declared a cease-fire, but some of their more intransigent members, led by Séamus Costello (who was later murdered), defected and formed the Irish Republican Socialist Party (IRSP) and the Irish National Liberation Army (INLA). The Officials, trying to cling on to the dominance they still retained in some areas of Belfast, found themselves fighting armed feuds against both the INLA and the Provos.

At last, a good six years after the crisis began, they dismantled what armed forces they still possessed, proclaimed an exclusive commitment to the ballot box, and renamed themselves Sinn Féin the Workers' Party (in the North, still more clumsily, they were called Republican Clubs the Workers' Party) and finally, in 1982, to the inexpressible relief of headline writers, the Workers' Party *tout court.*

Their claim to complete renunciation of violence has never gained full public acceptance, for two reasons, one good, one bad. The first is that a group still exists which carries out bank robberies, whose members do not belong to the Provos or the INLA or any other identifiable subversive group, nor yet to the ordinary criminal class. There are grounds for suspicion that these are the Official IRA, slimmed down.

The second, based on a conspiracy theory, deserves little consideration. Some excitable people think the Official IRA has merely gone further underground, building up large stocks of arms and biding its time to instigate, with the help of Moscow, a communist revolution North and South.

If stockpiles of arms do exist in any quantity, they are being held, not for a revolution but for a "Doomsday" situation: mass Protestant attacks on Catholic areas of Belfast following a British withdrawal. The Workers' Party have organised themselves, not for armed revolution but for the kind of work they did in the middle sixties, with the difference that nowadays they place more emphasis on parliamentary politics, and on building up support in certain influential quarters, than on street agitation.

The electoral successes of the Workers' Party in the North have so far been negligible, but in the Republic they have emerged as a serious challenge to the Labour Party for the leadership of the left. They won their first seat in the Dáil in 1981 and increased for one term to three in 1982. In part, these successes can be explained by their filling a vacuum created by Labour's weaknesses and lack of credibility, discussed below; in part, by their choice as candidates of men with long records of dedication to the tedious grind of local constituency work. But WP discipline and self-sacrifice go a lot deeper than that: they have about them an ethos which combines touches of the conspiratorial (natural enough in view of their origins), the hard left (acceptance of the "party line") and the monastic. As with communist parties, this ethos both attracts and repels. It attracts those with a taste for self-denial, both material and intellectual. Among the more comfortable sections of the middle class the Workers' Party have been making, and are likely to make, little progress; but they have gained, as well as votes from workers, sufficient support among intellectuals to suggest that, in at least some of the more cultivated Irish minds, the ascetic prevails over the chaotic. They have ensured for themselves considerable influence in certain trade union and media quarters, and rarely lack for high-powered advisers on any aspect of policy.

Behind their facade of rigid discipline, they are divided into factions like any other party. They have troubled many of their supporters by Moscow-lining (including support for military rule in Poland) and by voting with

Fianna Fáil in the Dáil. Some of them concede the incomprehensibility and implausibility of their current Northern policy, which calls ultimately for an all-Ireland socialist republic, but in the meantime seeks the restoration of majority rule in the North, tempered only by a bill of rights. They do not explain how these proposals can be reconciled. But it is probable that the Workers' Party will continue to make electoral gains in the Republic unless the Labour Party, at present in crisis, somehow manages to resolve its problems.

Like so much else in Irish society, Labour gained fresh vigour in the sixties. New members flocked in, attracted in part by Labour's adoption of more radical policies, in part fired by the progress of the Civil Rights movement in the North and by an optimistic misreading of the events of 1968 in the United States, France and Czechoslovakia. They called for a "New Republic"; their leader, Brendan Corish, declared that "the seventies will be socialist" and said that he would not serve in a coalition with Fine Gael. In the general election of 1969, that *annus mirabilis*, they gained their highest percentage ever of the vote, nearly 17 per cent. (That proportion has fallen at every subsequent election, and in 1982 went down to a mere 9 per cent; their share of the vote in Dublin working-class constituencies has been hit even harder).

The "New Republic" euphoria did not last long. Hot on the heels of the general election came the boiling over of the Northern pot, followed by the arms crisis. At their annual conference in Cork in 1971, Labour dropped their opposition to coalition. But it was on the Northern question, and related issues in the South, that the Labour leaders showed themselves most prone to panic, and even paranoia. They persuaded themselves that the root cause of the Northern troubles was a conspiracy between Fianna Fáil and the Provisional IRA, and that arms were being smuggled into the country for a *coup d'état*, not for use in the North. The *coup d'état* theory was mere fantasy; as to the other proposition, there was unquestionably collusion between the Provos and some prominent members of

Fianna Fáil, but the idea that this caused the Troubles could be entertained by nobody with the smallest sense of chronology.

Left-wingers suspected that several Labour leaders seized on the Northern question as an excuse to reverse policies distasteful to them, above all that on coalition. That is not quite fair. Their horror at the atrocities committed by the Provos was genuine, and so was their distrust of Fianna Fáil. But these sometimes took ludicrous forms. Their denigration of Fianna Fáil extended even to Lynch and others who could not reasonably be suspected of the remotest sympathy with terrorism; and one or two of them were not above smearing as Provo sympathisers people who merely disagreed with their analysis of the Northern crisis, or protested when civil liberties were threatened.

Abandoning the synthesis of nationalism and socialism propounded by the party's founder, James Connolly, Labour adopted instead what is now called the "two nations" theory (originally, the "two-nation" theory, denounced by John Redmond in 1913). According to this proposition, the Northern Protestants constitute a separate nation, with "national" rights, of which the chief is the right of self-determination. This theory, which of course rejects a prime, non-sectarian tenet of Irish republicanism, is superficially comfortable, and far more popular among the middle class than the working class; but paradoxically its more articulate proponents belong to the left: in Labour, to some extent in the Workers' Party, in a new party, the Democratic Socialist Party, founded in 1982 by Jim Kemmy, deputy for Limerick East, and in groups of the lunatic fringe like the British and Irish Communist Organisation. Not by accident, its identification with Labour came at a time when that party was throwing away its working-class base in Dublin.

Of more practical effect was the weak stance which Labour now took in the Dáil on the question of civil liberties. Civil liberties inevitably came under threat from the beginning. Street protests, occupations of buildings, refusals by juries for whatever reason (sympathy or intimidation) to bring in guilty verdicts, all led to one instalment of emergency legislation after another. Most people accepted certain of the measures, like the introduction of the non-jury special criminal court (it has three judges, unlike the one-judge "Diplock courts" in the North), as regrettable necessities; others were harder to justify.

Clearly, what was needed in the Dáil was an important party which would challenge the introduction of measures which infringed existing rights, but with the defection of Labour from the cause of civil liberties, the Dáil no longer contained a major party committed to their defence. Indeed, Labour as well as Fine Gael members — especially during the tenure of office of the 1973-77 coalition government — positively gloated over the harshness of the measures introduced. At the same time important Labour figures participated in veiled (and some not so veiled) threats to the press, while all three main parties delighted in enforcing a rigorous control of broadcasting, and in bullying the Radio Telefís Éireann authority and its executives. Labour's record in this sphere destroyed one aspect of its credibility.

Nor did the party have much credibility on the other great issue of the time, Common Market entry. Officially Labour, like the trade unions, opposed entry and argued against it in the 1972 referendum campaign. But several of its leading members wholeheartedly and publicly advocated Irish membership.

Labour did deserve some credit for ensuring that a debate of sorts took place, and for raising a small voice to point out that entry affected the question of political and even military neutrality. But that voice went for the most part unheard. Fianna Fáil, Fine Gael and the farmers' organisations carried out a campaign based on arguments which were often both dishonest and irrelevant. It concentrated heavily on the advantages for agriculture. The farmers were promised a bonanza, and for some years after our entry they did indeed benefit from an improvement in prices. Moreover, the state as a whole has been a large net beneficiary from EEC transfers under the common agriculture policy and other schemes.

But in general the farmers have suffered several difficulties and set-backs, some caused by an inflation rate greatly in excess of that of most of our EEC partners, others by greed and recklessness. Instead of devising coherent agricultural and land-use policies of our own, governments allowed the farmers to suppose that from now on Santa Claus would arrive every day of every year. Over-investment bordered on the insane. Prices up to £4,000 an acre were paid for land which, in a good year, might yield a return of £300. It needed only a couple of bad years to plunge over-borrowed farmers into the most terrible difficulties. Some had gone in so deep that in the end banks, and the Government-sponsored Agricultural Credit Corporation, moved to seize their farms. But if the farmers were blameworthy for so foolishly committing themselves to borrowings which they could not fund, the banks which lent them the money deserve an even greater share of the blame: some blame also attaches to the Central Bank for failing to impose restraint.

Nor are farmers more prone to greed and folly than the rest of human kind. The country at large was persuaded that EEC entry would solve all our economic problems: that from now on we would enjoy limitless and unending growth and prosperity. By encouraging this belief, the political leaders incurred the guilt of inculcating immature and unrealistic attitudes in the people. They were also guilty of not promoting sufficient debate on the two other compelling reasons, besides agriculture, for entry.

The first was industrial. Having abandoned the old policies of protection and self-sufficiency, it was considered imperative that we should attract foreign investment. For this, access to the enormous West European market was a powerful inducement. But more recently the question has been penetratingly raised as to whether we might not have done much better by promoting the growth of native instead of foreign industry.

The second, and most important reason of all was political. Even after independence we had continued to live in Britain's shadow, always conscious of the enormous disparities in population, wealth and power between the two countries. The EEC, in which the smaller countries can, if they take their opportunities, exert an influence out of proportion to their size, offered us a new and gratifying role in the world. As it turned out, this role has often been filled with credit, and at times, as during FitzGerald's presidency of the Council of Ministers, with distinction.

But such things have their price. The founders of the European Community did not envisage it as merely a trading bloc; they saw it as a first step towards political integration or federation. And political integration implies defence integration, as we have seen, more or less clearly, since we joined. One might say that both Britain and Ireland went into the EEC dishonestly, "with their fingers crossed", for the first country and its leaders entirely oppose political integration, and the second deluded itself that it could obtain all the benefits of membership, including the political benefits, while pretending to remain neutral and evading the defence implications. All these contradictions meant that plenty of trouble was in store.

Chapter Nine

Although they pride themselves on their realism and common sense, the British are as much prisoners of their history, and their myths, as any other people. It has not been easy for the world's first industrial power and the rulers of the world's greatest empire to come to terms with the position of Britain after the Second World War: that of a country of the second rank, in danger of being reduced to the third rank.

By the beginning of the twentieth century Britain was in relative, perhaps absolute, industrial decline. Her income from foreign investment and her predominance in services like banking, insurance and shipping — both advantages closely tied to her possession of the empire — served to conceal her true state and to maintain living standards at home, but helped at the same time to bring about a position, which ultimately reached the proportions of a calamity, in which domestic industry suffered intolerably from lack of investment and modernisation. Her losses in two world wars in blood and treasure were colossal, and those who fought in the second, or endured it at home, have given ample testimony of the universal feelings of depression and exhaustion which prevailed in 1945. In the years that followed she rapidly divested herself of her empire, but not for a long time of a deep-seated belief that she remained an imperial power, with imperial rights and obligations. ("Not for a long time" is an understatement; for some people that should read "not at all." When a

British diplomat in Buenos Aires heard the news of the Argentine invasion of the Falkland Islands in April 1982, he exclaimed: "They can't do that to a first-class power!")

Certainly for two decades after the war — and to some extent to this day — Britain kept up the pretence of being a world power, without the resources to sustain the role. As late as the middle sixties Harold Wilson thought the country needed a military presence "east of Suez". Britain still maintains a large and costly army in West Germany. She remains a nuclear power, relying on expensive and out-of-date weapons and on a strategy dictated by the Americans, at some cost to her conventional forces. Twenty years ago the former American Secretary of State, Dean Acheson, offended the British by saying that they had lost an empire and not found a role.

In 1970 Edward Heath came to office convinced that he had found Britain's new role: in industry, in diplomacy and in defence. He was a man of complex and unusual character: arrogant, impatient, petulant and peremptory (strange qualities in a former Conservative chief whip, for a chief whip needs above all to be a conciliator), and he seemed a model representative of the new-style Tories (his origins were near the bottom of the lower middle class, and he had been a scholarship boy at Oxford before the war). Moreover, he was celibate (as prescribed by Francis Bacon for those who hold great office) and single-minded.

Heath advocated what then seemed simplistic right-wing economic policies, similar to the latter-day "monetarist" and "Supply-side" economics of Margaret Thatcher and Ronald Reagan; and he shocked his supporters by reversing his industrial policy and showering public money on "lame-duck" enterprises instead of leaving them to sink or swim. He never recovered the standing in his party which he lost by his many U-turns, but the backbenchers, if they had considered his career more deeply, would not have been so surprised. He had no real commitment to hard-line industrial or other policies; he was a pragmatist and a liberal. While at Oxford his anti-fascism had led him to campaign against an official Conservative candidate in a by-election.

He opposed capital punishment. In 1968, while in opposition, he dismissed from his shadow cabinet Enoch Powell, who had made a speech predicting that the presence in Britain of large black immigrant communities would cause "much blood" to flow. Powell afterwards became one of his bitterest opponents on the Irish and Common Market issues.

In his private life he resembled much more a representative of the aristocracy or the upper middle class than of the new men. He had a passion for music, and a fondness for good food and Scotch malt whisky. In his political attitudes he was fully in line with the Establishment, that all-important conglomeration of business, finance, academic life, the administration, politicians of all major parties, and the minority of the hereditary aristocracy which concerns itself with public life.

The Establishment was united on three points: first, British industry must be modernised and made more productive and efficient; secondly, as one means to this end, trade union law must be reformed to reduce strikes, go-slows and restrictive practices; thirdly, Britain must join the European Community and thus provide for herself a new role on the world stage. To these objects Heath added a fourth: a new departure in defence by means of an Anglo-French nuclear axis, which would reduce dependence on the Americans.

Wilson and his Employment Secretary, Barbara Castle, had tried to bring in a trade-union reform bill, but had to drop it because of the opposition of the unions and, within the cabinet, of James Callaghan. The Heath government managed to get an industrial relations bill through parliament, to the delight of the "union-bashing" right-wing Tories; but he dismayed these in 1972 when he held out to the unions a prospect of unprecedentedly close and continuous consultation with the government: to make them, as the comment went at the time, "another estate of the realm". His enemies marked this as another U-turn.

But Europe remained by far his greatest preoccupation, throughout his premiership and later. His greatest ambition — which he achieved — was to bring Britain into the Common Market. For this achievement, as for all such, a price had to be paid, or rather two prices.

One price, which offended the country at large but most particularly the Labour Party, was in terms of money: acceptance of the Common Agriculture Policy, which meant a financial burden for Britain as a food-importing country (though Britain obtained from the start substantial concessions in being allowed to import food from overseas, and she has since been granted considerable rebates of her contributions to the EEC budget). The other, which caused most concern in the Tory Party, was a dilution of parliamentary sovereignty. Once again, Powell was one of the most prominent in arguing against entry on these grounds.

After the imposition of direct rule and the despatch of William Whitelaw to Northern Ireland as Secretary of State, Powell made a taunting speech in which he showed how deep-rooted enmity can sometimes give insights into another's character. What, he asked, were "Willie's marching orders"; was he sent to Belfast to preserve the Union at all costs? Or to wheel and deal, to damp down fires, to keep Northern Ireland off the Prime Minister's back?

These questions went straight to the point of Heath's impatience and exasperation. He did indeed want the North off his back, and as quickly as possible; the "marching orders" he gave Whitelaw contained instructions neither to maintain the Union at all costs nor to dissolve it, but they most certainly included an injunction to make haste, finish the job and get back soon to the real action in London.

This desire for excessive haste led to numerous mistakes, mistakes just as fatal as those caused earlier by the delay of two and a half years. The first mistake was one of the most calamitous, for it damaged Whitelaw in the Tory Party and at the same time revived — just when the British and Irish governments most needed to co-operate — suspicions in Dublin of British double-dealing and bad faith.

Whitelaw, rich, amiable and self-confident, with half a political lifetime as an "operator" and conciliator behind him, was Heath's closest friend in politics. The latter gave him an extraordinarily free hand in tactics, and also with money. But Whitelaw's first significant move could not have been undertaken without the direct approval of the Prime Minister.

This move was the negotiation, in the early summer of 1972, of a cease-fire with the Provisional IRA, whose leaders Whitelaw flew to London for talks in the house of one of his junior ministers, Paul Channon. In order to obtain the cease-fire and to stop a hunger strike in Crumlin Road Prison, Belfast, he granted IRA and other "political" prisoners and internees "special category" status.

At first, the cease-fire looked like a triumph for Whitelaw. Later, the events of this time were seen, more truly, as disastrous. The former Secretary of State (later deputy Prime Minister under Margaret Thatcher) himself said that he had made a dreadful mistake. Pressed for an explanation of why he had made such a false move, one of his most senior officials told me that the negotiations were not serious or substantive: "It was a case of letting the dog see the rabbit."

Statements like these, made with considerable benefit of hindsight, are best taken with several grains of salt. Few people then (though there were very important exceptions) saw very much wrong with negotiating with the Provos. Their aim of taking over both parts of the country by force had not yet emerged, even in their own minds; rather, many ascribed that design to the Stickies. British Army officers negotiated with them; so did the SDLP, who had persuaded them to call an earlier cease-fire; so did prominent clergy; so, for that matter, had Harold Wilson in Dublin the previous year. Indeed, sporadic negotiations have continued ever since at various — though usually very low — levels. This continued even during the 1980 and 1981 Long Kesh hunger strikes, when contacts were maintained between British officials and Provo representatives outside the prison, at a time when the British refused, supposedly as a matter of principle, to talk to the prisoner designated by the others as their commanding officer. There is at least a distinct possibility that not only were the Whitelaw negotiations seriously meant, but that if the cease-fire had held, further talks would have taken place.

During the cease-fire, I discussed these events with one of the most influential Conservatives, a man a long way to the right of Whitelaw, a man, also, with a long-standing interest in Northern Ireland. He astonished me by describing one of the Provo leaders, Daithi O Conaill, as "a latter-day Michael Collins". In saying this, he echoed the view of many British leaders in 1921, when they thought that by negotiating with Collins, the chief of those then in arms against them, they would ensure that any deal would "stick". It was not quite so simple then, and it was very much less simple in 1972, for to hold such a view in relation to the Provos showed a rather cavalier attitude towards Irish representative democracy. In particular, British flirting with the Provos outraged Lynch. The British, who had warned him — the elected leader — against meddling in the affairs of Northern Ireland, were talking to people who threatened Irish democracy, who made his own position unstable, and who were all too favourably regarded by an uncomfortable number of people in his own party.

But euphoria over the cease-fire, and talk of Michael Collins, did not last very long. It was quickly broken by the Provos, and the breakdown was soon followed by a dramatic action by Whitelaw: the reduction of the no-go areas in Belfast and Derry. Operation Motorman was launched before dawn one cool summer Monday morning, and within a matter of hours British army personnel and vehicles had demolished all the barricades and established control of the targeted areas. They met with almost no resistance, made few arrests, and caused only one fatal casualty. The imminence of the operation had been signalled clearly to the Provos, the SDLP (who made no objection) and the press. Ships carrying men and vehicles to Derry lay off the coast a full day, in plain view of anyone who cared to watch. In Derry, particularly, Provos on the wanted list — including one who had taken part in the London talks — slipped quietly over the border into County Donegal.

The cease-fire and the negotiations had had at least one effect quite unintended by the Provos: since these had held talks with the British, their great rivals the SDLP felt that they could also talk to them without fear of losing support in the Catholic community. ("I felt," Gerry Fitt told me, "a great ripping and tearing in the region of my collar. It was the SDLP sliding off the hook.") Then the breakdown of the cease-fire, followed by Motorman, closed off the "Provo option" — supposing that a Provo option had ever really existed — and opened the way for the deployment of Whitelaw's grand strategy, in which the SDLP would play a key part.

But Motorman also had the effect of completing the appearance, which had been gradually taking shape since August 1969, of Northern Ireland as an occupied country and especially of Belfast as an occupied city. While Whitelaw vigorously and rapidly — too rapidly — pressed on with a political settlement designed to unite Catholics and Protestants, people "on the ground" took more note of circumstances far too certain to divide them further. These may be discussed under three heads: the role of the British Army, the activities of the terrorist organisations, and the almost complete division of Catholics and Protestants — again, particularly in Belfast — into geographically distinct communities.

After internment and its "Five Techniques" sequel, and after Bloody Sunday, it was certain that many Catholics would never regard the British Army as other than enemies, and although no comparable incidents occurred in the ensuing decade, they continued to have grounds constantly for suspicion, and often for anger. The commonplace sights of Belfast in the early seventies included army vehicles driving at speed through the streets, their occupants training weapons on passers-by (this activity has since much diminished): sandbagged and armoured observation posts; soldiers stalking through lanes and gardens and patrolling the balconies of complexes of flats; the army operating a variety of undercover enterprises (in one case a laundry, and according to popular legend, massage parlours), counting milk bottles, rummaging through dustbins, recording all movement in and out of certain streets; soldiers detaining and questioning people on their way to or from work; very frighteningly, the army beaming from helicopters powerful searchlights capable of illuminating a whole street; at worst, the shooting of innocent civilians including children. The number of killings has not been large, and some of those responsible have been tried and punished, but every death increases Catholic alienation.

In our age of violence much of this kind of thing is common practice in many countries. Anyone who has a secret will be wise to assume at a minimum that his telephone is tapped, and that a computer check on his car number will reveal to some interested authority all sorts of information about him. But in Belfast one of the obvious effects of such activities is to increase the sense of harassment felt by many ordinary Catholics — who, it may be remembered, are also simultaneously intimidated and wooed by the Provos and the INLA.

In the countryside, this period saw an increase in Provo activity (which emphasised the importance of the movement of arms and explosives across the border, and gave rise to many loud Unionist complaints about terrorists escaping to "sanctuary" in the Republic) and the introduction into Northern Ireland of members of the Special Air Service (SAS). In those days — long before their dramatic and ruthless ending of the occupation by terrorists of the Iranian embassy in London in 1980, and their exploits in the Falklands War in 1982 — little was known about the SAS. It was rumoured that their previous occupations had ranged from cutting throats in Kenya during the Mau Mau insurrection to napalming villages in Oman. Their very presence in Northern Ireland was not admitted until several years after it was first disclosed by the present author and another *Irish Times* journalist, Conor Brady, in 1972.

Even now, all that is known with certainty is that they have engaged in undercover operations in areas where the normal forces of law and order rarely penetrate. Some of these operations consist of no more than collecting information; an officer, Captain Robert Nairac, engaged in this work in South Armagh, was abducted, taken over the border and killed. Many Catholics suspect that they have "set up" Provo and IRA leaders to be killed by Loyalists; some indeed suspect that the British Army, and the RUC, have provided information which helped Loyalists to carry out various acts of violence; and at the extreme, attempts have been made to pin the blame on the SAS for atrocities committed not only by the Loyalists but also by the Provos. In the Belfast ghettos, many firmly believe these allegations, even in instances where the real culprits were subsequently apprehended and shown to be, for example, Provos or UFF men. (In the case of the RUC, it has often been alleged that senior officers have leaked information to Loyalist politicians, and even to Loyalist terrorist organisations; but one of their highest-ranking officers denied this to me with some vehemence).

Whatever the truth about SAS activities in South Armagh and elsewhere, their mere presence, coupled with the sense of fear and harassment felt by urban Catholics, serves to keep Catholic suspicions constantly alive. And suspicion is felt more widely than just within the North: to a good many people it looked as if the British Army was using Northern Ireland as a training ground for techniques to be used in the case of civil unrest, possibly connected with race, in Britain itself.

According to an authority on these questions, this was true only in the earliest years. He comments as follows:

> In the beginning it was both disruptive for the army, in NATO terms, but also interesting in terms of dealing with civil strife. But as the years went by it got more and more disruptive and less and less interesting. The disruption, which reached a peak in 1975, was gradually ended through longer army

tours and Ulsterisation. But in terms of developing new techniques, any benefits to be got had been got by the mid-seventies; no innovations, few experiments since then.

While Catholics, and to a much smaller extent Protestants, in the ghetto areas ran the danger of having their doors kicked in or even of being shot by soldiers, both sides suffered far more from the onslaughts of the terrorist gangs — and not just from attacks by Catholics on Protestants, or Protestants on Catholics, but also from the tyranny of the gangs in their own areas. Even after Motorman, it remained — and still remains — unsafe for the people of the ghettos to cross them. For informing, terrorists impose the death penalty; for alleged minor crimes, they inflict such punishments as tarring and feathering, shooting off kneecaps, or dropping heavy weights to break a man's legs.

Much of the indignation provoked by the campaign of violence has centred, somewhat misdirectedly, on the casualty rate. But by comparison with countless other instances of civil strife, this has been relatively low. In thirteen years, just under 2500 people — a grand total composed of members of the security forces, members of violent organisations and innocent civilians — have been killed; in no single year did the number killed exceed five hundred, and in only one year did it exceed the number killed in road accidents in Northern Ireland. (The total killed by violence is not confined to Northern Ireland, but includes people murdered as part of the troubles in various incidents in the Republic, in Britain and abroad). Much more significant in effecting the alienation of the communities from each other, and in creating a general atmosphere of misery and fear, has been the nature of the violence, which has combined, uniquely, examples of crass and brutal stupidity, ingenious refinements of cruelty, and sheer nastiness.

Leaving aside the more important and spectacular political assassinations, which call for separate mention, it is worth recalling at this point some of the more horrible crimes, especially those which were most nakedly sectarian, with little or no colour of having been committed for the sake of some cause. The atrocities have included the murders of parents in front of their children, the murder of a child in front of his parents, and the shooting of a teacher in front of a class of children.

In the border areas the Provos have simply waged war on the local Protestants, usually on the pretext that those they murdered were members of, or connected with, the security forces. This is indeed true of Protestant males of military age in those areas, but it does not of course justify the murders; and many people have been murdered who had no connection with the security forces. It must have taken a strange mental feat to claim, as was done, that a murdered woman census taker was an agent of the state machine of repression. Even more appalling was the machine-gunning of a mini-bus full of Protestant workers on the way home from their mill; the driver, a Catholic, was ordered to take to his heels.

On the other side, an early specialty was the slitting of the throats of Catholics, picked more or less at random, who happened to be on the streets of West Belfast late at night. ("We killed a lot of the wrong people," one of the Loyalist leaders told me casually; later the Loyalists concentrated their fire, equally chillingly, on prominent members of the IRSP.)

In one outstandingly horrible case, a woman who had transgressed the code of the UDA was beaten to death by other women while her daughter, aged six, hysterically knocked at the door of the room, out of which she had been locked. In an even worse case, a gang of Protestants murdered a handicapped teenage boy, then raped and shot his mother in the bed on which his body lay. A terrified lodger in the house escaped through a skylight; he had earlier offered to show the killers his Bible to prove he was a Protestant.

The Loyalist organisations were able to say that at least they had not authorised this particular outrage — but their activities had helped to make it possible. The Provos have an even stronger line in self-righteousness. When they killed a little boy in the midst of his family — by bad aim: they meant to kill his father — they issued a statement of apology to the family. When they attacked a party of dog fanciers in the La Mon restaurant outside Belfast with incendiary bombs, literally burning several people to death, it was claimed on their behalf that the bombs had gone off prematurely and that they had intended the building to be evacuated.

It is distasteful to dwell on these horrors, and unnecessary to moralise; it is more tempting and perhaps a little more profitable to speculate on the connection between the rise and fall in the rate of violence and the effects, real or intended, of the most spectacular atrocities on political developments.

Every attempt at a political settlement has been accompanied by increased violence from one or both sides, but usually from the Provos. One cannot be certain, but it is at least a reasonable speculation that this has more than once been deliberately organised to alienate the Protestants and provoke reprisals from these or from the security forces which would in turn alienate the Catholics: in short, with a view to destroying hope of political progress.

If this was indeed the intention behind occasional escalations of violence in the North, they have certainly had considerable success. The same cannot be said of the various bombings carried out in the Republic by the UVF and UDA, and in Britain by the Provos, the INLA and, in the early part of the crisis, by the Official IRA. These were intended partly as reprisals and partly for political ends: in the first case, to discourage the people of the Republic from taking too close an interest in Northern affairs, in the second, to instil fear in British people so that they would support the movement for withdrawal of troops from Northern Ireland. There is no evidence that either of these aims succeeded, but in the British case the atrocities have had one very obvious effect, namely, to increase a pre-existent sense of disgust or an alienation from things Irish. They have also had the effect of making life just a little more uncomfortable for Irish people living in Britain, but this has not resulted — as the terrorists doubtless hoped — in any increased support for themselves among the Irish in Britain.

While violence within the North reached its highest point during Whitelaw's tenure of office as Secretary of State, there was also occurring, sometimes violently, mostly quietly, what came to be described as "the greatest movement of population in Europe since the immediate post-war period".

Scores of thousands of people — perhaps as many as a hundred thousand, or more than one-fifth of the population — moved out of the "mixed" areas of Belfast and out of districts where they constituted a minority: Catholics moved to purely Catholic areas, Protestants to Protestant. This happened to a lesser extent in smaller urban and some rural districts, but scarcely at all in middle-class areas; the places by far the most significantly affected were where the Belfast working class lived. There had always been ghettos in Belfast, but also places where Catholics and Protestants lived cheek by jowl. In the sixties quite a determined effort had been made to create integrated new working-class estates; now within a couple of years working-class Catholics and working-class Protestants separated themselves almost totally from one another.

Much of the movement was voluntary — people felt safer and more comfortable "among their own" — but much intimidation accompanied it. This might take the form of a bullet in the post, a painted scrawl on the wall, or a knock on the door, followed by advice to get out within twenty-four hours. Sometimes the warnings took more terrible forms. Shots were fired into the houses of couples involved in mixed marriages, and in one dreadful case, two young Protestant brothers were murdered simply because they had Catholic girlfriends.

The human misery involved is all too easy to imagine: the destruction and loss of hasty removals, the transfers from good modern houses into slums, the abandonment of friends of half a lifetime; frequently it meant a virtually complete separation from close relations of a different religion. As so often in Belfast, the tragic and the grotesque were hideously intermingled. One day I happened by chance to be in the house of a Belfast city councillor when a middle-aged couple came in with a sad and extraordinary story. Their elder son, a boy of nineteen or twenty, had been tried and imprisoned for the murder of a Catholic. As a sort of atonement, both had become Catholics and in consequence had to move from their Protestant housing estate into a "mixed" area. But now the Protestants were being driven from this area and their younger son, still a Protestant, found his life threatened. Could the councillor find them somewhere safe to live? Alas, he feared he could not.

Suspicions have been voiced from time to time that the population movement was actually encouraged by the authorities, who wanted to move all Catholics out of East Belfast and all Protestants out of enclaves where they split up the Catholic majority areas in West Belfast. East Belfast is now almost exclusively Protestant, except for a tiny Catholic enclave, the Short Strand; nor are Catholic businesses readily to be found there, for Protestant bombs took care of these at an early stage: one Catholic businessman had his entire property there, nineteen separate premises, bombed.

Protestants, however, continue to live in large numbers in West Belfast, and they protested strongly at threats to the Shankill Road and Sandy Row, streets sacred to their culture and mythology. The authorities denied any intention of demolishing those streets or moving Protestants out; but the Protestants may well have got it right. For one thing, separation and knowing where one stands appeal greatly to the military mind, and the British Army possesses countless neatly coloured maps. For another, one can safely assume that British contingency plans leave nothing out and that they include, as one of their "worst case" options, the repartition of Ireland. The more than one hundred thousand Belfast Catholics would pose the biggest problem in a repartition; and a homogeneous, easily defended enclave would seem a better bet than another massive movement of population, possibly accompanied by much loss of life and destruction of property.

The point here, however, is the effect of the population movement on the participants — or, as one might better call them, the victims. Many were naturally embittered at the disruption of their lives. Many who were children then and are now adults must have as one of their most important formative memories the traumas of the move. Adults and children alike, they became the prey of the respective gangs in the Protestant and Catholic ghettos — to be, like the other ghetto inhabitants, tyrannised over, or indoctrinated, or inducted into the appropriate organisation, or some combination of the three.

Again, it must be remembered that in spite of numerous attempts at reform, employment in Northern Ireland remains very far from integrated, and education, with unimportant exceptions, not integrated at all. In any case, for much of West Belfast especially, such a thing as employment hardly exists: in the worst areas, unemployment among male school leavers approaches 100 per cent. Great numbers of young Catholics, and young Protestants, grow up without ever coming into normal personal contact with anybody from the other tribe. The implications of that need no elaboration.

Such were the ominous circumstances in which, from the summer of 1972 until late 1973, Whitelaw worked for a political settlement which would reconcile Protestants and Catholics, and gain the approval of Dublin.

Chapter Ten

Not only did the British, earlier guilty of damaging delay in repairing the state of affairs in Northern Ireland, now incur the guilt of excessive haste; they also made a further mistake in that, having previously done too little — usually nothing at all — for the Northern Catholics, they now pursued a policy too favourable to them, and fatal to the Unionist leader, Brian Faulkner.

The phrase "The Irish Dimension" first appeared in a British Government green paper published in the autumn of 1972. The British declared that they wished to "bind" the Catholics to the institutions of the state; but they acknowledged that in order to do so it was necessary to dilute the concept of allegiance. Not only would it be necessary to bring the SDLP, as representatives of the Catholics, into government; the SDLP could come in and nevertheless retain their allegiance to the concept of an all-Ireland republic; furthermore, the creation of all-Ireland institutions was envisaged. This last was later proposed in the form of a Council of Ireland which in fact never came into existence, but which would have had not only a rudimentary all-Ireland parliament composed of representatives of the Dáil and a Northern Ireland assembly, but also executive powers of its own. These executive powers were left undefined, but were intended to include an oversight of security.

These terms — the foundation of the Sunningdale agreement of December 1973 — did not of course appear at first in their full clarity. When the green paper appeared one of the Unionist leaders at Westminster told me with great complacency that he found it entirely satisfactory; he thought "The Irish Dimension" (admittedly a fairly vague idea at this time) a meaningless phrase.

The SDLP and the Lynch government in Dublin had much better reason to find the British proposals satisfactory. They entered enthusiastically into negotiations, and from this point onwards the British kept them very closely informed, usually in advance, of their proposals. Relations, recently so chilly, soon became warm, even excessively cosy. Little changed when Lynch lost his Dáil majority in a general election early in 1973 and a Fine Gael-Labour Coalition Government, with Liam Cosgrave as Taoiseach and Garret FitzGerald as Minister for Foreign Affairs, took office in Dublin (Lynch went so far as to arrange a meeting between Heath and Cosgrave before the latter took office).

Though assured of SDLP co-operation — at a price — the British had to put together the other pieces of the Northern jigsaw. They knew that they could rely on the small, non-sectarian Alliance Party; they still had to face the problem of who would represent the Unionists, who must after all constitute the majority in a Northern assembly and executive.

Faulkner stayed out of favour in Whitehall for some little time after his intemperate reaction to the fall of Stormont. The British were prepared to entertain the idea of helping other Unionist leaders to "emerge" — one of their favourite words. They flirted for a while with Paisley, but Whitelaw concluded within a matter of a few months that only Faulkner could lead the Unionists into the new settlement. When some of his advisers urged him to take Faulkner's name off the list of possible Unionist leaders, he refused, saying that he would merely "leave him on the shelf for a while". Whitelaw was right in his belief that he would have to deal with Faulkner, but the latter, by the time he was fully restored to favour, had made one or two serious mistakes of his own which better relations and more self-confidence might have helped to prevent.

New legislation provided for the election of an assembly and the formation of an executive to which power would be devolved in instalments. Several Unionist parties and factions fought the assembly elections of 1973, but Faulkner fairly successfully fought off the challenges of his main rivals, Paisley, Craig and Ernest Baird, the leader of a third splinter party. However, Faulkner and the main-stream Unionists unwisely committed themselves against sharing power with "republicans" — and many of their supporters, and all their Loyalist rivals, included the SDLP in this category. The British, by contrast, were well satisfied. Although the opening of negotiations with the SDLP provoked further defections from Faulkner, he had enough seats to ensure, in coalition with the SDLP and Alliance, a commanding majority in the assembly.

Faulkner, more than other politicians, depended on the goodwill of the British, and came under more pressure to reach accommodation. In the words of Gerry Fitt, "Wee Brian can have sixty per cent of something or he can have a hundred per cent of nothing." He got his 60 per cent all right, in the form of a Unionist majority on the executive (called for the time being the "executive designate") but what was the "something"? It soon emerged that there would be something for the British, something for the SDLP, something for Dublin, but precious little for wee Brian.

British haste and lack of sensitivity in this period had their origins chiefly in domestic political considerations. Heath cared little for Faulkner's internal difficulties and did not scruple, at the subsequent Sunningdale Conference, to bully him into concessions which he thought unwise. Heath's relations with the unions had once again deteriora-ted, and he wanted Whitelaw (who might have appreciated the delicacies of Faulkner's position better) back in London quickly to use his powers as a conciliator. In the event he got the worst of both worlds, translating Whitelaw from Belfast before his work in Northern Ireland was completed, but too late to make any significant impact on relations between the Government and unions — and too late, specifically, to prevent a strike by the miners. British insensitivity was also seen in attitudes towards the Republic, as in the quarrel over extradition which was to follow; but where it now wreaked most damage was in failing to strengthen Faulkner's leadership of the Protestant population.

The formation of the "executive designate" was only the first part of what was meant to be a three-part procedure. The second was the Sunningdale Conference of members of the Executive and of the British and Irish governments; the third was to be the setting up of the Council of Ireland.

Faulkner had several clear objectives at Sunningdale, including concessions which he hoped to obtain from Dublin and the SDLP and matters on which he hoped not to have to concede. Chief among the latter ranked his view of the Council of Ireland, which he wanted to be a harmless "talking shop". The concessions he sought were the recognition by the Republic of the constitutional position of Northern Ireland as part of the United Kingdom, extradition from the Republic of persons wanted for questioning about terrorist offences in the North, and support by the SDLP for the security forces. He considered these the minimum terms under which he could keep his fragile party united and gain the support of a majority of Protestants; and he assured me, in a conversation a few days before he went to Sunningdale, that he had every confidence of success.

The SDLP, for their part, had not the smallest intention of agreeing to such terms. They — and Dublin — were eager to obtain meaningful all-Ireland institutions, and they laid particular emphasis on the point that the Council of Ireland should have an oversight of security. They also believed, probably wrongly, that the challenge from the Provos and other extreme elements to their position as leaders of the Catholics obliged them to take a maximalist position.

The Sunningdale Conference was held from 6 December to 9 December 1973 in a civil service college easy to guard and isolate. The Thames Valley police took an obvious pride in their job of guarding; the organisers, one suspects, enjoyed an equal pleasure in their success in isolating the press, who worked in a separate building and stayed in hotels often several miles away. While the politicians argued, through day and night sessions — breaking off one evening for a trip to London and a bibulous dinner in Downing Street, at which sentimental songs were sung — scores of journalists engaged in all-night poker games or scrambled, in a manner hallowed by custom, for liquid refreshment in the hotels. In one hotel the overpriced beer ran out. In the absence of real news, wild rumours flew about and were as often as not believed or half-believed. The BBC reported the imminent breakdown of the conference.

At last, late on the evening of Sunday, 9 December, we were summoned to a conference room and handed the documents detailing the terms of the agreement. The most rapid and cursory reading showed the extent of the victory gained by Dublin and the SDLP. I said to my neighbour, Maurice Hickey, political correspondent of the *Evening Herald*, "It's the jackpot!" Hickey agreed; Liam Cosgrave did not. At this conference, he said, "there were no winners and no losers".

Whatever about winners, there certainly was one loser. This was of course Brian Faulkner, who now (1 January 1974) formally took office as Chief Minister of the new executive, with Gerry Fitt as his deputy. The executive survived until 27 May, a period of just under five months. It collapsed during a strike organised by the Ulster Workers' Council (UWC) and it has become received wisdom that the UWC — or the UDA, which closely associated itself with the strike — brought down the executive. The claim is as plausible as that of the Provos to have brought down Stormont, but no more accurate. The executive, like its predecessor, was dead long before the official obsequies; and, again as in the case of the older

Stormont, the causes of its death must be traced in its genesis.

But if the previous Protestant government and parliament foundered because they never sought, much less gained, Catholic support, the new assembly and executive went down because Faulkner and his moderate adherents could not command sufficient Protestant support. Though he tried, gamely enough, to "sell" the Sunningdale provisions to the Unionist Party, it was clear from the beginning that he had very little to sell.

Essentially, what he had to sell consisted of half a paragraph in the Sunningdale communiqué. Paragraph Five contained two declarations, printed side by side in the text, from the Irish and British governments. The Irish agreed that Northern Ireland could not cease to be part of the United Kingdom without the consent of a majority of the inhabitants; the British declared that in the event of a vote in the Six Counties in favour of a united Ireland, they would accept and support the decision. Looked at from a diplomatic viewpoint, here was a highly sensible and acceptable compromise on the constitutional position, allowing Faulkner on the one hand to deny the existence of any explicit or implicit threat from the Republic, and the Dublin Government on the other to claim that the British had gone farther than ever before towards making what came to be known as a "declaration of intent" in favour of Irish unity. As things turned out, however, the second argument was never put forward with any force; more seriously, subsequent events diluted if they did not altogether remove any benefit Faulkner might have gained.

On the question of extradition, Faulkner succeeded only to the extent that the Conference agreed to set up a joint law enforcement commission comprised of British and Irish jurists, including one from Northern Ireland. The proceedings of this commission, when it met, were marked by fundamental disagreement between the Southern members on the one hand and the British and Northern members on the other.

The members appointed by the Dublin Government

shared the opinion that extradition for political offences would contravene the Constitution. They proposed as an alternative the formation of an all-Ireland court composed of judges from North and South to try terrorist offences. The British and Northern members refused to accept the constitutional argument and, in the commission's report, made plain their preference for extradition. A compromise was reached providing for the passage of legislation in the Dublin and Westminster Parliaments allowing for the trial of "terrorist type" offences in the jurisdiction in which a suspect is apprehended, regardless of the location of the alleged crime.

Very little use has since been made of this legislation, partly at least owing to difficulties in obtaining evidence (Northern courts in such cases rely heavily on confessions, Southern on forensic evidence). Difficulties regarding evidence would have prevailed even if extradition had been agreed: some years later a very senior officer of the RUC told me that his men had files on scores of persons now living in the Republic who had committed crimes in the North, but that they had not sufficient evidence to prosecute more than half a dozen of them. This, however, is not how matters appear to the average Unionist, who has it firmly rooted in his folk consciousness that the Republic swarms with fugitives from Northern justice, whose extradition is refused for political reasons. Extradition has become a catch-cry, and in 1974, Faulkner's failure to make rapid progress on the question hammered another nail in his political coffin.

But the greatest anomalies, and Faulkner's greatest weakness, derived from security, the position of the SDLP, and the Council of Ireland — questions interlinked in such a way as to make it appear briefly that the SDLP had played their cards with exceptional cleverness. In order to obtain their support for the security forces, it was necessary to press ahead with the establishment of the all-Ireland body, and a meeting with that object in view was held as early as February 1974. It seemed extraordinary, at a time when Faulkner's position was already visibly crumbling and far more pressing troubles required discussion, to see ministers from North and South discussing quite petty details of which powers should be handed over by the Dublin government and the Northern executive to a new body. But what infuriated even moderate Unionists was the consideration that SDLP members had been allowed to take their seats in the executive while still withholding full support from the security forces. Their anger grew when they saw some of the SDLP ministers spending what seemed an excessive amount of time in Dublin, discussing Northern affairs with the government there.

The Alliance Party showed themselves even more agitated than Faulkner himself about the delicacy of his position, and accused the Southern government and people of lack of understanding, complacency, and insensitivity to Unionist rights and fears. Their cries drew little response from a puzzled public, or from a government which vied with the SDLP in its claims to have achieved the British declaration in Paragraph Five. In some respects, Dublin complacency eerily echoed British complacency.

It was, however, British complacency and thoughtlessness, coupled with the long-standing tendency of British Governments to regard any cobbled-up "solution" as something permanent and no longer to be bothered about, that would soon deal the executive an irrecoverable blow. This came with the first of the two Westminster general elections of 1974. But before that happened another massive blow had already been struck.

This came from the Republic, when Kevin Boland, one of the Fianna Fáil ministers who had resigned in the crisis of 1969-70, brought a court action challenging the constitutionality of Paragraph Five as infringing Article Three of the Constitution, which claims the right of the Dáil to jurisdiction over Northern Ireland but puts it in abeyance "pending the reunification of the national territory." Boland lost his case, but Faulkner took fright at the defence entered by the Irish Government's lawyers, namely, that the declaration in Paragraph Five did not dilute the force of Article Three. This argument might have appeared better fitted for medieval theologians than modern lawyers and politicians, but it looked real enough to Faulkner, for it made Unionists demand what, in that case, was the value of the Irish government's assurance to them in Paragraph Five. He flew to Dublin for talks with Cosgrave and other ministers, was given reassurances that Dublin stood by the principle of "unity only by consent", and went home to present them to his suspicious supporters in as good a light as he could.

His old adversary, Edward Heath, now took the front of the stage. Having driven Faulkner from office once, he now, though without wishing to do so, did something which would ensure his removal from office a second time. Beset by economic difficulties including the first oil crisis of the seventies, challenged by a miners' strike, with industry on a three-day week, anxious for a new mandate and believing that he had the perfect issue on which to fight an election, he went to the country in February. He lost, though very narrowly, and when he failed to make an alliance with the Liberals, Wilson returned to office at the head of a Labour minority government. In a second election a few months later, Wilson improved his position somewhat, but Labour's control of the House of Commons remained precarious all through their tenure of office under Wilson and his successor James Callaghan, which ended with their resounding defeat by Margaret Thatcher in May 1979.

Heath, in his headstrong way, refused to see or believe how calamitous the consequences of the two election defeats had to be for himself and his faction of the Tory Party. The Conservatives notoriously treat unsuccessful leaders harshly; he had to go, but he tried to cling on, unreasonably. Had he gone quickly and gracefully, Whitelaw in all probability would have succeeded him; while he stayed, Mrs Thatcher's supporters had the time to organise her challenge. She won the leadership with the help of her own courage and iron will, and of a clever campaign led by her great friend and confidante, the war hero and veteran parliamentarian Airey Neave.

Heath's obstinacy and misjudgments, in the first 1974 election and later, had several profound effects for both Britain and Ireland. For one thing, they paved the way for the accession to the Tory leadership and eventually to the Premiership of a most extraordinary woman: extraordinary in the first place for having come to the top without ever having shown much knowledge of either the economy or world affairs, and having held in her career but one cabinet job, that of Education Secretary; more extraordinary still, as would be seen, in her actions as Prime Minister. For another, they marked the departure from the Conservative Party of an equally remarkable man, and one equally inimical to Heath. In the first 1974 election, Enoch Powell counselled the electorate to vote Labour on the issue of the Common Market; in the second, he had himself re-elected to the House of Commons as Unionist member for South Down, and thenceforth he exerted a strange influence, sometimes divisive, sometimes hypnotic, on the Unionists.

By calling the February election when he did, Heath also gave birth to another long-lived misconception. Much the same people who think, wrongly, that the Ulster Workers' Council brought down the executive think that the National Union of Mineworkers brought down Heath. They did not, and could not: only the voters, in a demo-cratic election, could do that. But Heath, by fighting on the phony "who governs?" question, brought the myth into being. As to the immediate effect on Northern Ireland of that election, it is not too much to call it catastrophic.

The election did nothing less than take away most of Faulkner's legitimacy. Moderate Unionist candidates loyal to him failed to win even one of the twelve Northern Ireland seats at Westminster. Anti-Faulkner Unionists and Loyalists took eleven of the twelve. Somewhat later this loss of legitimacy was confirmed when he lost the leadership of the Ulster Unionist Party and had to form his own, notably unsuccessful, Unionist Party of Northern Ireland (UPNI); of more immediate concern was the restiveness or open desertion by Unionist members in the assembly, and evidence of disaffection by members of the executive, whose proceeedings were leaked to the UWC and other organisations. Meanwhile, Provo violence continued, and though the British, not the executive, were responsible for law and order, this was used by his enemies as an example of the ineffectiveness of his rule.

In April, Cosgrave and FitzGerald went to London for talks with Wilson and his Northern Ireland Secretary, Merlyn Rees. The British leaders offered the Irish reassurances which the sardonically minded might compare in value with the reassurances which the Irish themselves had so lately given Faulkner on the constitutional question. The British would stand behind Faulkner to the last ditch; they would repress violence from all sides; they believed in the soundness of the executive and its future.

The Irish leaders professed satisfaction with the guarantees they had received, and confidence in British firmness. I shared neither their satisfaction nor their confidence. I spent the next few days in London, inquiring into the extent of British determination to support Faulkner, and found, without surprise, that no such determination existed. The British, meaning Wilson and Rees, believed that he could not last much longer unless his luck changed, and they did not foresee his luck changing. Perhaps, they suggested, the SDLP might agree to abandon, or in some way water down, the Council of Ireland, so offensive to Unionists. What did the provision for "executive functions" mean anyway? Not, you understand, that we think even that could save the executive. And as for ourselves, what can they expect us to do? It's really up to those chaps over there. One could call it a very extreme example of the time-honoured British "arm's length" policy; or, put more simply, "goodbye".

Not fully understanding the feebleness of the British position, but convinced of their capacity to topple the faltering executive, the UWC in May embarked on a strike, or "constitutional stoppage" as they called it, designed to bring normal life in Northern Ireland to a halt.

The UWC was partly an organisation spontaneously

sprung from the Protestant workplaces, which of course included the major industries and the huge electricity generating station at Ballylumford, outside Belfast. They owed their origin in part to a former body, based on the Belfast shipyard, called the Loyalist Association of Workers, but they were very heavily infiltrated, to put the case at its mildest, by the UDA, and supported by a number of Loyalist politicians, notably William Craig.

They — and the UDA — had examined the question of Protestant power, and found it wanting in two respects, political and military. They judged Faulkner to have lost his legitimacy as the Unionist leader, but he still commanded a majority of sorts in his assembly. They did not have the power, in confrontation with the British Army, to bring about a new régime by insurrection; and in any event — with the exception of the "independence" faction of the UDA — they wanted Northern Ireland to remain part of the United Kingdom. Where then did their power lie? Why, in the "industrial muscle" of the Protestant workers, and their ability to stop industrial production and services.

They were very strongly organised in the power station (their trump card, as they saw it) as well as shipbuilding and engineering; in other industries they were relatively weak. Outside Belfast they had some support from farmers, who blocked roads with tractors, but in general they were by no means as convinced of their power and prospects of success as the terrified ghetto Catholics, who laid in supplies of tinned food and candles. They knew that in order to give the appearance of massive support for the strike they would have to rely heavily on intimidation, overt and implied, and from the first morning detachments of UDA men, wielding clubs, appeared on the streets. They still had two adversaries to fear: one was the regular trade union leadership (workers in Northern Ireland are very highly organised, in Irish and British unions); the other was the British Army.

The unions opposed the strike with considerable courage and adherence to principle. Len Murray, Secretary of the British Trade Union Congress, went to Belfast and personally made a brave but hopeless effort to lead a handful of men to work. But much larger numbers of workers stayed at home, either because they approved of the strike, or because of intimidation, or simply because they found it the most convenient course of action (why try to go to work, risking clubs, bombs and bullets, only to find no buses to take you there or back?). That left the Army, and the Government behind the Army. Not only the executive but Whitehall, the ultimate authority, had come under challenge. How would it respond? Would it respond at all?

From Dublin, Cosgrave advised Wilson to "hose them off the streets" (the club-wielding UDA men) and clear the way for people to go to work without fear. But Wilson never had any intention of ordering the Army to use hoses, or for that matter guns. Instead, he went on television and denounced the Protestants, describing them as "spongers on British democracy". Almost immediately, cars (using petrol rationed by the UWC on a voucher system) appeared in the streets, carrying little bits of sponges attached to windscreen wipers and radio aerials. Their drivers knew that Wilson's petulant speech meant victory for them.

Three days later Faulkner resigned. The executive died politically with him, and direct Westminster rule was reimposed.

So the Northern Ireland executive fell, in circumstances of discredit and confusion. A great pity. In this account of it I have concentrated on the unfavourable aspects, and in particular on those which blighted Brian Faulkner's prospects from the start, to the extent almost of expressing the opinion that it never had any chance of survival. But this is far from certain. For all its weaknesses, it is at least possible that it might have survived — but only provided that a reasonable arrangement was worked out on the security question (which will be discussed in more detail later) and that no deadly blow was struck to Faulkner's legitimacy, as happened in the election of February 1974.

Before its corpse grew cold, voices were raised which

declared the sharing of power between Protestants and Catholics a failed experiment, unworthy of reconsideration let alone repetition. This is nonsense. Power-sharing within the executive itself worked for the most part admirably; most ministers, as well as one can judge given the short period involved, did their jobs well, and they established excellent personal relationships with one another. More widely, the Sunningdale agreement with all its contradictions and ambiguities — one may dare to say, *because* of its contradictions and ambiguities — put up some of the signposts to an ultimate settlement between Britain and Ireland. A pity, indeed, that it lasted less than five months. And a great pity that, as we shall see, the lessons to be gained from its establishment, its course and its downfall were so badly learned.

Chapter Eleven

I have only twice seen Whitehall in a state of near-panic. The first occasion, and the more understandable, was the aftermath of Bloody Sunday, when the British Government feared a state of outright civil war coupled with Southern involvement. The second, and more surprising, was provoked by the fall of the executive.

The nervousness which prevailed in Whitehall that week was all the more inexplicable considering that, in the event, direct rule was restored quite rapidly and smoothly and the North settled down again to some sort of stability. What did the British have to fear? They knew that embryonic plans existed for the setting up of a Protestant provisional government which might, in certain circumstances, have declared a form of independence while still proclaiming loyalty to the Crown. Such a declaration would almost certainly have brought about the full-scale civil war which the British had feared since the second decade of the century. But the downfall of the executive, removing at one stroke power-sharing and the Council of Ireland, both detested by the Loyalists, had also removed the threat (however seriously it might be taken) of the most extreme use of Protestant power.

In the Republic, and among Northern Catholics, a different and harsher view was taken of British attitudes. To most Catholics, North and South, it appeared as if the British had backed down from a confrontation with the Unionists, just as they had done in the pre-independence period. More specifically it appeared to them that the British Army had simply refused to intervene.

This view was reinforced indirectly by evidence, which subsequently continued to accumulate, of British intelligence activity in the Republic, and particularly at this time by the strange case of the brothers Kenneth and Keith Littlejohn, who had been employed to infiltrate the IRA and who were both imprisoned for a bank robbery in Dublin. In fact, intelligence activities had little to do with the case. Spying is one of the world's great growth industries, and Northern Ireland had long been a happy hunting ground for agents of various colours and countries. The American Central Intelligence Agency, whose pretence that they do not operate in allied countries is a lie, had long been active there and had established contacts with the IRA; the allegation, made in a New York court case in the autumn of 1982, that they had even been involved in gun-running, has been neither proved nor disproved. That British agents have long been active in the Republic, going so far as to suborn members of the security forces, is no cause for surprise and has little bearing on political/military activities in the North; but in 1974 consciousness of dubious if not actually hostile British intelligence activities did have a bearing on public perception of events there.

At its extreme, the perception was that the Army had disobeyed Wilson's orders to move against the UDA street patrols during the strike. That seems to me one of the unlikeliest hypotheses. It is far more likely that no such orders were ever issued. In all probability Wilson sought military advice as to the courses of action open to him, and if he did so the Army would have advised him against military action. That still leaves open the question whether, on the one hand, Wilson judged at any stage that anything useful could be achieved by the use of force, or, on the other hand, he contemplated the effects on the prestige of his own Government of allowing the executive to fall. In the Republic, however, people recalled Bloody Sunday, internment and other incidents — and the unwillingness of the British Army to fight on two fronts.

139

Cosgrave was furious. Initially he laid all the blame for the disaster on the British, who in his view had lied to him and FitzGerald and had breached their undertakings to himself and others by failing to back the executive, if necessary by force. He said privately that now they had lost the will to govern Northern Ireland they should declare their intention to withdraw and hand over to all-Ireland institutions, providing the latter with a financial subsidy for twenty years. He was all the angrier because he believed that almost half a century earlier his father, William T. Cosgrave, had been manoeuvred by the British into a position in which he was forced to recognise the Northern Ireland boundary, and into giving the first Free State administration a more "pro-British" complexion than was truly the case.

History notoriously repeats itself when we fail to learn its lessons. In the twenties, as Cosgrave recalled with some bitterness, the infant Fianna Fáil Party had accused his father, unjustly, of "selling out" on partition; now Fianna Fáil would have another opportunity of presenting itself as the "patriotic" party. Unfortunately for him, he allowed this to happen again when he and his ministers very quickly stopped blaming the British and instead blamed the Provisional IRA for the collapse of Sunningdale.

They made matters worse for themselves by adopting attitudes towards the SDLP which betrayed a curious ignorance of elementary psychology. One or two of those who had eagerly claimed a share of the credit for the gains made at Sunningdale now put it about that they had warned the SDLP against seeking too much; and meanwhile, the SDLP leaders who had been received with great warmth and hospitality in Dublin while the executive lasted now found their welcome very much cooler. The Dublin ministers would have shown more sense had they made their earlier welcomes cooler (when the SDLP might have done better to stay away) and the later welcomes warmer (when the SDLP needed shoulders to cry on).

The SDLP had in fact already made a belated effort at compromise. While the strike was actually in progress they and Faulkner had renegotiated, and considerably diluted, the provisions of the Sunningdale Agreement relating to the Council of Ireland. This renegotiation was a painful business, achieved only after one of the SDLP ministers was dissuaded with difficulty from resigning. The party found it hard to abandon or even dilute their beloved "Irish Dimension" and never fully appreciated that its force depended less on institutional expression than on their own presence in government *accompanied by recognition of their aspiration to Irish unity.* They also worried, naturally enough, lest a willingness on their part to make concessions should lose them their powerful electoral position and increase support for the Provos and other extreme parties. My own view at the time was that they were unwise to make any concessions since the executive was doomed anyway. In the event it had no immediate effect on their electoral support in the North or their enormous popularity in the Republic.

If the SDLP would have many more traumas to endure in the coming years, so would the Unionists; but in the aftermath of the strike the more extreme Unionists were of course rampant. Moderate Unionism seemed all but dead, and talk of Protestant power, industrial muscle and ability to make the North ungovernable, was in every mouth. But the Loyalists failed almost entirely to capitalise on their victory. The organisers of the strike distrusted the political leadership, with the exception of William Craig, but they made no serious attempt for a long time to replace it with new leadership or new ideas.

Instead, they luxuriated in the myth of "Protestant power", a myth expressed in dangerous and illusory ways. The real strength of the Northern Protestants lies in their fundamental rights as individuals and as a community; their willingness to fight with whatever means they have at their disposal (political, terrorist, industrial or any other) against what they see as an assault on their rights is important but secondary. Their power, including their industrial power, would be formidable in the face of an onslaught on their rights from the South, but no such onslaught is in prospect. Those who think they can frighten the British by threatening to make Northern Ireland ungovernable are grossly mistaken, as more recent events have proved abundantly. Strikes against direct rule administrations in 1977 and 1981 — the first conceived by the UDA, the second by Paisley — failed dismally. Even in 1974 it was laughable, if also pitiable, to hear threats to close the Belfast shipyard, which the British Government owns and, in view of its huge losses, wishes it did not. Since then the British have allowed Northern manufacturing industry to come close to collapse. In 1974 the North had an unemployment rate of 6 per cent. Since then the rate has quadrupled or worse; one must take into account that the figures are not directly comparable (because of early retirement, youth employment schemes and so forth). The Loyalist strikes have doubtless caused permanent losses of jobs and investment, thereby helping the North's cup of misery to overflow, but they have discommoded the British by little more than making them liable to pay more social welfare money.

But in 1974 one British politician had what amounted almost to an obsession with Protestant power, and he was the one who, with the reimposition of direct rule, mattered most: the Secretary of State, Merlyn Rees.

Rees (later Home Secretary, and one of James Callaghan's closest friends) is an archetypal Labour politician of the war generation, educated but intensely conscious of his working-class roots, an organisation man who likes the hard graft of party in-fighting, home affairs, policing and associated matters. He had come to office imbued with several — related — prejudices which affected his conduct of affairs. He knew the Dublin politicians well but considered most of them frivolous and incompetent, and derided their seriousness on the question of unity. He disdained the intellectual right wing of his own party, who happened to be the same "Gladstonian and Asquithian Liberals" who favoured a united Ireland; and he did not greatly care for the middle-class, too-clever-by-half SDLP. At the same time he had an intense personal dislike of Paisley, while he had a fondness for the Protestant working class, in whom he fancied a resemblance to the Welsh mining community in which his origins lay; and he hoped, by displaying sensitivity to Protestant feeling, to prevent the Protestant workers from falling under Paisley's leadership.

Rees toyed for a while with a plan to hold a new assembly election, to see whether it might give him the opportunity of forming another executive, including Catholics but without any provision for a Council of Ireland. He soon abandoned this course of action. He chose instead to hold an election for a constitutional convention which under an appointed chairman — the Lord Chief Justice, Sir Robert (later Lord) Lowry — would discuss and report on its own proposals for the governance of Northern Ireland; the last word would of course remain with Westminster. The election was held accordingly in 1975 when the moderate Unionists were still reeling and the right wing had their tails up; and it gave the extreme Loyalists and the anti-Faulkner Unionists — now in an alliance in which Paisley overshadowed the weak official Unionist leader, Harry West — a clear majority. However, the weakness of the moderates was counterbalanced to some extent by divisions among the hardliners; these at the time were split into several different groups, of which the most important belonged to the loose alliance under West; in reality, as future elections would prove, only two really mattered, the Official Unionists and Paisley's Democratic Unionists.

Lowry and Rees set about exploiting the divisions within, and between, the Official Unionists and the DUP. Opinions vary as to the skill and application with which they did so. They seemed to me to work extremely hard; they certainly worked very closely together, and Rees's appearance of maintaining a lordly isolation in Stormont Castle was a pose; but one of the shrewdest and best informed journalists thought them "too damned aloof. Lowry could have done a lot more of the sleeves rolled up in smoke-filled rooms — that kind of thing."

At any rate, they soon found a way of exploiting the

Loyalist divisions — with the help of an unexpected ally. This was William Craig, hardline Home Affairs Minister of the *ancien régime,* opponent of O'Neill and Faulkner, founder of the Vanguard movement, who had paraded (unarmed) men, talked of independence and declared that Protestants would "shoot to kill" if provoked. Though a man of considerable personal qualities, he seemed an unlikely moderate. He shared the general Unionist resentment that the power-sharing executive had been imposed by Whitelaw, but he believed thoroughly that Northern Ireland should be allowed to run its own internal affairs. He was of the opinion that the British would grant devolution only on condition of some form of power-sharing ("partnership" was the new catchword), that the Dublin Government's determination to face down the IRA was genuine, and that the Republic did not pose a serious threat to the North's separate existence.

Personal, and political, dislikes also coloured his views. On the one hand he was uneasy about the alliance with Paisley; on the other, he deplored the influence wielded at Westminster (where he himself sat for East Belfast until he lost his seat to a Paisleyite in 1979) over the leader of the Unionist MPs, James Molyneaux, by Enoch Powell. Some called Powell "Jim's Svengali"; Craig saw him as an ignorant busybody. He cared nothing for his huge reputation as a parliamentarian, but vehemently disliked the way he influenced Molyneaux and some others in favour of a policy of "full integration" with Britain — a proposal he viewed as a cul-de-sac, since he was certain the British would never grant it.

Craig came forward with a proposal, not for formal power-sharing, but for "voluntary coalition" — precisely what Rees and Lowry wanted, but infinitely stronger coming from such a source. The arguments over this proposal became the most interesting feature of the convention's deliberations; but they took place, not on the floor in public, but at private talks and committee meetings closed to the press. Rees and Lowry began to entertain hopes of real progress when the DUP showed considerable interest;

but Paisley and his associates quickly backed away in some confusion, with contradictory statements and unconvincing denials. It could not be proved that the Big Man himself had ever contemplated coalition with "Republicans", that is to say Catholics, though it is certain that some of his party had discussed the proposal seriously.

In all this the DUP, and the Loyalists and Unionists generally, displayed rather poor political sense. What Craig could see, and they could not, was that they thus threw away the opportunity of a masterstroke. A scheme of voluntary and *temporary* power-sharing — with no all-Ireland institutions, and with members of an executive obliged to take an oath of loyalty to the Crown — would have been accepted by the Alliance Party, and would have gravely embarrassed Dublin and the SDLP. If the latter had accepted such a scheme, they would have put themselves at the mercy of the Loyalist majority; if they had rejected it, they and not the Loyalists would have put themselves in the light, as Westminster saw it, of "wreckers" and intransigents.

They therefore looked on in some relief as the convention wound up its affairs early in 1976 with the production of a majority report which showed how little the Unionists had learned from all the troubles. It proposed, in brief, a return to the old Stormont system, with some safeguards for Catholics; and it was rejected, as it had to be, by the British.

Wilson resigned suddenly as Prime Minister and was succeeded by James Callaghan; Rees, who organised Callaghan's campaign for election by the Labour MPs, became Home Secretary, and the former Defence Secretary, Roy Mason, replaced him as Northern Ireland Secretary. Rees would not be remembered for his political achievements (though at least one moderate Unionist said: "He was the one Brit who gave us the chance to say how we should run our own affairs, and we blew it") but for what he did in the field of law and order, in which he left a lasting but contradictory, and in some instances fatal, legacy.

Rees ended internment and set a date in 1976 after which all those convicted of terrorist offences would be treated as ordinary criminals; to house them, a vast new prison complex was built at Long Kesh beside the compounds where those previously convicted remained — some still remain — in conditions appropriate to prisoners-of-war. This was the policy of criminalisation.

Hand in hand with "criminalisation" went "Ulsterisation". This meant that the police, not the Army, would be the chief force for the maintenance of law and order in all its forms. The third leg of the tripod would be "civilianisation" of the police.

These policies have had some considerable successes, but also striking failures. From the beginning they were riddled with contradictions. "Ulsterisation" and "civilianisation" cannot be fully reconciled in the absence of an effective militia acceptable to Catholics. The Ulster Defence Regiment is not such a militia; it is very far from being either effective or acceptable; and the RUC itself has gained only partial acceptability among Catholics. It has few Catholic officers and gets few Catholic recruits, and soon after "Ulsterisation" was introduced, a spate of well-documented reports began to appear which showed, beyond any serious doubt, that grave ill-treatment had been inflicted on suspects in police hands, especially in the RUC interrogation centre at Castlereagh in East Belfast. Whether this derived from excess of zeal or had approval at a very high level is uncertain, but the latter is much more probable. In recent years such practices have ceased or at least become far less common. The present Chief Constable, Sir John Hermon, has convinced most people of his determination to stamp out misconduct among the police; and the RUC have had considerable success in bringing to justice Loyalists guilty of murders and other crimes often committed several years before their apprehension. Nevertheless, Catholic fears and suspicions of the police remain an important irritant.

The contradiction involved in "criminalisation" was that it occurred while Rees, through senior officials, was negotiating with the Provos in the fruitless hope of obtaining a lasting cease-fire. To talk to the Provos is to call in question the legitimacy of the state, a point never lost on any Dublin government (Irish governments, through officials or intermediaries, sometimes negotiate concessions for "subversive" prisoners, but they never admit that they have any status other than that of ordinary criminals, and they never negotiate with them on political issues). In 1972 Whitelaw had negotiated politically with the Provos; and he also, in order to stop a hunger strike in Crumlin Road Prison, Belfast, conceded a demand for "special category" or "political status" for convicted IRA prisoners as well as internees. Rees ended political status, but the Provos — with a great many Northern Catholics not normally their supporters, and not a few people in the South — simply did not regard and do not regard these prisoners as criminals, any more than they accept the legitimacy of the state which has imprisoned them.

As each Provo prisoner (soon INLA prisoners would join them) entered the "H-Blocks" in Long Kesh — officially the Maze Prison — he refused to do prison work or wear prison clothing, remaining in his cell, wearing only a blanket and being denied privileges. Eventually hundreds of men were "on the blanket"; and after a series of running fights with warders they began the "dirty protest", in which they refused to empty their slops and smeared excrement on the walls of their cells. It was only after the "blanket protest" and "dirty protest" had failed to gain the prisoners political status or practical concessions that they embarked, against the wishes of the IRA leadership, on the hunger strikes of 1980 and 1981.

These in their time would have disastrous effects on the whole complex of Anglo-Irish and North-South relations, and would see the inauguration of a new era in the relationship between the Provos and politics. But in the period in which these events had their origins, the late seventies, the new era that mattered was the new era in which Britain was living.

Of course the British had been living in this era ever since the war and the end of Empire. Under both Tory and

Labour Governments, through many changes of policy, the underlying economic decline had continued, neither reaching a climax (as appeared to some) during the first oil crisis of the seventies nor being arrested by the discovery and exploitation of British North Sea oil; indeed, one of the most startling milestones on the road to ruin (to quote the noted economist Wynn Godley) was not reached until 1982, when Britain recorded a deficit in trade in manufactured goods, the first in peacetime. But hitherto Britain had at least lived for most of the time under stable governments of both major parties which enjoyed secure parliamentary majorities.

It was otherwise with the Government of James Callaghan, who succeeded Wilson as Prime Minister in 1976, recalling Rees to London as Home Secretary and appointing Roy Mason as Secretary of State for Northern Ireland. This Government, like its predecessor, had little economic policy beyond persuading the unions — successfully for some years — to accept pay increases which lowered real living standards because they trailed far behind the inflation rate; it had little foreign policy, in large part because of continuing Labour suspicion of the EEC, reflected in non-co-operation which often amounted to obstruction; and, after the failure of the constitutional convention, it had no Irish policy. Worst of all, however, from the Irish viewpoint, was its lack of a certain parliamentary majority. Callaghan did not fancy his electoral chances sufficiently to take the usual way out and call a general election, so in order to cling to office, he made deals (or had others, usually his parliamentary right-hand man Michael Foot, make deals) with minor parties: the Liberals and the Unionists. These manoeuvres created great resentment in Ireland. They gave the Unionists a new focus — though a divisive one — to replace the Stormont which they had lost and could not have back again. Under the skilled guidance of Powell they played the Westminster parliamentary game cleverly, taking all they could and giving in return as little as possible in the way of support for the Labour Government. In their biggest achievement they obtained a promise that the number of Northern Ireland seats at Westminster would be increased from twelve to seventeen.

Such concessions did not save Callaghan. In the end the Unionists chose as inconvenient a time as possible to withdraw their support, thus helping to force the general election in which the Conservatives won an easy victory in May 1979. They strengthened, unintentionally, the "integrationist" wing of the Unionist Party, led by Molyneaux with Powell at his elbow. This caused considerable friction, but mostly underground, between the "integrationists" and "devolutionists"; the latter maintained a majority in the party, though devolution remained off the agenda for several years longer.

The new Secretary of State clearly had no instructions, and no desire, to undertake important political initiatives. Harold Wilson in his day had tried to establish a rapport with Irish politicians by telling them, in a well-intentioned but irrelevant way, that more Irish Catholics lived in his Merseyside constituency of Huyton than in any of theirs. Roy Mason, sometimes known as "the Barnsley Brawler" because of his political style, began his conversations with them, as with everybody else, by telling them that he had started work in a coal-mine at the age of fourteen. The SDLP disliked him personally and complained that he was unresponsive to their representations about police behaviour (this was the age of the Castlereagh events). They also thought he much preferred the company of Unionists to theirs. Whatever about Unionists, he certainly liked the company of soldiers: in his previous job, that of Defence Secretary, he had got along famously with the generals.

In his three years of office Mason had two moments of glory. One came when he persuaded an American sports car manufacturer, John De Lorean, to set up a factory near Belfast. The factory had some initial success and employed at one stage over two thousand people, but the venture collapsed in 1982, simultaneously with the arrest in the United States of De Lorean himself on charges of trafficking in drugs. It had cost something in the region of £100 million in British public money.

Mason's other great moment had come earlier, in the summer of 1977. In her Silver Jubilee year Queen Elizabeth showed herself to her subjects in every region of the United Kingdom. By her own desire — according to the official account — her itinerary included Northern Ireland. But a royal visit to Northern Ireland posed enormous problems of security and politics.

In 1921 her grandfather, King George V, had driven, un-harmed and indeed unthreatened, through the streets of Belfast to open the first parliament of Northern Ireland, which sat, before the construction of the parliament building at Stormont, in the City Hall. But although he did so before the end of the War of Independence, at a time when a state approaching civil war prevailed in the North, the threat to his granddaughter's safety fifty-six years later was incomparably greater.

The political dangers were no less ominous. The monarchy, in Britain an instrument of unity and healing, in Ireland represented one of the most formidable symbols of division. George V indeed had gone to Belfast — at a time when the British Government of the day was making secret contacts with representatives of the Irish insurgents — with words of peace and conciliation. Elizabeth might speak sooth; she might work (and had worked) in small ways behind the scenes to smooth the path of those who sought a settlement; but unlike her grandfather she could offer no hint that anything of moment was in prospect. Most Protestants would regard her visit as some measure of support and compliment for them; most Catholics would resent it, and their representatives would boycott functions to which they were invited. And on all sides people would wait, most with anxiety, some with eagerness, for the response of the Provisional IRA.

In the event farce predominated — but farce with the usual Northern overtone of tragedy. The royal yacht arrived in Belfast Lough very early on a lovely summer morning, greeted, in addition to the customary manifestations of courtesy, by a barge draped with an enormous banner of welcome. This gesture, designed to appear charmingly spontaneous, had been arranged (in my presence) in the Europa Hotel late the previous night by officials of the Northern Ireland Office, to one of whom, a man of years and distinction, fell the duty of conveying the banner to the barge.

The Queen flew by helicopter from her yacht to the high-walled enclave of Government House (formerly the governor's residence) at Hillsborough, a few miles from Belfast, to meet representatives, not of the people of Northern Ireland but — with very few exceptions — of the Protestant and Unionist people of Northern Ireland. The affair did not begin auspiciously. On her arrival she looked unwell and unhappy; she had never travelled by helicopter before, and she had not enjoyed this unsettling experience. She was also, with good reason, extremely nervous. By her side strutted Roy Mason, looking completely master of the situation.

She made a sufficient recovery to spend most of the afternoon strolling around the grounds, being gracious to hundreds of people presented to her by Mason. The work was tedious, under a blazing sun, but at least the surroundings were pleasant. The same cannot be said of the campus of the New University of Ulster at Coleraine, to which the proceedings shifted on the second day of the visit.

This place had as a claim to royal favour little but the convenience in sealing it off from disturbance or threat. It consists of a handful of identikit modern buildings, situated on a desolate marsh, and its very existence is a reminder of Catholic grievance, for the choice under the O'Neill administration of Protestant Coleraine in preference to Catholic Derry as the site of the university had helped to bring the Civil Rights movement into being a decade earlier.

To Coleraine, however, the Queen went, to show an interest in the university's manuscripts and other treasures, to eat lunch, to make a speech, and to entertain various (again, of course, mainly Protestant) worthies at a garden party similar to that held at Hillsborough the previous day.

The guests did not enjoy themselves as much as they might have expected. Some dozens of them inexplicably fell ill, apparently with food poisoning, and had to go to hospital. The Queen, for her part, very obviously did not enjoy herself at all. When, for example, cameramen a few feet away — far closer than would have been permitted in Britain — disturbed her with lights and noise, her face assumed an expression which, had it been worn by one of her remoter ancestors, would have foreboded a quick trip to the Tower of London. The officials and police who swarmed all over the place appeared equally unhappy, and a good deal more tense. Like the Queen herself, they had excellent cause for nervousness.

Early that morning the *Irish News,* the Belfast Catholic newspaper, had received a telephone call claiming that a bomb had been planted somewhere on the campus, and had passed on the information to the authorities. These put it about that the call was a hoax (bogus calls are of course commonplace) and that a breach of the enormous advance security was out of the question. In fact they knew the call was genuine, and while the Queen peered at manuscripts and chatted with guests, police and soldiers searched feverishly for the bomb. They found it late in the evening, long after the Queen's departure from Coleraine. They continued, however, to deny the breach of the security screen, saying that the bomb must have been thrown from a nearby roadway — a claim both false and implausible.

The next morning the BBC reported — in a manner that left no doubt of the story's origin, "heavy briefing" from Stormont Castle — that Mason had personally advised the Queen to carry on with her programme at Coleraine. Plainly Mason was trying to get all the credit he could for taking a stand that could be praised as strong, courageous and so forth.

One can say in his favour that, after all, the Queen had arrived and gone away safely, that she had not passed within a quarter of a mile of the bomb, and that a cancellation of the day's programme would have meant not only a blow to the standing and competence of the authorities, but a massive affront to her own dignity. But Mason nevertheless stands accused of arrogance and irresponsibility amounting almost to recklessness. If the bomb had exploded, causing perhaps the death of a policeman or a soldier, *in the very presence of the monarch,* no one can say what consequences, in the shape of Loyalist anger and retaliation, might have ensued. Certainly the police made no secret of their anxiety in this regard.

The Queen's own feelings, especially under the strain of concealing the fear which plagued her throughout the visit, are easily imagined. In the helicopter which conveyed her from Coleraine back to the royal yacht her husband, the Duke of Edinburgh, squeezed her hand and said: "Well, dear, unless they torpedo the Britannia we've made it." There can have been few odder contacts between a sovereign and her loyal subjects.

The royal visit had some amusing sequels — amusing, at any rate, at a safe distance. Contrary to normal practice, not a single local person associated with it received an award in the next honours list. This looked very like a sign of royal displeasure. Elsewhere, the Buckingham Palace press office handled royal press arrangements. In Northern Ireland, the Northern Ireland Office took over. Their chief information officer appeared in the honours list; this wise man had taken his annual leave at the right time.

In the television pictures of the Queen's arrival at Hillsborough, with the gamecock Secretary of State all but taking precedence of his sovereign, many found matter for derision. Not so Roy Mason. He liked them so much that he asked BBC Northern Ireland to show them nightly when they played "God Save The Queen" at the close of the programmes. When the BBC refused he persuaded the commercial company, Ulster Television, to do so.

One more footnote: on the first day of the visit a very small riot occurred in the centre of Belfast. An Italian journalist asked Gerry Fitt why the Dublin-controlled police were preventing the Belfast Catholics from demonstrating their love for the monarch. Fitt, the most voluble of politicians, for once found himself without words.

Chapter Twelve

For the Republic, too, these were locust years.

They seemed far otherwise at first. After sixteen years of Fianna Fáil rule, ending in dissension and inertia, the coalition had come into office in 1973 with a gloss of imagination, vigour and reform. It had impressive-looking ministers, and considerable liberal, trade-union and media support. On the economic side, the benefits of EEC membership — which gave agricultural prices an enormous boost, thus also aiding the balance of payments — offset the damage caused by the oil crisis later the same year. FitzGerald as Foreign Minister flung himself eagerly into European politics, believing as he did that membership of the Community gave Ireland its best opportunity ever of developing a world role. In the course of this work he made for himself something of a European and world reputation, and was spoken of as a possible president of the EEC Commission. The first "renegotiation" of the terms of British EEC membership was carried out while Ireland held the presidency of the Council of Ministers, and the work of FitzGerald and Irish officials helped to achieve an arrangement between Wilson, then Prime Minister, and his EEC partners. With Sunningdale, new hope appeared for a settlement of the Northern crisis.

With hindsight it is possible to see that the feeling of dismay and powerlessness which the collapse of the Northern Ireland executive induced in Dublin had an almost fatally enfeebling effect on the coalition. But at the time this was not apparent: it did not seem to affect the government's legislative programme, and it certainly did not end its lengthy honeymoon with the media, which Fianna Fáil greatly resented.

The coalition set itself impressive goals on legislation, and achieved not a few. In the biggest success of the period, the Finance Minister, Richie Ryan, put through — in the face of determined opposition inside and outside parliament — a radical taxation programme, including a wealth tax. The Labour Minister, Michael O'Leary, had several reforming measures enacted, including bans on discrimination against women in pay and appointments. The Parliamentary Secretary for Social Welfare, Frank Cluskey, considerably extended the scope of the social services.

But successes like these counted for little by comparison with a series of deadly blows, many of them self-inflicted, suffered by the coalition in the period from 1975 to 1977.

When the Minister for Justice, Patrick Cooney, brought in a bill to legalise the sale of contraceptives, Fine Gael allowed a free vote of their deputies, but Fianna Fáil imposed a whip on theirs. Although the bill was a government and not a private member's bill, the Taoiseach, Liam Cosgrave, and the Minister for Education, Richard Burke, invoked the conscience clause in their favour and, with several other Fine Gael deputies, joined Fianna Fáil in the opposition lobby to vote the bill down. Fianna Fáil claimed, and many agreed with them, that Cosgrave's action made a mockery of the doctrine of cabinet responsibility. It angered some members of the coalition too: a small group of Fine Gael and Labour ministers held an angry meeting to consider resignation from the Government. Cooney dissuaded them; and only on the left-liberal wing of the Labour Party were calls heard for Cosgrave's resignation.

Fine Gael, the party of constitutionalism and law and order, treated the institution of the presidency in an outstandingly cavalier way. When President Erskine Childers died suddenly in office, the Government knew that a

Fianna Fáil candidate would certainly win an election held by popular vote. In an attempt to avoid an election, ministers quietly canvassed the name of the President's widow, Mrs Rita Childers. They hoped that her popularity and that of her late husband would force Fianna Fáil to accept her. Her candidature was not publicly announced, nor was it stated whether the Government had consulted her, but the plan quickly became public knowledge.

Any who might not have been in the know heard the proposal disclosed — and denounced — by the present writer and Michael Mills, political correspondent of the *Irish Press*, on a radio news programme. There is a time-honoured Irish custom of electing widows to fill their late husbands' Dáil seats, but to extend the principle to the presidency struck us as too Latin-American for comfort. Our comments may have had some value, but it is doubtful if the intervention was necessary. Fianna Fáil had no intention of accepting any candidate other than one put forward by themselves. They might, however, have suffered some embarrassment had the Government persuaded Mrs Childers to stand.

When it became clear that the candidature of Mrs Childers was not a practical proposition, Cosgrave made the rather weak gesture of handing to Lynch a sheet of paper bearing the names of three possible agreed candidates. Fianna Fáil curtly rejected all three, and gave him the name of their own candidate: Cearbhall Ó Dálaigh, a judge of the European Court, formerly a libertarian Chief Justice, and an enthusiast of the Irish language and culture. Amiable, modest and scholarly, he had almost every qualification for the presidency and only one defect: a near-total inability to communicate with the public, whom he bored, irritated and confused with polyglot speeches which expressed impeccable sentiments in impenetrable language. To avoid an election — their chief aim in the matter — the government accepted his nomination.

But they accepted him with ill-grace, which was visible in striking ways from the beginning. At the reception held in Dublin Castle to celebrate his inauguration the guests were taken aback by the inferior quality of the food and wine — though none of them, unlike Queen Elizabeth's guests at Coleraine, was reported to have suffered any subsequent ill-effects. Hardly had the new President taken up residence in his palace in the Phoenix Park (Áras an Uachtaráin, the former British Viceregal Lodge) when rumours became current in Dublin of bad relations between him and the Government. These bad relations soon came to a head.

The one part of the Sunningdale Agreement that had survived and, in a manner, flourished was the joint law-enforcement commission. Neither its members nor the two governments involved could agree on the best means of curbing cross-border terrorist activities. The Irish rejected extradition for politically motivated offences as unconstitutional and also, *sotto voce,* on political grounds (for any Irish Government would incur unpopularity if it handed people over to the RUC) while the British, for their part, had little time for Dublin's most favoured proposal, an all-Ireland court to try terrorist offences. However, the jurists on the commission, and the two governments, found little difficulty in accepting the principle of extra-territorial jurisdiction as a second best. Accordingly, legislation was passed by both the British and Irish parliaments providing for the trial of scheduled offences in the jurisdiction in which the suspect was apprehended.

An Irish President has few powers, but those he does enjoy are important. He may refuse a dissolution of the Dáil to a Taoiseach who has lost the confidence of the house; and he may, before signing a bill passed by both houses, refer it to the Supreme Court for a test of its constitutionality. President Ó Dálaigh exercised the latter power in the case of the Criminal Law Jurisdiction bill. The court, as expected, found in it nothing repugnant to the Constitution, but the President's action drew down on him the wrath of the Government. The Minister for Defence, Patrick Donegan, called him "a thundering disgrace" — addressing his remarks about the President (and Commander-in-Chief of the armed forces) to an audience of army officers.

Few doubted that the Minister's views were shared at a higher level. A contrite Donegan offered Ó Dálaigh an apology, which the President refused, demanding instead his resignation. Donegan offered Cosgrave his resignation; when the Taoiseach refused it, Ó Dálaigh himself resigned the presidency and retired to a cottage in County Kerry, where he died not long after.

No constitutional crisis ensued. Cosgrave shrugged off the incident, and calmly endured a minor humiliation when he accepted the new Fianna Fáil candidate for the presidency: Dr Patrick Hillery, Vice-President of the European Commission and a former Foreign Minister. He thus again avoided holding a presidential election which Fianna Fáil would have won.

But the consequences of the affair could not be dismissed as lightly as Cosgrave supposed. It shook the Government, and damaged its standing with the public. The Government had unquestionably behaved arrogantly, discourteously, and with scant regard for the dignity of the highest office in the country. Ireland lost a good man and a good President, who might even in time have learned the art of communication. The affair also left a regrettable stain on the career of Donegan, an excellent Defence Minister who had done a great deal for the army's morale, but who could not live down his attack on the Commander-in-Chief before an audience of men who held the President's commission. And a minor but ominous precedent was noted by the keen-sighted: this was the first time that two Presidents in succession were chosen by agreement, not by popular vote. It is all too probable that in future the politicians will go out of their way to try to confine the decision on who is to be President to themselves, instead of allowing the people their say.

The coalition might have survived these and other incidents reflecting on their style of government. They did not, however, survive the next crisis and their reaction to it. This crisis began with one of the most dreadful events of the whole troubled period: the murder in 1976 of the newly appointed British Ambassador, Christopher Ewart-Biggs, within sight of the gate lodge of his residence at Glencairn, outside Dublin.

It is unnecessary to dilate on the terrible and shocking nature of this event. The murder of an envoy — which represents also the murder of a guest — strikes at the roots of civilised life and relations between countries and peoples. It is a gross affront to the state and the people he represents, and in any circumstances it cannot but deeply embarrass the responsible authorities.

In this case the culpability of the authorities was particularly flagrant. A bomb had been placed in a culvert under the road, a couple of hundred yards from the Ambassador's house, and members of the Provisional IRA, who had taken up positions on a slight rise of ground nearby, detonated the bomb as the ambassador's car passed over it. All this happened under the noses of the gardaí and in broad daylight. Moreover, the subsequent investigation was abominably mishandled. A most extra-ordinary dispute broke out, and became public, among the detectives investigating the case, in which the validity of fingerprint evidence found at the scene was upheld by some experts and challenged by others. Nobody was brought to justice.

The Government, who throughout this period did — like their predecessors — too little to improve police equipment, training, leadership and general efficiency on the ground, reacted — again like their predecessors when faced with other crises — by introducing yet more emergency legisla-tion on top of the already enormous sheaf of measures available to them.

Somewhat to its surprise, the country discovered that it had been living for a generation under a state of emergency declared on the outbreak of the Second World War, and never rescinded. The Government now proposed to repeal that emergency but to declare a new one, arising out of the Northern troubles; and it recalled the Dáil in September 1976 for a special session to consider two new bills, an

Emergency Provisions bill and a Criminal Justice bill, which contained as their most controversial measures an increase in the penalty for IRA membership to seven years' imprisonment, and an anti-press clause which would make newspapers liable to penalties if they came under a vague and wide-ranging definition of encouragement of violence.

The first of these was not quite so ferocious as it appeared, though seven years for some misguided — or intimidated — youth, who might never have engaged in any violence, seemed a heavy penalty. For several years a special criminal court composed of three judges (as compared with only one judge in Northern non-jury courts) had adjudicated terrorist charges. These courts operated by the normal rules of evidence, with one important exception, and the public by and large accepted the necessity for non-jury courts. But organisations like the Irish Council for Civil Liberties were uneasy about the possible effects of the enactment of new measures on top of some controversial pre-existing ones. What this provision meant, in short, was that someone could be sentenced to seven years if a chief superintendent or higher officer gave his opinion that that person was a member of the IRA (the above-mentioned exception to the normal rules of evidence).

It was further proposed that suspects could be held for seven days (as in the North) without being charged, and without access to a doctor or solicitor. This was bound to cause controversy in view of the numerous reports of ill-treatment of persons held for seven days in the North. Even though the Government reduced the detention period from seven days to forty-eight hours, and allowed access to doctors and lawyers, the question of police behaviour arose later in the year anyway. A series of articles in the *Irish Times* disclosed the existence of a Garda "heavy gang" which ill-treated suspects in order to obtain confessions. These practices ended after public (and internal cabinet) protests; and from then on the police relied in the main, and with some considerable success, on forensic evidence in major criminal cases.

Protests within the cabinet — from FitzGerald and from

the Minister for Industry and Commerce, Justin Keating — had already caused the Government to water down the clause in the emergency legislation which caused it most embarrassment — that referring to press comment. Their intervention followed a remarkable gaffe on the part of Conor Cruise O'Brien, one of the staunchest supporters of the new legislation.

O'Brien, who to FitzGerald's annoyance retained the anomalous position of Labour party spokesman on Northern Ireland in addition to his official position as Minister for Posts and Telegraphs, and whose statements on the subject did not always meet with FitzGerald's approval, gave an interview to Bernard Nossiter of the *Washington Post* before the emergency legislation came to be debated in the Dáil. In the course of the interview he opened a drawer and produced a file of (mostly innocuous) letters which had appeared in the Fianna Fáil newspaper, the *Irish Press,* citing them as examples of what might be banned in future. Nossiter, a little bemused, went straight from the Minister's office to that of his friend, Tim Pat Coogan, editor of the *Irish Press,* and a storm erupted in the newspapers.

This incident, and the Dáil debates of September 1976, marked the end of the honeymoon between the coalition and the media which had lasted for well over three years. Ministers reacted with disbelief and petulance. Some blamed the IRA for all the country's troubles, and in one or two cases convinced themselves that behind the activities of the IRA lay a communist conspiracy. Thus obsessed — and almost ignoring the greater concerns of the public, namely the country's growing economic difficulties, high taxation, and discontent among farmers who saw their gains from EEC membership eroded by a high inflation rate — they handed Fianna Fáil a golden opportunity, which the latter quickly seized.

Fianna Fáil are a marvel among political parties. The noisy and unthinking "patriotism" of their more robust members compensates, in a way, for their lack of any coherent economic and social policy, sometimes praised as "pragmatism"; it also masks great shrewdness, flair for organisation, lust for power, and ruthlessness in their attempts to maintain a near-monopoly of patronage. Too accustomed to office, they usually put up dreadful performances in opposition, but it never does to underestimate them. The coalition underestimated them.

By 1976 only the most extreme of the coalition ministers still clung to the suspicions they had once entertained about Lynch's apparently feeble role in the arms crisis of 1970. Most had developed a respect for him and an understanding of his internal party difficulties. But they also believed that they could use the unhealed wounds of Fianna Fáil to their advantage.

Lynch disliked the word "bipartisanship", which in his view implied advance consultation on policy; he sought, instead, what he called "an agreed approach" or "a unified approach" among the three Dáil parties on the Northern question. This the coalition determined to deny him. They did not wish to concede him a share in the electoral benefits of their moderation on the North — so appealing to the middle classes, increasingly alienated from any interest in the subject by the continuing violence — or their vaunted successes at Sunningdale. They counted on Fianna Fáil's divisions and tensions increasing when Lynch went into opposition. In this estimate, they proved all too correct.

Lynch welcomed the Sunningdale Agreement, claiming that Fianna Fáil had paved the way for it. He might have claimed with more justice that he personally, rather than his party, had developed the policy of which it was the fruit, for Sunningdale fulfilled his demand to the British, made years earlier, for "quadripartite" talks. But he ran into trouble almost at once. Much of the party felt uneasy about Paragraph Five, which stated that Northern Ireland could not cease to be part of the United Kingdom without majority consent; and the defenders of the agreement failed to make sufficient capital out of the parallel provision, which declared that Britain agreed, in the event of consent, to support Irish unity. When Sunningdale was debated in the Dáil in 1974, Neil Blaney embarrassed Lynch by tabling a strongly anti-partition amendment to the Government motion of support for the agreement; and party opinion forced Lynch and his deputies to vote for the Blaney amendment instead of backing, as he would have wished, the Government line.

On going into opposition, Lynch had moved to consolidate his position in the party by appointing a kitchen cabinet of three bright young men: Séamus Brennan, General Secretary, Frank Dunlop, Press Secretary, and Esmonde Smyth, head of a backroom policy "think tank". At the grassroots level he oversaw the organisation of a series of regional conferences, youth conferences, policy conferences and the like. These produced little in the way of solid achievement, especially in the matter of policy; they were not designed to do so; they were dominated by Lynch supporters and designed chiefly to help maintain his grip on the party.

Unfortunately for him, another and deeper movement was going on concurrently within Fianna Fáil. Charles Haughey had no intention of sitting for ever on the back benches. He wanted office, and the dismay and discontent which followed the collapse of the Northern Ireland executive in May 1974 seemed to point a way to it. He said very little in public, but he accepted every invitation he received to attend and speak at party functions throughout the country — and he received a great many. There was more than a little incongruity in the spectacle of Haughey, the millionaire gourmet, used to living in a Georgian mansion amid antique furniture and works of art, embarking on the "rubber chicken" circuit, frequently in locations as dubious in decor and comfort as in gastronomy. Years later he told me that he had attended so many country dinners that he could readily identify which factory the chicken had come from. But it was well worth it. He found that he had retained his long-standing popularity among the rank and file, and that the same rank and file wanted a far "stronger" line on the North.

Others were finding out, if they did not already know,

much the same thing. They included Michael O'Kennedy (later Foreign Minister, later a European Commissioner) who in the autumn of 1975 produced — more or less out of the blue, but knowing that it was what the grassroots wanted — a policy document calling for a British declaration of intent to withdraw from Northern Ireland.

O'Kennedy and other advocates of this course argued that such a declaration would "concentrate the minds" of Unionists and cause them to look favourably on an offer from the South of negotiations to work out the shape of the new Ireland. O'Kennedy also cast doubt on acceptance of the principle of Northern consent to a united Ireland. Lynch had implicitly accepted this principle when he publicly supported Sunningdale, but it was viewed with disfavour by a majority of the party.

Lynch hedged desperately on the question of a declaration of intent. He tried to draw back from it as much as he could, reiterating his own view that the British should be asked merely for "a declaration of interest in Irish unity"; but he could not prevent it from being adopted as party policy. He was further obliged to acknowledge Haughey's increasing power in the party — manifested by his election as one of its vice-presidents — by inviting him back on to the front bench as spokesman on health and social welfare.

Spurred by these events, and by their successes in the quarrels over the presidency, Fianna Fáil were ready for action when the coalition overplayed their hand in September 1976. Their opposition to the bills introduced in the emergency session was of course tactical and partisan. Their concern for civil liberties did not exceed that of Fine Gael, and fell greatly below that of the liberal wing of the Labour Party. But they had good, if sometimes subliminal, points to exploit.

Fianna Fáil, when they enact and implement repressive legislation, customarily do so with an air of firmness combined with apology, conveying the impression of bowing to distasteful necessity; their spokesman on justice, Gerry Collins, was a master of this art. The coalition, by contrast, gloried in what they were doing, forgetting the old Irish dictum that "it's only a sin if you take pleasure in it". At this time the magnitude of the Provo threat to the stability and even the survival of the Republic's institutions had not yet been fully perceived, and even had that been the case, many would still have thought the measures proposed to meet the threat excessive. On top of all this the Fianna Fáil front-bench security and Northern affairs team, augmented at his own insistence by Haughey, did an impressive job of parliamentary opposition. And the press, for the first time in that parliament, were ready to be impressed, wanted to be impressed. Praise for the coalition gave way to newspaper articles describing Fianna Fáil as a useful opposition and a credible alternative government.

It was a turning-point for the parties — and for Haughey, who rode out in an adamantine way the attacks of coalition ministers. These could not accuse him of gun-running, since he had been acquitted on that charge in the courts, but they revived the embarrassing and unanswerable charge that money voted for relief of distress in the North while he was Finance Minister had been mysteriously diverted into the funds of the Provisional and Official IRA. This blot on his record also, of course, caused disquiet in his own party; but in 1976 its attempted use by the coalition was rightly seen as diversionary and irrelevant.

Against the advice of some of his ministers, who wanted to wait until the autumn, Cosgrave called a general election in June 1977. The coalition suffered a devastating defeat. Fianna Fáil came back with a majority of twenty seats, the highest ever, in a chamber of 148 members. For the coalition it was an inglorious end to a sad chapter which had opened so brightly.

The reasons for the coalition's overwhelming defeat will be discussed in the next chapter, but before doing so, it is necessary to accord FitzGerald credit for his attempts to develop new policies in the area of North-South and Anglo-Irish relations. Unlike most of his colleagues, he did not react merely with dismay to the powerlessness of Ireland *vis-à-vis* Britain, revealed so luridly by the fate of Sunningdale and the duplicity which accompanied it. Sharing Cosgrave's hereditary distrust of Britain, he more than anyone had always viewed Common Market membership as a means of getting out from under the British shadow, and even as an instrument which perhaps, in time, might help to solve the "national question". So far little had been achieved beyond a friendly though useful interest. Statesmen like ex-Chancellor Willy Brandt of West Germany and the late President Georges Pompidou of France reminded the British from time to time that they had an eye on them, but this hardly amounted to "internationalisation" of the Northern question. Now, during 1975 and 1976, partly at the instigation of John Hume, FitzGerald moved quietly to establish another and more promising "dimension": the American dimension.

Hitherto the American contribution, and especially the Irish-American contribution, had been mainly negative. Millions of Irish-Americans, far more than their cousins at home, retain an ancestral hatred of England. The flight of their forebears from the stricken homeland during the famine of the 1840s forms an important part of their folk memory. They blame Britain for centuries of oppression of Ireland, and they view Britain as occupying a part of Irish territory by force and in opposition to the wishes of the Irish majority. From 1970 onwards they contributed large sums of money to the Provisional IRA through "front" organisations in the United States, and these contributions continued from year to year in spite of constant appeals from Lynch and others and in spite of the setting up of organisations like the Ireland Fund, designed to divert Irish-American dollars into more useful channels, like support for the arts in Ireland.

The new policy built on developments like the Ireland Fund, but went a long way beyond them. In addition to FitzGerald and Hume, those who chiefly devised it and carried it into effect were Seán Donlon, Assistant Secretary for Anglo-Irish Affairs in the Foreign Affairs Department, later Ambassador in Washington, later Secretary of the Department; and Michael Lillis, Counsellor at the Irish Embassy in Washington, later Assistant Secretary for

Anglo-Irish Affairs in the Taoiseach's Department. The initiative enjoyed quiet behind-the-scenes support from Lynch.

On the American side, support for the policy relied heavily on the moderate mainstream of Irish-American Democratic Party politicians, led by the "Four Horsemen": Senators Edward Kennedy and D.P. Moynihan, Speaker T.P. O'Neill of the House of Representatives, and Governor Hugh Carey of New York. Rational though its objectives and conduct were, it also exploited sentimental Irish-American feeling, which is usually most in evidence around St Patrick's Day, and not by coincidence its two most important public statements were issued in each case on 17 March, the first in 1977, the second in 1981. The first set out its purposes: condemnation of the Provisional IRA, an appeal to Irish-Americans not to give financial or other support to violent activities in Ireland, support for the peaceful reunification of Ireland, and a quiet hint to Britain that powerful people in the United States would not countenance any policy in Northern Ireland which would derogate from the rights of the Catholics. The second announced the formation of the "Friends of Ireland", a body still led by Kennedy and O'Neill but now including important figures in the Republican Party; and its launching coincided with the appearance of the new Irish-American President, Ronald Reagan, as guest of honour at a luncheon in the Irish Embassy.

Reagan on that occasion showed that he was as sentimental about his Irish roots as any roisterer in a South Boston bar. His eyes glistened as he accepted a scroll tracing his descent from medieval chiefs. For himself, he offered little beyond an overflowing goodwill; in practical terms much less than his predecessor James Carter.

In 1977 Carter had made an apparently dramatic, but in the event almost completely ignored, offer of American economic aid to Northern Ireland, conditional on a settlement acceptable to all parties involved. But the value of the "American dimension" does not rest on specific practical proposals, economic or otherwise; it rests, paradoxically, on the exaggerated value which the United States and Britain place on their alliance. Britain is America's staunchest ally (some would prefer to say, most craven satellite) in Europe. American rulers deplore anything that threatens to act as an irritant to the "special relationship"; the Irish question is such an irritant, and Ireland has sufficient friends at court to make the reminder of the irritant constant. But should it ever come to a choice between Britain and Ireland in Washington, Irish ministers and officials know very well that Britain must come first. In trying to call in the New World to redress the balance of the Old, the Irish participants were playing a very big game, and that game has not always been played cleverly.

Chapter Thirteen

The 1977 election result frightened the victors more than anybody else. Lynch said publicly as soon as he knew the enormous size of his Dáil majority that he knew it would cause trouble. The day before the new government took office Michael O'Kennedy put it to me in the form of a paradox: "In a year's time the next election will look a lot farther away than it does now." He meant that Fianna Fáil were for the moment impressed by the brutality with which the electorate had treated the coalition, and knew the same thing could happen to them if they did not tread warily, but that they would soon forget the lesson. Lynch and O'Kennedy were right.

Why did Fianna Fáil win, and by such a margin? At first blush it looked as if the reasons were economic — discontent with inflation, unemployment, high taxation, which contrasted with the Aladdin's cave of bribes to the electorate offered by Fianna Fáil: repeal of wealth tax, removal of domestic rates, abolition of duty on vehicles up to sixteen horse-power, mortgage subsidies, promises of job creation on a vast scale. A deeper look suggested that a complex of feelings connected with the Northern question and style of government (the contraceptives bill débâcle, the Donegan-Ó Dálaigh affair, and all the other mistakes) mattered at least as much.

It was noteworthy that the ministers who lost their seats in the rout included Cooney and O'Brien, while the Finance Minister, Richie Ryan, the alleged author of the national economic misery, held his. Ryan, unfairly dubbed "Red Richie" and "Richie Ruin" by right-wing critics, is a difficult man, by turns conservative, puritanical, hot-headed and impulsive, but he had also shown himself conscientious and honourable, and he had made a fair success of steering the economy through a recession, protecting the poor to the best of his ability and resorting to as little in the way of deficit budgeting as the prevailing conditions allowed him.

Cosgrave was another victim of the defeat, but a willing one. He did not wait to be pushed, but resigned as leader of Fine Gael almost immediately after the election. FitzGerald was elected, unopposed, in his place. Brendan Corish also resigned as leader of the Labour Party and Frank Cluskey, formerly Junior Minister in charge of Social Welfare, was elected leader by a margin of only one vote in the parliamentary party over Michael O'Leary, formerly Minister for Labour. Justin Keating might have been a serious third contender but was not available to stand: he was yet another minister who had lost his Dáil seat. FitzGerald, somewhat like Lynch four years earlier but with much more success, plunged enthusiastically into the work of organisation, ensuring that his own people filled important party positions and strengthening his personal control. By contrast, no improvement appeared in Labour's organisation or popular appeal.

The victors for their part faced three problems: the perennial questions of the North and the economy, and internal dissent within the Fianna Fáil Party. The effects of the first and third of these would in the end prove disastrous for Lynch; his handling of the second — with George Colley as Finance Minister and Martin O'Donoghue as Minister for Economic Planning and Development — was disastrous for the country.

Fianna Fáil, on regaining office, immediately broke the old and cynical, but useful, rule that election promises become invalid the day after the election. There could indeed have hardly existed a less appropriate time for them to fulfil theirs. They had inherited from the coalition a manageable budget and balance of payments deficit; the economy had come through the recession with unemployment under 10 per cent and a declining rate of inflation (which during several years both before and after 1977 exceeded 20 per cent); no injection was needed in the way of a sudden and large expansion of consumer spending. On the contrary, since the Republic had notoriously a small open economy, exceptionally dependent on inflexible imports of energy and raw materials and also exceptionally vulnerable in good times to increased imports of consumer goods, the extra money which the new régime put into circulation by remission of taxes and other popular policies was much more likely to create industrial jobs abroad than at home.

The new Government, however, merrily presided over an uncontrolled — and soon uncontrollable — boom. At one and the same time it forewent revenue from the taxes it abolished, laid an extra burden on the nationalised industries by requiring them to employ extra unwanted and unproductive staff, allowed and even encouraged inflationary national wage agreements, ran bigger and bigger budget deficits, and borrowed abroad, sometimes on unfavourable terms, to finance current expenditure. Within two years the state of the public finances had got totally out of control. And so far from alleviating unemployment, these policies were certain to increase it, for two reasons: they made Irish unit costs less competitive, and they ignored the problem caused by a striking increase in population. (This last problem was somewhat hidden by an extraordinary decision by the coalition to abandon, on grounds of saving the cost, a census due to be taken during their term of office. The population of the Republic, long stable at about three million because emigration took away the surplus, had begun to grow again in the sixties and by the end of 1982 stood at roughly three and a half million).

A new panacea quickly appeared in the shape of the European Monetary System, which Ireland joined — while Britain stayed out — in 1979. It was argued that participation in the EMS, dominated by the Deutschmark, would have the magical effect of reducing Irish inflation rates to German levels. This never happened, and the move produced some unforeseen disadvantages. So far from appreciating, as Ireland expected, against the dollar and sterling, the EMS currencies depreciated, strikingly so when the second recession of the seventies hit Western Europe, and was aggravated by the policies pursued by the Thatcher and Reagan administrations. Oil prices, denominated in dollars, rose to even dizzier levels. However, the effective devaluation of the Irish pound (*punt*) helped exports, and was probably inevitable in any case.

A more curious, and lasting, disadvantage was that the split between the *punt* and sterling created for the first time a monetary border in Ireland. It caused great inconvenience in border areas, where people had for generations been accustomed (in spite of ineffective customs barriers) to free trade; and it added a new weapon, the apparent worthlessness of the Irish currency, to the Unionist arguments against uniting Ireland.

The Government's misdirected economic policies probably had as many social as economic disadvantages. For many years — ever since economic development had begun in earnest in 1959 — the country's increased prosperity brought with it the concomitants of selfishness and corruption, the latter usually on a small scale, the former more insidiously threatening the social and political fabric. But the 1977 government, with its something-for-nothing philosophy, greatly accelerated the most unfavourable social trends, at incalculable cost to the national psyche.

As the puritanical W.T. Cosgrave and Eamon de Valera had understood, freedom requires order, discipline and responsibility, and in the absence of these virtues it cannot flourish. In the sixties and seventies, but most particularly after 1977, they seemed things of the past. Tax avoidance and evasion became more widely practised, with professional people among the worst offenders. The middle classes resented having to pay high rates of income tax

173

when those better off than they were exempted from property taxes. Farmers could not see why they should have to pay income tax at all. Workers who enjoyed industrial "muscle" or secure employment, especially in the public sector, resolved that their incomes should at least keep pace with inflation, no matter who else might suffer.

Social welfare fraud increased, particularly in rural areas, and sometimes as part of a tacit conspiracy between workers and employers to defraud the state. Individuals and communities were encouraged to believe that nothing they happened to enjoy should be taken from them: for example, they were led to suppose that if a factory closed down the Government, regardless of the state of the national or world economy, would immediately conjure another enterprise out of thin air to employ those who had lost their jobs. Yet at the same time an important part of the people's genuine living standards was being eroded.

In the countryside, arterial drainage destroyed scenery and wildlife at enormous cost and with only tiny gains in land reclamation. Pig slurry killed the fish in lakes once famous for their bounty; abandoned cars polluted celebrated beauty spots; hideous bungalows with mock-suburban gardens strung themselves along the rural roads. In the cities, and especially in the capital, dereliction and ugliness prevailed on a scale previously unthought of. Infrastructure everywhere was neglected, with the single exception of telecommunications. Roads fell to pieces under the weight of the increased traffic, and local authorities had no money to repair them.

The spillover of the Northern troubles made violent crime, mostly bank robberies, commonplace. Ordinary criminals, as well as some who had learned their trade in terrorist gangs, found firearms easier to obtain, and used them in gang warfare on a small scale. Mafia-style "families" developed a flourishing trade in heroin, accompanied by extreme violence; gangsters attempted to murder the head of the Garda forensic science laboratory, who was seriously injured but later recovered.

It was pitifully clear that the police — several of whom

were murdered during this period — lagged behind the criminals, "ordinary" and "subversive". They did not have sufficient modern equipment or well-trained officers, and they greatly lacked the resources to penetrate criminal organisations since so much of their manpower had to be devoted to the protection of those most at personal risk, like diplomats.

Even at the most basic level of police activity, they were slow to learn the lessons of the assassination of Ewart-Biggs. They failed to prevent a bomb being placed in the boat — which they were guarding — of Earl Mountbatten of Burma, a member of the British royal family and a war hero. The bomb exploded as he was sailing in Donegal Bay, killing him and killing or seriously injuring several other people; a member of the Provisional IRA was later convicted of the murder. (A little earlier, shortly before the British general election, there had been a third sensational murder of a distinguished Englishman. Members of the INLA attached a bomb to the car of Airey Neave, another war hero and a close friend of Margaret Thatcher, which exploded and killed him within the precincts of the House of Commons).

Yet during all this period, co-operation between the security forces on the two sides of the border continued to improve — as they had been improving ever since 1972 — — and bore fruit. Computers, helicopters, electronic surveillance techniques, in addition to improved communication between the Garda and the RUC, mattered a lot more than the television shots of army vehicles careering along the little border roads. The commitment of large numbers of troops and police to the Republic's border areas undoubtedly helped to prevent a breakdown of law and order in those areas, such as had threatened to occur in 1971 and 1972, and to some extent to contain the terrorism in the border areas of the North. Lynch's and other governments resented the constant British and Unionist calls for the introduction of extradition, since they held, rightly, that their commitment exceeded that of the British in the North.

These developments in security co-operation later had potentially useful consequences in the political field, but at the time they added to Lynch's embarrassment, and contributed to his downfall. Lynch faced a situation, in the North and in Britain, highly unfavourable to him, and damaging to his attempts to maintain cohesion in his party and in the country. He had to listen to the complaints of the SDLP about the Callaghan Government's flirtations with the Unionists, and about the conduct of Roy Mason, who, in their view, was to Northern Catholics and their rights what Henry VIII was to monogamy. He longed for a British government — any government — with a secure majority which would allow it to take its eyes off a parliamentary stalemate and set the political process moving again in Northern Ireland. But when the general election of May 1979 brought to office a Tory Government with a thumping majority, he found himself confronted by a Prime Minister, Mrs Thatcher, more committed to the maintenance of the Union, and less sensitive to the wishes of Dublin, than any of her predecessors since the crisis had begun. An admirer of Enoch Powell, and closely in sympathy with him on Ireland and many other issues, she pronounced herself "four square for the Union" and went back to the tired old assertion that Northern Ireland was an internal United Kingdom matter. Thus neither the Labour Government nor its Tory successor offered Lynch an opportunity to make the semblance of political progress which might have offset his mounting party difficulties.

The chickens of 1977 had come home, as Lynch had foreseen, to roost. Too many backbenchers, underemployed and with little or no hope of preferment, had plenty of time to plot and cabal; and they had a ready-made alternative leader in Haughey. Himself underemployed as Minister for Health and Social Welfare, Haughey maintained and developed his close and friendly contacts with the disaffected backbenchers and with the party organisation, and openly derided the Lynch-Colley-O'Donoghue economic policies.

After two years the gilt had worn off the 1977 ginger-bread. The bribes were forgotten; inflation and unemployment remained. The voters deserted Fianna Fáil in the European elections of 1979, and later in the year Lynch lost two by-elections in his own Cork backyard. He was obviously tired and despondent, and his wife was pressing him to lay down the burden of office. He may well, as he put it about, have earlier set the date of January 1980 for his resignation; in the event, he went a little sooner.

In the summer of 1979, Haughey's supporters organised a barely concealed plot, led by a caucus known as the "Gang of Five", to force Lynch out of office and to make Haughey his successor. Their trump card was the current lack of electoral success, but they chiefly used the question of security co-operation as a stick with which to beat Lynch: they made their loudest complaints about overflights of the Republic's territory by British military aircraft, and alleged that agreement had been reached to allow the British an air corridor, or free flight zone, which they could use as they pleased.

Lynch for his part convinced himself that Colley, not Haughey, would win a leadership election; so did Colley. They were wrong. In December 1979 a bitter campaign in the Fianna Fáil parliamentary party took place — led for Colley by Desmond O'Malley, Minister for Industry and Commerce and Lynch's own favourite for the succession, and on Haughey's side by the ablest of the dissidents, Ray MacSharry. Haughey won, though narrowly, the vote for the leadership.

He hardly had a chance to enjoy his triumph. No Irish leader, with the possible exception of Faulkner, ever had less of a political honeymoon. As his price for remaining in the cabinet and thus maintaining a semblance of unity, Colley demanded and obtained his own retention as Tánaiste, and a say (effectively a veto) on the nomination of the Ministers for Defence and Justice. Not content with this, he made a public speech in which he said that recent events in the party — meaning the plot against Lynch — absolved him of any need for expressing loyalty to

Haughey as the party leader: in other words, he and his faction claimed the right to try to bring Haughey down whenever they judged the time right.

When the Dáil came to debate his nomination as Taoiseach, the opposition parties mounted an even fiercer attack on him. The arms crisis and the misappropriation of public funds were dragged into the debate. Both FitzGerald and Cluskey attacked him as being unfit for the office, FitzGerald (who later apologised for his excessive rancour) speaking of his "flawed pedigree".

The bitterness was intentional, but it had, if anything, the opposite effect to that intended. Some of FitzGerald's advisers thought mistakenly that a number of Fianna Fáil deputies might abstain or even vote against Haughey's nomination as Taoiseach. They underestimated Fianna Fáil discipline, maintained through so many crises on the sound old political principle that those who do not hang together, hang separately. The nomination went through the Dáil.

Haughey retained — he had little option — most of Lynch's Cabinet. He allowed himself the satisfaction of dismissing O'Donoghue (whom, however, he brought back to the front bench two years later) and the Minister for Agriculture, James Gibbons, who had given evidence against him in the arms trial all those years ago. He gave the agriculture portfolio to MacSharry, and rewarded several of his own faction with junior ministries. Some of these were shrewd enough politicians of the second rank, but the appointments of others were greeted with derision, for they had little to recommend them beyond an unsophisticated and meaningless "verbal republicanism".

O'Donoghue's departure seemed to signal a new and much more restrictive fiscal policy, and in January 1980 the delighted economic commentators saw Haughey as bearing out this view when he gave a stern address on television warning that the country had been living beyond its means, and calling for retrenchment. But in the eighteen months of his first term of office he pursued exactly the opposite policy. Borrowing to cover current expenditure deficits accelerated; foreign borrowing grew eventually to

178

some five billion pounds, and the interest on the national debt swallowed up the entire annual revenue from income tax. Pay settlements in the public sector got completely out of hand. The Government sanctioned new spending projects of the most dubious kind, like the construction of an airport on a foggy mountain near the Marian shrine at Knock in County Mayo.

Haughey and a succession of finance ministers tried to justify this *volte-face* by claiming that borrowing was, in effect, both limitless and harmless so long as our international credit stood good. In Haughey's favour, it may be said that he had inherited a dreadful economic situation, brought about largely by an ill-timed reflation, and that he now faced another world recession. But it is hardly possible that he had somehow made himself believe in the virtues of reckless and doubtfully productive borrowing in contradiction of all his previous views. The explanation of his conduct lay not in the economic but in the political sphere. His plan was to hold a general election as soon as possible, and by obtaining another majority for Fianna Fáil, to establish the control of the party which he now so manifestly lacked. But first he wanted to make some progress, of as dramatic and visible a kind as he could, on the Northern question. Meanwhile he would do nothing to alienate the electorate — and electorates are easily alienated by lengthy and disruptive strikes by public service workers.

Haughey's attitudes and policy on Northern Ireland at this time appeared to differ radically from those of Fitz-Gerald — and of Lynch. Lynch and FitzGerald favoured reconciliation of Protestants and Catholics in the North — ideally, a return to a form of power-sharing — and the "American dimension". Haughey considered attempts at any further internal settlement in the North futile — he described Northern Ireland as "a failed political entity" — and he neither understood nor cared for FitzGerald's efforts to broaden the context by enlisting the aid of either the EEC or the United States. He believed that the best approach to a settlement was a bilateral one between the Irish and British Governments.

In reality, both approaches have validity, and are not beyond the wit of man to reconcile. Haughey was right to reject the notion of a purely internal settlement, not so much for the reason that appealed to Fianna Fáil — that it might prop up the Union — as for the simple fact that the unworkability of internal settlements had already been abundantly demonstrated (it has been further demonstrated since then). But any ultimate settlement must of necessity include reconciliation within the North, must indeed rest on a tripod of *rapprochement* between Ireland and Britain, between North and South, and between the two communities in the North.

Haughey, however, was determined on new departures; if he made serious mistakes in pursuit of his objectives, it has to be said of him that he set about his business with more than ordinary courage and resolution.

He had to work from a political base so unsound as to be almost untenable. Like Lynch, he enjoyed a huge parliamentary majority, but majorities are not everything. Half his Cabinet felt themselves in much the same relation to him as Antony to Brutus. Lynch made comments about him in private which were as mordant as those FitzGerald made in public. His relations with most of the media, with many important officials, and with a significant part of the Establishment, were terrible. The business community, remembering his good record as Minister for Finance, at first welcomed his accession to power, but turned against him because of his failure to control the public finances. As to leading journalists, academics and opinion-formers generally, most greatly prefer FitzGerald, and would disagree profoundly with the present author's insistence on laying the chief blame for the scuttling of bipartisanship on the 1973-77 coalition.

It has been said that if power corrupts, lack of power corrupts also. Long exclusion from inner counsels, humiliation at the hands of Lynch and others, had forced Haughey into excessive reliance on his personal friends, few of them well-fitted to advise him on great affairs, and had increased the tendency to pride, introspection and excessive self-reliance of someone who had always seen himself as a man of destiny and acted accordingly. Unreceptive to advice and warnings, he was least disposed to heed, as he was least likely to get, useful briefing and guidance from the quarter that could have done him the most good; for he and FitzGerald regarded each other with open dislike.

Characteristically, one of his first serious mistakes occurred in the area of American policy, when he tried to remove Seán Donlon from the position of Irish Ambassador in Washington and translate him to the United Nations. The furore provoked by the leaking of this news obliged him to abandon the move.

The furore was understandable. Not only was Donlon a personal friend of Lynch, FitzGerald, John Hume, Edward Kennedy and other powerful persons: he more than any other official was identified with the fiercest condemnations of the Provisional IRA and their Irish-American fellow-travellers, and with attempts to reduce American fund-raising for the IRA. Many believed that the attempt to remove him meant an easier line on the extreme Irish-American organisations, and cited as evidence the contacts between these organisations and Neil Blaney — who, it was rumoured at the time, might soon rejoin the Fianna Fáil Party.

These theories remained unproved. As to the Blaney question, it was certain that, if proposed at that time, his readmission to the Party would have been vetoed by the faction led by George Colley, Desmond O'Malley and Seamus Brennan (who having quarrelled with Haughey, resigned as Secretary of the Party, won a Dáil seat at the 1981 general election, and became one of the most determined of the anti-Haughey group). Besides, it was altogether inconceivable that any Taoiseach could turn a blind eye to Provo fund-raising in the United States.

A likelier explanation lies in Haughey's simple desire to have a man of his own in the job — or, failing that, at least to exclude a close friend of FitzGerald from such a crucial position as Ambassador in Washington. FitzGerald himself believed that Haughey just did not understand either American internal politics or the possible advantages for Ireland of an "American dimension".

FitzGerald's assessment was probably correct; and Haughey could be accused of the same lack of understanding with regard to Europe. His subsequent actions seemed to show that he viewed the EEC almost exclusively in terms of securing material gains for Ireland, and that he had no great grasp of Community policy or ideology. His downgrading of the American and European contexts may in part be attributed to the perhaps exaggerated emphasis he placed on trying to work out a Northern solution in co-operation with Britain. He clings very closely to Fianna Fáil mythology and culture, and accepts a Fianna Fáil view of history which stresses heavily the successes of the party, and most particularly the successes of de Valera, in obtaining concessions from the British in bilateral negotiations. And this Fianna Fáil version of history postulates, *inter alia*, that Ireland has gained more from Conservative leaders and governments than from the Liberals or Labour.

Chapter Fourteen

Mrs Margaret Thatcher is a woman of high intelligence and capacity, who believes firmly in herself, works very hard, and has a lifelong record of getting her own way by determined struggle and strength of will. She has well earned the nickname "the Iron Lady", conferred on her by the Russians. She is also a person of extreme narrowness of vision, ignorant of the world, intolerant of opposition, and lacking the quality of imagination which enables the more sensitive to understand the views and aspirations of those different from themselves in class, nationality and other respects. The grocer's daughter from a dim provincial town, on her way through life picked up all the prizes: an impressive university career, a rich husband, a seat in parliament, in the end the premiership itself. She has walked with kings and queens and not lost the common touch — because she never had it.

Much as Haughey identifies with the rural "verbal republican" wing of Fianna Fáil, she is very close to the Tory foot soldiers, above all the new breed, who spring mostly from the lower middle classes and fear and dislike the aristocratic "old gang" almost as much as they fear and dislike the workers. Not for her the patrician disdain of a Macmillan or the European enthusiasm of a Heath; her genuine delight in Tory conferences, her feeling of being among her own folk, cannot be mistaken.

And her own folk, in the conference halls of Blackpool and Brighton and in the House of Commons, respond to her with equally genuine warmth and loyalty. Her supporters — usually authoritarian, very right-wing in their social and economic views, more than a little racialist, and suspicious at best of the Irish — think that Heath let them down when he accepted a doubly alien, aristocratic and European, embrace. They know she will not.

Sharing their prejudices, and determined to reverse the decline of Britain by pursuing policies strikingly different from those of all her post-war predecessors, she set about remaking the country in her, and their, own image. She has a semi-mystical notion (akin to that of Powell) of the race and the nation, and, at a more basic level, is capable of delivering ill-thought-out lectures on the virtues of family life. Her economic ideas are equally old-fashioned: behind the voguish jargon of Thatcherism, Friedmanism, monetarism and Reaganomics lies nothing more than an attempted reversion to the ideas and policies which were universal in the capitalist world in the pre-Keynes era. Again like her supporters, she believes in strict enforcement of the law, with little concern for the forces of social unrest. At home, unlike the great majority of the House of Commons, she favours capital punishment; abroad, she promotes fierce opposition to communism, a friendly disposition to South Africa and right-wing régimes, and unfailing support for American leadership of the Atlantic alliance.

Like most of her faction of the Conservative Party — and, to be fair, like most British politicians — she takes a view of the EEC greatly different from that of the European mainstream. In political terms she saw it almost as an appendage to the North Atlantic Treaty Organisation — which meant, in effect, an appendage to the United States. She was of course correct in viewing the political and defence elements as closely interlinked, but (as with British leaders in pre-entry days) she displayed no interest in achieving some measure of European independence from the United States. On the economic side European leaders, tired of the near-boycott of the Community under Labour, welcomed the return to power in Britain of a Conservative Government. They were somewhat disappointed, for the disruptive and unco-operative British attitude continued under the Tories; Mrs Thatcher made virtually annual attempts to renegotiate the terms of British membership, and since the autumn of 1982 Britain has been making her most determined effort so far to destroy the common agriculture policy.

It was not likely, however, that any British leader in the closing decades of the twentieth century could pursue the policies Mrs Thatcher favoured in their full vigour; and with two notable exceptions she found herself obliged to tread a more moderate and cautious course than she would have wished. One exception was economic policy, in which she continued to adhere to severe retrenchment while unemployment climbed to well over three million. The second was the amazing Falklands affair.

That her policies in other areas were likely to turn out somewhat less rigid was signalled from the start by the composition of her cabinet. It would have been impossible for her to confine her choice to Tories of the new breed, since insufficient numbers of these with the appropriate experience existed; and she had also to maintain party unity, which meant giving, at least at the beginning, a considerable share in power to the moderates or "wets". In addition, most of those with large reputations at home and abroad were members of the worldly-wise "old gang". To the Home Office went Willie Whitelaw, to Defence another former Northern Ireland Secretary and a man of similar stamp, Francis Pym, to Employment James Prior, to the Foreign Office Lord Carrington and Sir Ian Gilmour. Over her years of office the composition of the Cabinet changed radically and it became very much more right-wing, but not all the changes resulted from fixed policy on the part of the Prime Minister. Some indeed were part of a reshaping to make it more to her own liking (as when she replaced Prior with the hardliner Norman Tebbit) but some were voluntary, some the consequence of accident or crisis, and some the symptom of a general rightward drift in the administration.

The Thatcher faction had often derided Heath for his

policy U-turns, but necessity forces policy changes on all administrations. Mrs Thatcher's first climbdown occurred on the issue of Rhodesia, one of the last and most troublesome imperial hangovers; it was watched with intense interest in Ireland.

Rhodesia had been ruled, illegally, for several years by a minority white régime. The British tried to promote an "internal settlement" under which the whites would retain most of the power under a black puppet Prime Minister. Under pressure from African and other foreign opinion, and from two powerful guerrilla organisations based in neighbouring countries, the internal settlement proved impossible to sustain.

At first Mrs Thatcher angrily resisted these pressures and imprudently declared her support for the existing régime, but she soon quite suddenly changed her attitude and gave her blessing to a new settlement which ousted the puppet Premier and brought to power the leader of one of the guerrilla movements. She did so under persuasion, almost certainly from the Americans, very probably from Queen Elizabeth, but chiefly from Carrington.

The affair of Rhodesia, now called Zimbabwe, encouraged Irish politicians to believe that British policy on Ireland could change in an equally sudden and radical way. They knew that knowledgeable British politicians of all parties, and high officials of the Foreign Office, considered a united Ireland the best possible ultimate solution; Carrington had told some of them privately that he himself shared this view, and they placed particular faith in Carrington, both because of his obvious competence and because of all the "old gang" he was much the closest to the Prime Minister and had proved that he could help to change her mind on one important issue.

Nobody watched these events more keenly, or believed in Carrington's influence more faithfully, than Haughey. He reasoned that the British could be brought to see that an "internal settlement" in Northern Ireland had no more chance of success than one in Rhodesia. His first task was to re-establish the Republic as Britain's partner — her *main* partner — in the search for a Northern solution. This aim he now set about achieving, and in fact did achieve, at meetings with Mrs Thatcher in London in May 1980 and in Dublin in December 1980.

Much controversy and confusion still surround these meetings, largely because of the intense partisanship which Haughey inspires, partly because of the combination of secretiveness and contradictory statements which followed the Dublin meeting. A surprising number of people continue to deny that they contained any real substance, but there are logical explanations for the achievement, the confusion, and the ultimate failure of the Haughey-Thatcher relationship.

Haughey believes almost messianically in his abilities, his force of personality — and his destiny. This is one of the reasons why he has few close associates at his own political and intellectual level, and why many politicians and officials find it hard to work with him. In Mrs Thatcher — a self-made woman, as he is a self-made man, and a firm believer in her own destiny — he thought he had found a kindred spirit.

He took exceptional care not to offend her politically, and almost absurd pains to please her personally. At the personal level, he flattered her on her good looks — as well as telling her that the way into the history books was not to take a few points off the inflation rate, but to solve an age-old source of contention between neighbouring countries. Having apparently heard that she had a fondness for nice things, he presented her at their London meeting with a Georgian silver teapot. (A common friend told me about the purchase of the teapot before the meeting, and the *Irish Times* published the story. A high official, obviously at the Taoiseach's instigation, asked the newspaper to suppress it. Whether this was done because of his love of secrecy, or for fear of being laughed at, I have never found out).

At the political level he ignored the first Long Kesh hunger strike, which was in progress at the time of the Dublin meeting in December 1980; and he did nothing to impede a feeble round of talks between the Secretary of State, Humphrey Atkins, and the Northern political parties, though he did not conceal his opinion that they were futile. Much more significantly, from the time he took office in December 1979 he intensified, instead of reducing, security co-operation on the border, and the British — who had feared a reduction in activity by the Irish Army and police — took favourable notice. Their fears were groundless anyway, for it bears repeating that terrorist activities on the border pose more of a threat to the Republic than to Britain, and no Taoiseach could ignore them; in the event, British gratitude was short-lived.

All his careful preparations could not obviate the problems of misunderstanding and irreconcilable attitudes. On the British side I suspect that (on much the same principle which holds that Ireland does better out of the Tories) Mrs Thatcher and quite a number of other British leaders like dealing with, in their own crude terms, "hardliners who can deliver" — delivering being viewed as very much a one-sided business. On the Irish side Haughey was mistaken in supposing that Mrs Thatcher either shared or could be quickly brought to share the favour shown by much of the British Establishment to abolishing or watering down the "guarantee" of the permanency of the Union; for Mrs Thatcher does in fact believe in the Union and in the guarantee.

Since Haughey himself did not believe in the validity of the guarantee to the Unionists, he addressed himself to the question of Britain's centuries-old and permanent interest in Ireland: the strategic question. He knew that, the war-time experience notwithstanding, Irish neutrality — certainly vis-à-vis Britain — is humbug: no Anglo-Irish accord, past, present or future, has ever been contemplated which materially contravenes British defence interests. But he also knew that there is in Ireland, and not least in his own party, a widespread sentimental attachment to the idea of Irish neutrality. He also knew that Mrs Thatcher was passionately, not to say belligerently, interested in the subject of defence.

He therefore decided to dangle in front of the Prime Minister the possibility of an Anglo-Irish defence pact; but he had also to leave himself the option of denying that such a pact was contemplated. This was one reason for secrecy; others will be discussed later. Mrs Thatcher expressed considerable interest in the defence pact idea — an interest by no means unanimously shared by the British Establishment — but she does not seem to have grasped the point that the possibility was brought forward not to supplement, but to substitute for, British sovereignty over Northern Ireland.

To emphasise the firmness of the axis, and the importance of the talks, Mrs Thatcher brought with her to the meeting in Dublin a whole gaggle of Cabinet ministers — including the Chancellor of the Exchequer, Sir Geoffrey Howe, who was understandably puzzled as to what he was supposed to be doing in Dublin. The joint communiqué issued after the meeting represented a triumph for Haughey. It was agreed that the two leaders should meet again in mid-1981, and that in the meantime top officials would hold "joint studies" on all aspects of Anglo-Irish relations, including future joint "institutional arrangements"; the joint studies, and future prime ministerial and ministerial talks, would concern themselves with the "totality of relations" within the two islands.

In Haughey's view the Dublin meeting and the communiqué established, as he had wished, the two Governments as the chief arbiters of a Northern settlement, with his Government as an equal partner. More controversially, he believed — though he did not say so publicly — that the reference to "totality of relations" constituted a dilution of the guarantee to the Unionists, since it had to comprehend the Northern question.

Some thought at the time that refusals by Mrs Thatcher to enlarge publicly on the details of the talks, coupled with exaggerated claims for their achievements by Haughey and his associates, derived from a Machiavellian plot to inspire in the Unionists the impression of conspiracy and imposition, with a view to turning their minds towards the

Republic and away from Britain. Some Unionists thought, or professed to think, that the purpose of the talks was to devise means of expelling them from the United Kingdom. Ian Paisley had an angry meeting with Mrs Thatcher, who assured him of her commitment to the Union; he called her a liar.

There were in fact three reasons for secrecy, and none of them had to do with plots against the Unionists. The first, the defence question, has already been mentioned; the other two concerned only Haughey, but were equally pressing from his viewpoint.

The first was "the principle of consent", which a little later became the new vogue phrase, meaning the Unionist guarantee of veto on the constitutional position of Northern Ireland. Fianna Fáil had long been ambivalent on the question of consent. Did it mean the decision of a majority of Irish people, or did it mean (as Lynch had appeared to imply, and his successor to deny) that unity could come about only by the consent of a majority in the North? Haughey did not want to be seen, especially within his own party, as going down the same road on which Lynch had encountered so much trouble. He may have exaggerated the power of the "green" Fianna Fáil hard-liners, but in any case they belonged to his own faction of the party and he was close to their thinking.

Here was a lamentable example of the ills that flowed from the collapse of bipartisanship and the antipathy between Haughey and FitzGerald. Fianna Fáil exaggerated the achievements of the Dublin meeting; Fine Gael and Labour belittled them. The terms of the communiqué, coupled with a little more frankness towards the public and a serious attempt to harmonise the approach of the two leaders on the question, could have provided firm ground from which to move forward; instead, both sides continued to treat the North as a partisan issue.

The Haughey-Thatcher meeting planned for mid-1981 never took place, because precisely at that time Haughey lost a general election and FitzGerald succeeded him as Taoiseach. When FitzGerald met Mrs Thatcher in London in the autumn, Haughey tried to lay down unreasonable criteria by which the success of their talks should be judged: he insisted that the minimum achievement for FitzGerald should be agreement on the establishment of an Anglo-Irish parliamentary council. FitzGerald, for his part, ordered the publication of some pieces of paper, described as the "documents" arising from the joint studies at civil service level, for the ostensible purpose of reassuring the Unionists that they contained nothing sinister. The documents were certainly sufficiently anodyne for this purpose; they were also uncommonly brief, and to anyone with knowledge of the workings of top officials the exercise bordered on the absurd. I put it to the most eminent of retired Irish public servants that he himself would never have dreamed of including in an official document anything with the remotest potential for controversy if he foresaw any danger of its being published; his reply consisted of a sharkish grin. It seems likely that the real reason for their publication was not a desire to reassure the Unionists but a determination to prove, as the documents showed, that Haughey had accepted the principle of consent. Haughey tried to claim that a difference of substance existed in the forms of words used by himself and by FitzGerald, but this claim rang rather hollow.

The reference to "institutional arrangements" gave no cause for secrecy, though it did give rise to exaggeration — and caused FitzGerald and other critics of the talks to fret about the implications. Before the joint studies were set up officials from both countries had studied the arrangements for close co-operation that prevail, for example, in the Benelux countries, in the Scandinavian countries, and between France and West Germany. In one crucial respect, at least, Britain and Ireland differed radically from all these cases, especially the last. France and West Germany are roughly comparable countries, used to treating with each other as equals. It is far otherwise with Britain and Ireland, with their enormous differences in population, wealth and power, and their long history of domination of one by the other. FitzGerald, with his fondness for the multilateralism of the EEC and the enhanced power which small countries can derive from it, feared that Anglo-Irish "institutional structures" would be far too one-sided. In the event, "Anglo-Irish councils" at ministerial and civil service levels turned out, at least for the time being, to mean no more than the kind of ministerial and official meetings which would have taken place anyway.

Haughey and his associates, by contrast, used the phrase "institutional arrangements" for propaganda, and made of it a good deal more than it was worth. His Foreign Minister, Brian Lenihan, in a radio interview, transformed "institutional" into "constitutional", suggesting a new agreement on the constitutional status of the North. They claimed that the negotiations had brought Irish unity "measurably" closer, and Haughey himself hinted at some kind of breakthrough within a year.

Haughey made a very grave mistake by trying to "oversell" his gains. He should have stood firm on the communiqué, the terms of which favoured him so greatly, on the progress implicit in the British recognition of a "unique relationship" between the two countries, and on the British (and of course Irish) determination to continue joint consultation on Northern Ireland regardless of what uproar it might cause there. It is doubtful if the exaggerated talk in Dublin greatly impressed the Irish public; on the other hand, it offended Mrs Thatcher, who delivered a stinging rebuke to Haughey when he met her early in 1981 at an EEC summit meeting. But by then the Anglo-Irish relationship had already begun to sour, for reasons for which Haughey could not be blamed.

Many of Haughey's mistakes in his closing months in office were the fruit of his obsession with the forthcoming general election. (This applies also to the economy. In these months the calamitous condition of the public finances was ignored, accounting principles abandoned, and crazy proposals for Government expenditure approved; the Fianna Fáil Party behaved in much the same way, and in the actual election campaign was alleged to have overspent its budget by a sum approaching a million pounds).

Haughey had set March or April as his target date for the general election, after which he knew he would have to adopt more stringent economic policies, but after which, also, he hoped to implement the next phase of his Northern policy.

In this phase, as he saw it, he would move from dealing with the British to dealing with the Unionists. And by the Unionists he meant Paisley, for he was as convinced as the Big Man himself that Paisley would shortly emerge as the undisputed Protestant leader. Paisley's response to the Anglo-Irish talks — denouncing the British, raising private armies and seeming to move towards a policy of independence for Northern Ireland — did not worry Haughey; on the contrary, he welcomed any signs of alienation between Britain and the Unionists and Loyalists; but he was concerned about his unpopularity among the Unionists, and his lack of contacts with them. He tried to open up a channel of communication with Paisley through a common friend, but he steadfastly refused, though pressed many times on the subject, to say what, in his conception of a new Ireland, he meant to offer the Northern Protestants. He contented himself with saying — and he repeated this both in and out of office — that the Republic would make them a most generous offer when they came to the negotiating table.

The Unionist reply was that they had no intention of coming to the table at all, but Haughey remained confident that a combination of alienation from Britain and the attractions of what he meant to offer would bring them round. However, not only could he do little or nothing until after the general election — bringing him as he hoped, his own mandate — but he also had to conceal the nature of the proposals he contemplated, for they were controversial in the extreme and he feared resistance to them in his own party. This was his third and perhaps greatest reason for secrecy.

Essentially, Haughey had in mind something like a resurrection of the "Boal plan", a proposal put forward many years earlier as an alternative to Sunningdale by Desmond

193

Boal, a distinguished Unionist lawyer and at one time a close friend and political adviser to Paisley. Boal had proposed a transfer of sovereignty from London to Dublin, with the all-Ireland Government disposing of only the most essential powers, like foreign policy, and with the largest degree of local autonomy — greater, in effect, than the powers of the old Stormont — reserved for a local, and necessarily Unionist, Government in the North.

The Boal plan in its crudest form would have meant revived Protestant domination over the Catholic community within Northern Ireland. It would raise horrendous problems of security and finance, but it would satisfy the fundamental nationalist demand in so far as it would end British political involvement in Ireland, while at the same time constituting a new kind of recognition of the Northern right of self-determination. Moreover, it powerfully attracted some influential figures in the SDLP. These believed that in the course of time it would remove the Protestant "siege mentality" and that they could accept Protestant domination in the belief that, as one of them told me, it would wither away of its own accord in a generation or two. Besides, it might not be beyond human capacity, within its general framework, to devise means of protecting the Catholics' civil rights, and to make satisfactory all-Ireland arrangements on security.

But it was the Provisional IRA, not the Loyalists, who pulled the rug from under the Haughey-Thatcher relationship. After their years of "blanket protest" and "dirty protest" had failed to achieve for them political status or any other concessions, a number of the Provo prisoners in Long Kesh (and some members of the INLA) tried their last resort, a hunger strike, in the autumn of 1980. They did so against the wishes and advice of the Provo leadership. The hunger strike ended before Christmas, without loss of life but in circumstances of confusion and recrimination, with the prisoners claiming that the British had made concessions which they repudiated when the fast ended.

The prisoners and their leaders in the prison were determined on another hunger strike. The IRA leadership continued to be ambivalent but when early in 1981 they saw that the prisoners were resolute, the most influential of the Northern Provo leadership decided that on this occasion they would not try to persuade them against it, but would instead extract from it all the benefits they could in the way of sympathy and propaganda. They succeeded beyond all their expectations.

During the spring and summer of 1981 ten men died on hunger strike in Long Kesh, while Catholics in the North and to a lesser extent in the South watched their sufferings with a mixture of anger and admiration, and increasingly blamed the British for refusing to compromise.

In so far as the timing of the second hunger strike was directed towards influencing Irish electoral politics, it was aimed at the Republic and specifically against Haughey, whose many reasons for wanting an early election included a desire to hold it before any of the prisoners died, with the incalculable consequences their deaths might bring. As a launching pad for an election, he convened the Fianna Fáil Ard-Fheis in February. But the conference had only gone through its preliminary stages when a dreadful fire in the Stardust Club, a discotheque in north central Dublin, in the early morning of St Valentine's Day, killed forty-eight young people. The disaster shocked the whole country, but Haughey, in whose own constituency it occurred, felt it as a personal blow. He postponed the Ard-Fheis — and the election.

On the heels of this calamity came another unforeseeable event, which gave the Provos the political foothold which they had long sought and lacked. This was the death of Frank Maguire, Nationalist member of the Westminster parliament for Fermanagh and South Tyrone, at the age of fifty-eight. It was followed by the first of two massive British blunders; the Government, instead of delaying the necessary by-election as they might have done, arranged for it to be held at once. The Provos seized the opportunity thus handed to them by putting forward one of the hunger strikers, Bobby Sands, as a candidate.

Traditionally in the two Westminster constituencies

where there is a small majority of Catholics over Protestants — Fermanagh and South Tyrone, and the neighbouring Mid-Ulster — Unionists win unless an agreed Catholic or Nationalist candidate can be found, a circumstance which gives great leverage to extremists. By running Sands, the Provos wrong-footed the SDLP, who found themselves in an almost impossible dilemma. Aside from the bullying and blackmail to which other potential candidates could expect to be subjected, the SDLP if they opposed Sands would stand accused not only of the ancient sin of vote-splitting, but also of inhumanity — a strange enough accusation in all conscience, considering its source, but containing some plausibility, since Sands's backers claimed that his election would save his life. But to fail to put up a candidate would mean relinquishing political leadership, if only in one area, to the Provos. It would damage the SDLP with moderate Catholic and Southern opinion. It would also mean an enhancement of their unpopularity among Unionists, especially since in the border areas, including Fermanagh, the Provos at this very time were carrying on a campaign of assassination of Protestants on the pretext that the people they murdered were, or had been, or had some connection with, members of the security forces. After much agonised argument, and faced with a revolt among their supporters in the constituency if they opposed Sands, the SDLP decided not to contest the seat. Sands defeated a Unionist in the election but died shortly afterwards, the first of the ten hunger strikers to die.

The British reaction had a disastrous effect on Catholic opinion in the North. They changed the electoral law to prevent other prisoners from contesting elections, and they went on to hold a second by-election in Fermanagh and South Tyrone. Again the SDLP stood aside, and the seat was won by Owen Carron, who had been Sands's election agent.

Frantic efforts to find a formula for ending the hunger strike had been in progress before the death of Sands, and they intensified when the prisoners began to die. The mediators included some who had been instrumental in ending the previous fast, along with a variety of new faces (SDLP and other local politicians, British ministers and officials, members of hunger strikers' families, even outside bodies like the International Committee of the Red Cross). The efforts of the mediators were greatly impeded by confusion as to who could agree a settlement, what they would settle for, and whether they would trust the British to "deliver" on any deal. It was accepted — though not necessarily, and certainly not publicly, by the Provos and their "front" organisations — that the British would not concede political status; but the prisoners' "five demands", of which the most important concerned refusal to wear prison clothing and perform ordinary prison work, were in themselves negotiable. The issue was further complicated by Provo insistence that any settlement should involve talks between the authorities and the man elected by the prisoners as their "commanding officer".

This condition the British adamantly refused to concede, making it an issue of principle. That stand lacked credibility, since contacts between IRA representatives and British officials and military officers have continued at various times and at various levels through hunger strikes, assassination campaigns, and onslaughts on the security forces. It is of course conceivable that Mrs Thatcher did not know this fact; if she did, she ignored it. She maintained a position of complete intransigence on concessions to the prisoners, even when mediators came to believe that they had reached a basis for settlement with junior ministers in the Northern Ireland Office. One of the ministers went so far as to tell mediators that he agreed with one specific set of proposals, but "there is a lady behind the veil".

Her inflexibility increased anxiety in the Republic, where an ugly new word, "destabilisation", came into common currency as sympathy and support for the hunger strikers — and by extension for the Provos — grew. International opinion also became concerned, and anti-British feeling swelled among continental radicals and, inevitably, among Irish-Americans. Irish government sources had estimated the amount of money collected by Provo sympathisers in the United States in 1980 at less than two hundred thousand dollars, as opposed to a record of between one and a half and two million dollars in 1972. In the first six months of 1981, the amount exceeded a million dollars.

Haughey had a double concern: in general, the effect of the hunger strike on the climate of opinion in the Republic, and, in particular, the fear of losing seats to "H-Block" candidates if they intervened in the general election — which he could not long delay, and which in the end he was forced to hold while the crisis was at its height. He was among the many who begged Mrs Thatcher to compromise, sending her urgent private messages to say that Long Kesh would cost him as many as five Dáil seats. His pleas, like all the others, had no effect.

Chapter Fifteen

If the coalition had deserved to lose the 1977 general election on the issue of style of government, Fianna Fáil deserved to lose that of 18 June 1981 because of their financial mismanagement. That it ended almost in a dead heat may be attributed largely to the fact that a nervous electorate longed for stable government, and Fianna Fáil were the only party with any hope of forming a single-party administration. They could be beaten only by a coalition of Fine Gael and Labour; and Labour were committed to fighting the campaign on their own and coalescing with Fine Gael only if the two parties between them gained a greater number of seats than Fianna Fáil — and then only if a special delegate conference of the party allowed the parliamentary party to go into government. Labour fought a flabby and implausible campaign, putting forward policies radically different from those of Fine Gael, while leaving the coalition option open.

Fine Gael possessed one electoral advantage almost as compelling as Fianna Fáil's stable government line. Their leader, FitzGerald, according to the opinion polls, enjoyed far greater popularity and credibility than Haughey. The party naturally exploited their leader's high standing in their campaign publicity, but they lacked the courage to fight simply on this issue, and on that of Fianna Fáil's mishandling of the public finances.

The party leadership was divided between the "pure of heart" and those who wanted to offer bribes to the voters much on the lines of Fianna Fáil in 1977. A compromise was reached, more in favour of the latter than the former, so that Fine Gael fought the election on economic policies of the most contradictory kind. On the one hand they promised to "phase out" a budget deficit estimated at £800 million (which turned out more like a billion pounds); on the other they put forward proposals for sweeping cuts in income tax and for the payment to housewives of £9.60 a week. It may, however, be doubted whether the more level-headed among the voters ever believed either the Fine Gael promise to reduce taxes or the even more ridiculous claims by Haughey that foreign borrowing could continue indefinitely at the existing level, and that the inflation rate was only 10 per cent (it was in fact at its usual level, about double that figure).

Haughey's fear that Fianna Fáil could lose as many as five seats on the H-Block issue proved somewhat exaggerated. In the event they lost two seats to Long Kesh prisoner candidates in the border constituencies of Cavan-Monaghan and Louth; one of them, Ciaran Doherty, was on hunger strike and, like Bobby Sands, died shortly after his election. But those two seats made the difference between victory and defeat.

The National H-Blocks/Armagh Committee put up candidates in several constituencies. This committee was not, as many supposed, merely a Provo "front". Its local branches included, in addition to representatives of the Provos, the INLA and the extreme left, a number of quite prominent trade unionists and members or ex-members of the Labour Party; it also enjoyed the public support of some distinguished people in the literary and artistic world. Its successes, such as they were, pointed up a disturbing trend in Irish society, for it enjoyed far greater support in rural areas and certain working-class areas than elsewhere. The middle classes for the most part shunned the agitation; not a few of them privately agreed with Mrs Thatcher's intransigence on the issue. Nevertheless, the H-Blocks agitators had an opportunity to build on a fairly broad base of support, and to damage Labour as well as

Fianna Fáil; but Provo domination of the organisation and of the election campaign threw away most of that opportunity. The Provos, for example, insisted on running only hunger strikers and other prisoners as candidates when they could have chosen national (or powerful local) figures. They disapproved of the candidature of Bernadette Devlin McAliskey, and she stood down — but she campaigned vigorously for H-Block candidates, although on crutches and in pain after being very seriously injured in a murderous attack on herself and her husband by UDA gunmen, which had failed narrowly. Such was Provo bigotry that in one constituency they refused to campaign for an INLA prisoner candidate, because he was prepared to recognise the Dáil.

They made capital out of parading through the border constituencies the wives and children of hunger strikers, begging for their husbands' and fathers' lives, telling electors that they sought to "borrow" their votes for one election only. But — by contrast with what happened in the North, then and later — they misjudged the mood of the Southern electorate; and some of their other tactics were less clever. The voters of the Republic, much more conservative and much more closely bound to the political system than Northern Catholics, did not enjoy the spectacle of eggs and flour being thrown at the Taoiseach, or the burning of an English tourist bus near the border in County Leitrim.

The result of the election, for a chamber of 166 seats, was Fianna Fáil 78, Fine Gael 65, Labour 15, minor parties and independents 8 (including the two Long Kesh prisoners, who would not have taken their seats even had they been at liberty to do so). With two more seats, Haughey would have equalled the combined total of Fine Gael and Labour, and could have formed a government with the support of some of the independents; indeed, right up until the day the new Dáil met, he appeared to believe that he would be able to do so anyway, but the arithmetic was against him. Fine Gael and Labour cobbled up an agreed policy for a coalition government, and the Labour leadership (now under Michael O'Leary, since Cluskey had lost his own Dáil seat in the election) forced it through the mandatory special conference in the teeth of ferocious opposition from the left.

When the Dáil met, FitzGerald was elected Taoiseach by a majority of three votes. Among those who supported him were Joe Sherlock of East Cork, a former IRA man and the first member of the Workers' Party to win a Dáil seat, and Jim Kemmy of East Limerick, a former Labour Party member who, disgusted with what he viewed as bombastic and hypocritical nationalism, had embraced the "two nations" theory. Although the Northern question had become almost an obsession with him, the controversies in which he was later involved concerned altogether different issues.

FitzGerald at once set about tackling the enormous problems of the North and the economy with characteristic speed, vigour and optimism — admirable qualities, it may be observed in passing, not always matched by prudence or good judgment. But first he and O'Leary had to appoint cabinet ministers and junior ministers, and distribute patronage. They did so in a manner which fairly took away the breath of the country, which now saw a very unfamiliar FitzGerald.

In his allocation of ministries he showed unusual ruthlessness, discarding leading people who did not belong to his faction of the Fine Gael Party, and displaying no regard for regional considerations. He gave the vital Ministries of Finance and Agriculture to two men in their mid-thirties, John Bruton and Alan Dukes, and appointed a close personal friend, James Dooge, Foreign Minister.

Dooge is a world-famous hydrologist, better known as a scientist and academic than as a politician. (When the British cabinet discussed the Dublin appointments, and his profession was mentioned, the Lord Chancellor, Lord Hailsham, commented: "Aha! an indubitable wet." Mrs Thatcher was not amused). Since at the time of his nomination he did not hold a seat in either house of parliament, FitzGerald appointed him a member of the Senate.

He proved an excellent Foreign Minister.

Another close friend of the new Taoiseach, Alexis FitzGerald (not a relation), became special adviser to the government at a salary of over £30,000 a year. Other friends got government jobs, front-bench positions in the Senate and appointments as special advisers in government departments. Clearly FitzGerald meant not only to play the patronage game as assiduously as Fianna Fáil had traditionally done, but to maintain the strictest personal control of the government and the Fine Gael Party.

A good deal of factional dissent and muttering ensued, but nothing remotely approaching revolt; Fine Gael's tendency to "deference", analogous to that of the Tories in England, ensured that. It was otherwise with Labour. The left, already enraged by the decision to enter coalition and fearful that the party would lose its identity, were further incensed by their exclusion from office, and by the fact that their leadership also played the patronage game without mercy. They were given further food for discontent when Bruton, almost immediately after taking office, introduced an exceptionally severe budget as a first step towards rectifying the public finances.

Bruton displayed a commendable control of his brief, but he made some serious mistakes in his budgetary strategy — mistakes which foreshadowed grave trouble for the government. He concentrated on increasing taxes instead of reducing public expenditure; and the government entirely failed to devise a credible method of holding back public-sector pay increases, something urgently necessary because Fianna Fáil had allowed public-sector pay to get completely out of hand. Negotiations for a national wage agreement sputtered along for months, finally breaking down on the issue of the size of the general increase; then, to considerable public astonishment, the government conceded pay increases in the public sector roughly equal to the figure on which the general negotiations had failed, and higher than some settlements already "in the pipeline" in the private sector.

Fianna Fáil's stands on economic policy were at least

equally confused, and their divisions on the question rapidly came into the open. Martin O'Donoghue, although one of the architects of the giveaway manifesto of 1977, had become a convert to some degree of fiscal rectitude, and he and others publicly took issue with Haughey's continuing defence of unlimited borrowing. Haughey brought him back on to the front bench in January 1982 — just in time, as it happened, for another general election.

At this time all semblance of bipartisanship disappeared when Haughey bitterly criticised FitzGerald's initiatives on the related issues of the North and constitutional and social reform in the Republic.

The personal antipathy between the two men, and Haughey's conviction that only he could solve the Northern problem, made a bitter division certain; and the situation was not helped by the curious manner in which FitzGerald went about some of his initiatives, or by developments in Britain. At the time of the election the British government had made clear in subtle, and some not so subtle, ways their preference for FitzGerald as Taoiseach; then, from the autumn of 1981 onwards, they began another attempt to revive the policy which Haughey so deplored, that of trying to find an "internal settlement" in the North.

Early in the new government's tenure of office Haughey refused to allow Fianna Fáil to take part in an all-party committee on marital breakdown and family law, on the slender ground that FitzGerald had committed himself in advance to legalising divorce (a long overdue reform in any case). Then he fiercely criticised what came to be known as the "constitutional crusade", a discussion launched by FitzGerald on reform of the constitution, with particular reference to divorce and to the excision, or rewriting, of Articles Two and Three (the articles having to do with the claim of sovereignty over Northern Ireland). FitzGerald announced the "crusade" in a radio interview in September, with little sign of having prepared or thought out what he proposed, and with no attempt to obtain consensus. He imprudently criticised Southern society as "sectarian", a word which he amended to "confessional": Haughey dismissed the "sectarian" tag, and called FitzGerald's statements an exercise in national self-abasement. The two leaders seemingly agreed on only one constitutional matter, in that both supported a proposal to include in the constitution a ban on abortion.

That autumn Mrs Thatcher made a move which would have enormous implications for Northern Ireland, but was prompted purely by her internal cabinet considerations. She had decided that the time was ripe to purge the cabinet of malcontents, and promote to more powerful positions ministers closely in sympathy with her own views. Some of the "wets" she could sack; others, more influential in the Tory Party, she could only demote. Above all she had her mind set on removing James Prior from the job of Employment Secretary and replacing him with the hardliner Norman Tebbit, with a view to introducing new legislation to curb the powers of the trade unions. Prior resisted vigorously, calling in aid his considerable support in the cabinet; but he lost, and was obliged to agree to take the job of Northern Ireland Secretary. He did retain sufficient "clout" to be able to insist on the appointment as junior ministers of two of his own friends, Lord Gowrie and Nicholas Scott, but it was demotion, even exile.

Could he turn this defeat into a victory? The role of proconsul had made a stepping stone to greater things for others; perhaps he could repeat their success. He began to move almost at once, at first cautiously, then more rapidly, to devise new political institutions. In this he had the enthusiastic and able support of Gowrie, himself by birth (and partly by upbringing) a Southern Irish Protestant. Gowrie conveyed to nationalists the message that he had no objection to a united Ireland; both men hoped to exploit the divisions in the Unionist camp, both between the Official Unionists and Paisley and between the "devolutionist" majority and the "integrationist" minority within the Official Unionists.

Behind a smokescreen of press leaks, Prior was trying to

devise a scheme of what he called "rolling devolution", in which powers would be granted to an assembly and an executive stage by stage, conditional on what he called, in his final formulation, "cross-community support". In other words, it would have to include power-sharing (though he did not call it that) in some form or other. He also hoped to provide it with a built-in stability so that, unlike the 1974 executive, it could not be brought down in a sudden crisis. As to the "Irish dimension", he told a dubious SDLP, that already existed in the Anglo-Irish talks.

In spite of Mrs Thatcher's obvious preference for FitzGerald over Haughey, her relations with him started on an uneasy footing, for he called on her publicly (Haughey had done so only privately) to act on the H-Blocks crisis, and was rebuffed. But both sides took rapid steps to repair their relations, and when FitzGerald met Mrs Thatcher in London near the end of the year their talks went smoothly. FitzGerald seemed to have abandoned some of his own objections to institutions disproportionately weighted in favour of the British, and it was agreed to bring into being an Anglo-Irish council at ministerial and official level. But the British — almost certainly for fear of alienating the Unionists — refused for the time being to set up the third, interparliamentary tier. The advantage of creating such a body, of course, would consist in the possibility of nominating or electing to it politicians from Northern Ireland, thereby achieving a prime Dublin objective: the formation of an association which contained, however powerlessly or innocuously, an all-Ireland parliamentary element.

FitzGerald had long disagreed strongly with Haughey's coyness in the matter of offers and reassurances to the Unionists, and hoped to placate them with his "constitutional crusade" and the publication of the joint studies documents. He also looked with more favour than Haughey on the proposal to set up a new assembly in the North, from which members of an Anglo-Irish parliamentary body (and, he hoped, an all-Ireland parliamentary body) could be drawn. But he had to take into account the very acute fears and suspicions of the SDLP.

Over the years since the fall of the executive, the SDLP had become not only more Catholic, more middle-class and more rural, but in terms of Southern politics, more factionalised. It still had some Protestant members and some working-class members, but it had been greatly weakened by the defection of its former leader Gerry Fitt (who complained that it had grown too "green" for his liking) and of another working-class representative, Paddy Devlin. Hume, who had succeeded Fitt as party leader, retained his old friendship with FitzGerald, but he spent much of his time abroad as a member of the European parliament and his deputy leader — Séamus Mallon, a personal friend of Haughey — leaned towards the Fianna Fáil line.

FitzGerald's conciliatory attitudes had some effect on Unionist and Loyalist opinion. The more radical, like William Craig and the UDA, praised his initiatives. But most Official Unionists, and *a fortiori* Paisley, took the old line that the Protestants were being "sold out" in the Anglo-Irish talks.

Paisley, indeed, in his continued pursuit of the Protestant leadership, now adopted his most extreme attitudes so far. Using as pretexts the Anglo-Irish talks and the murder in November 1981 of the Reverend Robert Bradford, Official Unionist member for the Westminster constituency of South Belfast, he announced the raising of yet another private army — what he called a "third force" — with the declared purpose of opposing and killing IRA men on the border. Catholics regarded this action with alarm, but it is doubtful if Paisley ever went very far in the organisation of the "third force", or indeed if he ever intended more than bluff and bluster. He appointed a minister of his Free Presbyterian Church commander of the "third force" in the area where most murders of Protestants had occurred, but it appeared to take no action. Its most spectacular showing was a large parade in front of the television cameras, in the safe Protestant town of Newtownards, a long way from the border.

Extraordinary events at the beginning of 1982, unconnected with any of the issues which had brought Paisley so much popularity, brought him a temporary political setback.

Earlier, newspaper reports (the first appeared in the *Irish Independent)* and representations by Gerry Fitt had helped to bring about the prosecution and imprisonment of several members of a homosexual prostitution ring, the chief of whom was William McGrath, "housefather" in the Kincora Home in East Belfast, a home for boys in need of care. Other newspapers, principally the *Irish Times,* took up the story, and an amazing scandal began to be uncovered piece by piece.

As the disclosures went on, the scandal spread, with investigations and suspensions of staff at other boys' homes. The public read with horror and fascination of two suicides and one murder which might have had some connection with it. But the most sensational part of the story concerned the duration of the malpractices, and their political implications.

It appeared that improper practices, often of a horrifying kind, had gone on in Kincora and other boys' homes for up to twenty years. Numerous teenage boys had had prostitution forced upon them, being taken for this purpose to hotels not far away. Their exploiters were said to include British officials as well as Loyalist politicians and members of "paramilitary" gangs. McGrath himself was both a prominent Orangeman and leader of the Tara organisation, described by British intelligence as "a bizarre homosexual army". Further newspaper disclosures showed that investigations and calls for remedies over a period of several years by social workers, the police and a woman official of Paisley's church had been impeded and covered up. And the *Irish Times* revealed a close connection between McGrath and Paisley (who had recently led a noisy but ultimately unsuccessful campaign to "save Ulster from sodomy", ie to prevent the British law allowing homosexual acts between consenting adults from being extended to Northern Ireland). Paisley admitted the connection, but denied that he knew the nature of

McGrath's employment.

Prior rejected demands (from Paisley among others) for a public judicial inquiry, and set up a private inquiry instead. This inevitably provoked suspicions of a cover-up, for it needed little imagination to guess that the British might like from time to time to embarrass Loyalist politicians, but would wish to protect any officials of their own who might have been involved. These suspicions grew when most of the members of the private inquiry resigned before it ever met, saying that they had been misled about the state of RUC investigations into the affair. Police investigations continued, but the whole of 1982 went by without the appearance of any evidence that they were bearing fruit.

Meanwhile, what looked like deliberate delay and concealment provoked even more lurid suspicions. Could it be that not just officials, but high-ranking British army and intelligence personnel (of whose "Theban" proclivities so much has been heard) might have been involved? That would certainly give added colour to the constant allegations that, for instance, British intelligence had given Loyalist gangs information which helped them to assassinate certain Catholics.

Political repercussions, however, were felt almost at once, when the by-election to fill the South Belfast seat left vacant by Bradford's murder was held in March 1982. After a campaign marked by intense bitterness between the Official Unionists and the DUP, in which the former made use of the Kincora scandal to discredit the latter, the seat went to the Official Unionist candidate, the Reverend Martin Smyth, head of the Orange Order but a moderate as Orangemen go; the Alliance candidate came second, Paisley's man only third. The DUP had to fight on shaky ground, in a middle-class area and against good candidates of the other parties; nevertheless, the result represented a humiliation for Paisley, and showed that the Official Unionists could face him down if they found the courage to stand and fight.

A minor casualty of this by-election was the recently

formed Ulster Loyalist Democratic Party, an offshoot of the UDA, whose candidate fared disastrously.

The UDA's hopes of becoming a political force — somewhat analogous to those of the Workers' Party, but without the latter's renunciation of violence — seem unlikely to be realised in the near future. What once appeared a shadowy alliance with the Workers' Party, with a view to promoting working-class politics, has dwindled to low-level contacts; meanwhile, their violent wing has suffered several defeats by the police. They remain torn between their faint but lingering desire for a political role and the maintenance of a Protestant army to be brought into action in the event of civil war and independence.

For the people of the Republic, all these events were overshadowed by dramatic political developments in Dublin.

On 27 January 1982 Bruton, in pursuance of his policy of drastically reducing the deficit on current account, brought in a budget even more severe than that of the previous July. Its provisions included the removal of subsidies on milk and butter, and the imposition of a tax of 18 per cent on clothes and footwear. Jim Kemmy, who had hitherto supported the Government on most issues, revolted and voted, with other independents, against the budget. The Government was defeated — the first defeat of a budget in the state's sixty-year history — by one vote; the Dáil was dissolved after sitting for less than seven months and a general election was called for 18 February.

The coalition parties went to the country in daunting circumstances. The budget itself had been a perfect model of insensitivity and hamfistedness. It was bad enough that FitzGerald and Bruton — the one sprung from the comfortable upper middle class, the other from a millionaire family — should try to impose a tax on children's shoes when they depended on the votes of left-wing deputies, themselves working class in origin, who represented the poor and unemployed; but that the Labour Party's representatives in the cabinet could support such a measure, almost defied belief. The exercise smelled of arrogance and loftiness, and implied that the coalition were quite out of touch with the preoccupations of ordinary people. Besides, the inflation rate continued high, and they had manifestly failed to keep their promises to the middle class in the matter of tax reform, so that the budget seriously threatened almost everybody's living standards. On the night the Government fell, it looked as if they were headed for massive — and well-deserved — electoral defeat.

But almost from the start of the campaign, it could be seen that the Government's warnings about the state of the national finances had been brought home to the people, and that they would get credit for trying, however clumsily or misguidedly, to set matters right. Fianna Fáil canvassers reported, with some astonishment, that they had found the question of foreign borrowing raised on doorsteps in working-class as well as middle-class areas. Opinion polls showed that the budget had gained as much acceptance as disfavour. A lot of people quite admired its brutal honesty.

Fianna Fáil had excellent issues — inflation and unemployment, seen by the voters as more important than the budget deficit — to exploit. But they were terribly split on both policy and personalities. The anti-Haughey camp were also the fiscal rectitude camp; after fierce internal argument their view prevailed, and although they published an "alternative budget" this envisaged a deficit of the somewhat arcane figure of £713 million, the same as the coalition's projected deficit.

They were obliged to do this in order to retain any credibility, including credibility among financial interests, domestic and foreign. But Haughey (to the anguish of the orthodox, who had begun to think that a policy of stringency might gain votes instead of losing them) continued to cast himself in the role of the last of the big spenders. When he made brief campaign visits, by car and helicopter, to various parts of the country, he could rarely restrain himself from making commitments to further projects for public expenditure. Promises to develop this harbour, build that airport, nationalise the other factory, blew in the February wind.

Fine Gael took sufficient fright at the defeat of the budget to abandon the proposal to tax clothes and shoes, but for the most part they stuck to the path of financial rectitude. They fought the campaign with vigour and courage, spurred on by their increasingly high standing in middle-class areas and by the vast personal popularity of their leader. Not so Labour: they began the campaign with an angry meeting of their ruling body, the administrative council, which failed to resolve the question of whether, and on what conditions, they were bound to another coalition, and matters improved not at all during the campaign.

The leadership fought as committed coalitionists, the left on the opposite platform, claiming that no coalition pact existed at all. O'Leary, seemingly distraught by his party's irreparable dissensions, wandered through the campaign like a somnambulist, frequently appearing to be unaware of the issues and developments.

Provisional Sinn Féin ran seven candidates in the new election, with uniform lack of success. This contrasted sharply with a further advance by the Workers' Party, who increased their Dáil representation from one to three. (In the second election of 1982, they fell back to two seats, though slightly improving their vote). Fianna Fáil won both of the seats taken the previous year by Long Kesh prisoners in Louth and Cavan-Monaghan.

These gains, along with gains in Meath and Wexford where Labour wantonly threw away seats, should have been sufficient to give Haughey a majority, but they were partly offset by losses elsewhere, so that Fianna Fáil took only 81 seats instead of the 83 which would have given them an effective majority in the new Dáil. Haughey could rely on the support of Neil Blaney, still "independent Fianna Fáil" deputy for North-east Donegal, so that he found himself, tantalisingly, one seat short. Everything now appeared to depend on a young independent, Tony Gregory, who had been elected for Dublin Central on a platform of revitalising the rundown and poverty-stricken inner city. And so FitzGerald and Haughey each made his way to Gregory's constituency office at Summerhill, in the heart of the slums; O'Leary met him also, but in a hotel. All discussed with him the price of his support for a new government, but it was Haughey who struck the bargain.

This bargain, known as "the Gregory deal", was contained in a truly remarkable document, signed by Haughey and Gregory and countersigned by Michael Mullen, Secretary of the Irish Transport and General Workers' Union and a personal friend of Haughey. It agreed the rapid implementation of a number of large schemes for inner-city development, variously costed at from £80 million to £150 million. Either of these figures would be an amazing, perhaps a record, price for a single vote. But the deal could be justified by the argument that revitalisation of the inner city was an urgent, even desperate, necessity, which warranted the expenditure of larger sums still.

Meanwhile the Labour deputies re-elected O'Leary as their leader and proceeded, in defiance of the parliamentary arithmetic, to try to keep open the option of joining with Fine Gael in another coalition. The Workers' Party for their part called for "an alliance of the left" and complained that O'Leary ignored three requests for meetings to attempt to create such an alliance.

In Labour's absence the WP tried to set up a grouping consisting of themselves and the remaining two left-wing deputies, Kemmy and Gregory, but the divisions proved insuperable. Kemmy was determined to vote for FitzGerald as Taoiseach, though he had brought him down so short a time before; Gregory, for the most obvious reasons, favoured Haughey. The three WP deputies (and their ruling body, the ard-comhairle) had more ponderous problems to resolve, and nice calculations to make.

Their inclinations lay against Fianna Fáil, particularly the members of the "green" wing whom they blamed for the split in their movement in 1969-70 and the emergence of the Provos. Their attitude was reinforced by the election returns, which showed WP voters as, by and large, more favourable to Labour and Fine Gael (shown by their willingness to transfer second preference votes to them) than to Fianna Fáil. But they must have calculated that they had "lost" Gregory; and with all their three seats highly vulnerable in the event of another early election, they saw a powerful argument for putting in the party — Fianna Fáil — likeliest to stay in office for a considerable period.

Labour and others suspected them of not being completely in earnest on the question of a left-wing alliance. Although they had asked Labour to join — which must inevitably mean to lead — the alliance, continued adherence by Labour to coalition with Fine Gael would allow the WP to present themselves in future elections as the left-wing alternative.

The WP ard-comhairle met and decided to support Haughey in the vote for Taoiseach, but kept the decision secret. It also kept secret any divisions within the party on the decision. Labour, by contrast, displayed its sores even more openly than hitherto. When the administrative council met on the evening of 8 March the meeting was marked by furious and bitter argument. It lasted for six hours and ended, to the rage of the leadership, with a victory for the left and a renunciation of coalition.

These were savagely ironic developments. It had seemed during the election campaign that the left was irrelevant, that the only choice lay between the harsh puritanism of Fine Gael and the patronage and populism of Fianna Fáil. But the election result, a second "hung" Dáil, meant that the left, if it could come together, could hold the balance of power and could even hope, if it kept its nerve and fighting strength, to force a realignment in Irish party politics. In short, the result threw the ball to Labour — and they dropped it.

The majority of the parliamentary party seemed quite unable to see that if, immediately after the election, they had set about forging and leading a left alliance, they would first have tested the good faith of the Workers' Party; secondly, they might well have succeeded in joining

214

with them and Kemmy (and conceivably also with Gregory) in an arrangement to support, conditionally and for a fixed period, a minority government of either Fine Gael or Fianna Fáil; thirdly, they had the hope open to them that the strains thus imposed on the two big parties would in time force them to split and perhaps bring about a coalition of their like-minded elements. (On the right, opinion was against a coming together of the two main parties. Fine Gael had many prominent members who disliked coalition with even a moderate left-wing party like Labour, and altogether deplored any contacts between FitzGerald and Gregory or the WP). But Labour clung on too long in the vain hope of returning to office; and when their decision against coalition came, it came too late.

On the afternoon of 9 March the Dáil elected Charles Haughey Taoiseach for the second time by the unforeseen margin of seven votes. The three WP deputies, fortuitously locked out of the chamber, vaulted over the railings of the press gallery to reach the division lobby. It was a bizarre spectacle, but nothing to what would follow.

Chapter Sixteen

The year 1982 resembled nothing so much as the last act of *Juno and the Paycock*. From the fall of the coalition in January to the massacre at Ballykelly, County Derry, in December, when seventeen people were killed in the bombing of a discotheque by the INLA, misfortune followed upon the heels of misfortune to an extent which bewildered public and politicians alike. Through this year of calamities Charles Haughey, in the South, and James Prior, in the North, filled the helpless parts of Captain Boyle and Joxer. Nothing turned out right for them.

Machiavelli insisted that a prince must enjoy good luck, Napoleon looked for the same quality in a general. Haughey suffered, in nine months in office, a run of bad luck so consistent as to be astounding. In those nine months he could lay claim to only one success, in that the inflation rate at last fell sharply: by the end of the year it stood at 12 per cent and was plainly headed into single figures. But it was not government policy, and certainly not prosperity, that brought about the fall; it was produced by the depth of the economic recession. Every month brought news of more redundancies, and higher unemployment: by the end of the year the unemployment rate had reached 14 per cent.

In the North the true unemployment rate was probably double that figure, and the close of the year brought with it a chilling Northern statistic: employment in manufacturing industry there had fallen to a mere 97,000 persons, well below the total number of persons unemployed. But that was cold comfort for the struggling South.

Haughey was not even allowed to take office in March without having to fight off a challenge to his leadership of Fianna Fáil from the Colley-O'Malley camp. This challenge fizzled out in the face of appeals for party unity from a battery of weighty figures — and after a unique night-long series of telephone calls by his supporters, who used every technique of persuasion and pressure to discourage wavering backbenchers from opposing him. So intense was the pressure that at least one sensitive backbencher was reported to have broken down in tears. The dissident leaders, not at all tearful, bided their time to strike again.

He excluded all the dissidents except O'Malley and O'Donoghue from his new cabinet, and filled the cabinet and junior ministries mainly with his own friends. Few of these performed convincingly in office. He made his stoutest, and ablest, supporter, Ray MacSharry, Tanaiste and Finance Minister, but even MacSharry began his term of office with a *faux pas,* promising "bloom and boom" instead of the "gloom and doom" peddled by the coalition. His education in economic realities by officials of his department and of the Central Bank was rapid, and stern. There was no bloom, and no boom.

Instead, those who wanted diversion from the economic troubles witnessed an astonishing series of scandals. One of the most inexplicable concerned a country policeman, Garda Thomas Nangle, who was charged with assaulting a man in a public house at Dowra, County Cavan, not far from the border. When the case came to be heard in the local court in September the chief witness for the prosecution, the man allegedly assaulted, did not appear: he had been arrested early that morning by the RUC on the other side of the border, detained until the evening, and then released without having any charge preferred against him. It later emerged that this man's detention had been the subject of discussion between senior officers of the Garda Síochana and the RUC, and that the latter had decided to detain him in spite of advice from their local officers that

217

he was innocent of any wrong-doing. Garda Nangle is the brother-in-law of the then Minister for Justice, Seán Doherty.

The most amazing event of this period occurred in August, when a man later convicted of murder was arrested in the flat of the Attorney-General, Patrick Connolly. No suspicion attached to Connolly. He was a friend of the man concerned, who had been his guest on more than one occasion. But the Attorney-General's conduct, and Haughey's handling of the affair, were alike baffling. Instead of remaining in Dublin to help the police with their inquiries, Connolly left almost at once for London, and thence for New York where he planned to spend a holiday. He had informed the Taoiseach of his intentions, and Haughey, it seemed, made no objection.

In the midst of a public outcry Haughey recalled Connolly from New York (sending an official from the Irish consulate to meet him as he stepped off his plane) and, as soon as he arrived back in Dublin, accepted his resignation. At a press conference Haughey explained his mistake in allowing Connolly to leave the country at such a time by saying that the Attorney-General was an important constitutional officer, on whose legal advice the Taoiseach would himself normally rely. He described the affair, accurately, as "grotesque, unbelievable, bizarre and unprecedented". The initials GUBU were gleefully seized on by one of his old enemies and critics, Conor Cruise O'Brien, who pilloried in his columns in the *Irish Times* and the *Observer* these and other aspects of the government's performance which appeared grotesque, unbelievable, bizarre and unprecedented.

But so far as Anglo-Irish relations were concerned, by far the greatest disaster followed the Argentine invasion of the Falkland Islands in April. Ireland, then a member of the United Nations security council, supported a UN resolution demanding Argentine withdrawal, and the Irish ambassador, Noel Dorr, made an exceptionally strong speech condemning Argentina's breach of international law; Ireland also participated in EEC economic sanctions against Argentina. The international stances thus taken almost certainly did not reflect the views of a majority in the Republic; more to the point, as developments soon showed, they certainly did not reflect those of the majority of the Fianna Fáil Party. Haughey, from the beginning, adopted them with some reluctance.

A widespread Irish view was that the Falklands, a few thousand square miles of windswept bogland inhabited by some eighteen hundred persons of British birth or descent, were simply not worth fighting for. They lay three hundred miles from Argentina and eight thousand miles from Britain; the argument from geography was on the side of the Argentines. Moreover, Anglo-Argentine negotiations, which presumably had as their object the transfer of the islands to Argentine sovereignty had dragged on for many years. The vicious nature of the Argentine military régime was widely seen as irrelevant. On the contrary, when Mrs Thatcher despatched an enormous fleet with the apparent intention of retaking the islands by force, it was she rather than they whom many saw as a war-monger.

This view was reinforced in the most dramatic way when the British sank the Argentine cruiser *General Belgrano*, with great loss of life, at the beginning of May. Much as British people may dislike the argument, it is necessary in honesty to say that the torpedoing of the *Belgrano* — and to some extent the whole conduct of the war — were widely regarded abroad as quite shocking and unjustified. The British had warned Argentine vessels and aircraft to remain outside a two-hundred-mile "exclusion zone" around the islands, but the *Belgrano*, when sunk, was well outside that limit. More generally — as was pointed out at the time by some British commentators — one of the conditions of a just war is that the force employed should be proportionate to the end desired, and British conduct of the Falklands War by no means met this condition. By the time the islands were recaptured, the number dead on both sides equalled the entire population of the islands, and the cost on the British side amounted to at least one million pounds per head of population.

Several other aspects of the British handling of the conflict were regarded with distaste in Ireland. Britain's professed determination to uphold international law and deter aggression was seen as hypocritical: in Cyprus, for example, Britain had shown a singular lack of any such determination. Many saw the risk to the lives of the British troops and seamen involved as unjustified. In the course of hostilities the fleet was shown to be in large part ill-prepared and ill-equipped, and had it not been for the incredible stupidity and incompetence of the Argentine commanders, it is doubtful whether the islands could have been retaken without appalling casualties, if at all. (The stupidity of the military régime also affected their diplomacy, for before the reinvasion they received several excellent — from their viewpoint — offers of a settlement through the United Nations and otherwise, and refused them all. Had they shown more sense, they would have greatly embarrassed the British government, who as Irish people suspected — and subsequent evidence has tended to prove — were not negotiating in good faith, but *wanted* a military victory).

The resignation of Carrington, unjustly made a scapegoat for earlier mistakes, shocked Irish politicians rather than the public. They viewed his departure, rightly, as a grave loss to British politics and to the usefulness of the British contribution to world counsels.

It would seem that, like the Argentines, Haughey did not realise just how formidable a person he was dealing with in Mrs Thatcher. Had he done so, and had he also envisaged the possible effects on Ireland's international standing, it is unlikely that he would have embarked on the course he now set. It is also most improbable he would have acted as he did had not relations with Mrs Thatcher broken down during the H-Blocks crisis. But he had to face pressure within the Fianna Fáil Party, especially after the sinking of the *Belgrano* — which caused his Defence Minister, Paddy Power, to declare that the British were now the aggressors.

Reversing his earlier policy, Haughey now caused

Ireland to derogate from the EEC sanctions, and instructed Dorr to make a *démarche* at the United Nations with a view to obtaining a cease-fire. He thus made two serious mistakes. His statement on the UN *démarche* appeared to call for a cease-fire in place, which would have left the Argentines in occupation of the islands; he was obliged to explain that Ireland still nevertheless supported the original UN resolution calling for Argentine withdrawal. As for the sanctions move, this was a breach of Community solidarity, something no small nation should dare without good reason.

Of course Haughey had a perfect right, as leader of an independent country and in all probability in consonance with the views of a majority of those under his jurisdiction, to act as he pleased and as he judged right. (I am often reminded, when considering Anglo-Irish relations, of the remark of an obscure but stalwart American, one Mr A. Hitler, about the time the United States entered the Second World War: "Let the other fellow change his name.") But regardless of the rights and wrongs of the issue, he would have been better advised to do and say as little as possible; and as to his declared reasons, they carried little weight.

First, he claimed that when Ireland supported sanctions these sanctions were designed to back up diplomatic moves and not military action. But in fact at the time Mrs Thatcher's warlike preparations were already in train, and anyone who supposed that she did not mean to carry matters as far as needs might dictate, gravely misjudged her.

Secondly, he sought to justify his actions by alleging that to support Britain by maintaining the sanctions would amount to a breach of Irish neutrality. But aside from the inherent weakness of the argument, his own attitude on neutrality was, to put it kindly, both puzzling and inconsistent. At various times, in and out of office, he seemed to rank neutrality high as a principle and also a practical matter, recalling Irish moves in the past to try to obtain a nuclear-free zone in Europe and citing the advance of the anti-nuclear movement in West Germany and elsewhere. Yet it was he who had shown, at the time of his Northern Ireland talks with Mrs Thatcher, that he understood the necessity of taking into account British defence interests in an Irish settlement; and it was he who, in a speech in Washington in March 1982, seemed to suggest that Ireland should become more closely tied to the Western alliance, of which the Republic was already part to all intents and purposes, at least in the political sense. (When questioned by journalists, Haughey denied that this was a correct interpretation of his speech, but it may be observed in passing that both he and FitzGerald, in different ways, had abused the "American dimension". Haughey embarrassed the Americans by calling publicly for pressure on the British; earlier, FitzGerald had embarrassed them equally by asking them, also publicly, for intervention on the H-Blocks issue; on that occasion, however, both President Reagan and his then Secretary of State, Alexander Haig, made private representations to the British. The interventions by both Haughey and FitzGerald made some of those at home who genuinely believed in neutrality, wonder whether the dangers of the "American dimension" might not exceed its advantages; for what if the Americans made some kind of military demands on the Republic in return for their good offices with the British?).

The greatest miscalculation, however, concerned British political and public opinion. British people by and large have very little interest in Ireland, but they do understand that acts of terrorism are repudiated by the great majority of Irish people, including the vast majority of the half-million or so natives of the Republic living in Britain. This was different: here was the elected Irish Government seemingly stabbing them in the back. Anti-Irish feeling grew at all levels. Trade and tourism suffered — not for the first time. Support swelled in the Conservative Party for a move to deprive Irish-born people of their right to vote in Britain.

The Falklands affair was detrimental to political developments within Britain, and on their implications for

Ireland. It made Mrs Thatcher and the Conservative Party — now overtly Unionist — enormously popular. Her government's policies had not only brought about a fearsome increase in unemployment, to a real figure of about three and a half million, but they had ruinous effects on manufacturing industry. Large parts of the country had become, like Northern Ireland, "de-industrialised". Although inflation fell in 1982 to 6 per cent, it was clear that sterling was over-valued (largely attributable to North Sea oil) and that devaluation could be avoided only by keeping interest rates high. The long-term economic outlook, when the oil resources are depleted, was deplorable. Yet the government was massively popular — and it enjoyed much of this popularity with the working-class people, whose jingoism should not be underrated.

In 1981 it had appeared that the new Social Democratic Party, in alliance with the Liberals, would "break the mould" of British politics, and destroy the two-party system. The SDP and Liberals had had several spectacular by-election successes. Now, under the impact of the "Falklands factor", the alliance faltered.

Curiously enough, the SDP, full of the ex-Labour "Gladstonians" and "Asquithians" once derided by Merlyn Rees, had so far failed — and have not yet succeeded — in devising any coherent Irish policy, or even of demonstrating that they understood very much about the issues. The same holds true of the Liberals. The advocates of a united Ireland have done much better, in the recent period, with Labour. The latter party had long been torn between a number of totally irreconcilable policies, ranging from the near-Unionism of Roy Mason to the straightforward "troops out" line of Tony Benn. At their annual conferences of 1981 and 1982 a compromise was reached — and backed by all factions of the party — on a policy in favour of a united Ireland, somewhat fudging the issue of "consent".

Domestically, too, Labour had been in deep trouble, failing, under the feeble leadership of Michael Foot, to resist attempts by the extreme left to impose their will on the party. The Bennites reached their highest point of influence at a special conference at Wembley in January 1981; this decided that the party leader and deputy leader should henceforth be elected not by the parliamentary party but by an "electoral college" in which the trade unions would have 40 per cent of the votes, with 30 per cent each for the MPs and the constituencies.

This ridiculous arrangement was the proximate cause of the departure from the party of the leading right-wingers who then proceeded to form the SDP. It did not, however, have the effect desired by the Bennites, for at the annual conference in the autumn Benn narrowly failed in the election for deputy leader, being defeated by Denis Healey. From this point onwards the right wing, the centre and the moderate left rallied against the Bennites, capturing from them positions of influence within the party. By the time of the next annual conference they presented a much more plausible appearance of unity and good sense, and they did tolerably well in by-elections towards the end of the year. Labour, however, remained committed to absurd policies, notably withdrawal from the EEC.

The Falklands affair naturally delighted the Unionists and their guru, Enoch Powell. The latter warmly congratulated Mrs Thatcher — to her intense pleasure — on her resolution. He takes the view that the people he now represents in South Down are exactly the same people as those of his native Birmingham. If Mrs Thatcher was willing to do so much for a handful of people at the ends of the earth, what would she not do for a million Unionists on her own doorstep?

While Powell and his faction favoured integration, Prior pressed ahead with his plans for devolution. His problem was the SDLP, whom he tried to persuade to contest the assembly election in October, and to take their seats in the assembly once elected. But the SDLP were irreparably divided between abstentionists and those who wished to sit in the assembly, reserving their position on further co-operation.

Finally they reached a compromise: it was decided that

the SDLP would contest the election but refuse to take their seats. Not only was this a blow to those who argued that nationalist parties had always suffered in the past when they adopted a policy of abstention; it also failed to unite the party, for some of the leading figures, who would have preferred a total boycott, refused to take any part in the election.

For all this the SDLP bitterly blamed Prior, whom they accused of completely abandoning the "Irish dimension" and of planning to create something at Stormont which, in the unlikely event that it worked at all, would mean the restoration of Protestant domination. The election results showed that they had even better cause for bitterness. The Official Unionists emerged as always the largest party in the assembly, closely followed by Paisley's DUP, with the SDLP third and Alliance (whose successful candidates included several Catholics) fourth. But the most shattering result was that for Provisional Sinn Féin, who obtained 10 per cent of the total vote. This meant that probably 30 per cent of all the Catholics who turned out voted for the Provos. The Unionists took this as meaning that a high proportion of Catholics were willing to vote for terrorism; the really serious effect, however, was on the SDLP, who now for the first time found themselves facing a real Provo electoral challenge. They themselves were partly to blame, both for their misguided policy of abstention (shared by the Provos) and for the hostages they had given to fortune by failing to contest the two by-elections in Fermanagh and South Tyrone in 1981. Their decision to contest the election but not take their seats resembled the Judgment of Solomon — supposing that Solomon had actually had the baby sliced in half. But they had good grounds for their anger with Prior, who by holding the election created not one but two monsters: Provo electoral credibility, and the Unionist assembly itself.

Once in the assembly, the Unionists behaved like children playing a game of "parliaments". The proceedings began with a Byzantine intrigue over the election of the presiding officer, which ended with the defeat of the

Official Unionist candidate by an unlikely combination of the DUP and Alliance; subsequent proceedings were equally absurd. But along with the absurd went the sinister, as the Unionists showed (with some astuteness) an embarrassing determination to gain for their assembly some power, or the semblance of power.

The whole affair did nothing for Prior's political reputation, and subsequent events did even less to convince the Catholics of British good faith. A Unionist assemblyman brought a successful court petition to unseat Séamus Mallon on the ground that he was a member, appointed by Haughey, of the Irish Senate (an unwise section of the legislation setting up the assembly had excluded members of "foreign" legislatures). When the Labour leader of the Greater London Council, Ken Livingstone, invited two Provo assemblymen to London, the Home Secretary banned them from entering Britain. This was another propaganda victory for the Provos, who could plausibly claim that when they tried to engage in normal political activity, they were prevented.

The Catholics were further alienated by strange activities on the part of the RUC. Over the years, but particularly under its present Chief Constable, Sir John Harmon, this force had made spectacular advances in both efficiency and fairness. It had restored normal policing in at least some areas; it had brought successful prosecutions against great numbers of Loyalist terrorists. With the help of informers it had "penetrated" the Provisional IRA and the INLA, as well as Loyalist organisations, with great success. But its successes were dearly bought, and very controversial. In at least one case one of the worst murderers and gangleaders was granted immunity from prosecution for turning informer or "supergrass".

Even more controversial was the "shoot to kill" policy, which seemed to show that the authorities, in the absence of real political movement, were ready for open war. On several occasions the police chased and shot up cars containing unarmed members of the Provisional IRA or INLA, killing the passengers. It was alleged that these actions were carried out by an "SAS-type" unit set up within the RUC for the express purpose of killing Provos and INLA men. They were unanimously deplored by nationalist leaders of every shade, and by Catholic clergy; Unionists, however, saw little wrong with them. Clearly the two communities were very far apart in their thinking, just as they were segregated in their schools and places of residence.

Meanwhile the Republic faced its third general election in less than eighteen months. When the Dáil reassembled in October Haughey's bad luck remained as consistent as ever. One of his deputies died, one suffered a serious heart attack, so reducing his parliamentary representation by two. Haughey lost a confidence motion and had to seek a dissolution. He then had to contest an election as leader of an openly divided party, having just fought off, with difficulty, an attempt within his parliamentary party to pass a motion of no confidence in him. In addition, he faced not only the enormously popular FitzGerald but a Labour Party which, in consequence of an extraordinary and paradoxical upheaval, had suddenly found unwonted self-confidence and fighting strength.

It started with a massive blunder by O'Leary, who resented the way in which he had been obliged to fight the last election without an arrangement for coalition, and who wanted to fight the next with a greater degree of freedom. He therefore proposed, at the party's annual conference in Galway, that if the opportunity again arose for Labour to coalesce with Fine Gael, the decision should be made by a joint meeting of the parliamentary party and the administrative council, at which he assumed he would have a safe majority for coalition. His proposal was opposed not only by the committed anti-coalitionist left, but by the former leader, Cluskey, and the trade unions. It was defeated and the conference instead resolved that the question should be decided, as before, by a special delegate conference.

O'Leary brooded for a few days, then abruptly resigned his position without consulting the rest of the leadership;

he also resigned from the party, joined Fine Gael and successfully contested the general election the following month as a Fine Gael candidate. One might have expected his departure to fling an already shaky Labour Party into total disarray, but it had exactly the opposite effect. Cluskey and two other obvious contenders stood down from the ensuing leadership contest, and the parliamentary party elected as their new leader Dick Spring, a barrister aged thirty-two, who had been a member of the Dáil only since June 1981, had held junior office in the short-lived coalition, but was still recovering from terrible injuries received in a car crash. He had no sooner become party leader than the Government fell and he had to abandon medical treatment in order to fight the general election. He made an immediate, and highly favourable, impact on the party and the voters; although himself strongly and openly in favour of coalition, he was liked by almost all sections of the party, while the public found him attractive, modest and level-headed.

The main contest, however, lay between Haughey and FitzGerald once again. It was Fianna Fáil who now espoused a stringent fiscal policy and pay restraint in the public sector: they had cut back somewhat on public pay rises, and had published a rather flabby economic document entitled "The Way Forward", under which slogan they fought the election. During the campaign the Government published the public expenditure estimates for 1983, making a virtue of restraint. Labour adopted a policy of massive state expenditure to create employment. Fine Gael stayed almost completely silent on policy questions: they relied on FitzGerald's popularity, on clever constituency organisation, on marketing techniques — and on the opinion polls, which showed that they enjoyed greater credibility on all the major issues, even stable government.

Beaten on the issues, and discredited by their internal divisions, Fianna Fáil tried two diversions. The first concerned the proposal to hold a constitutional referendum to insert in the constitution a provision to forbid abortion. The intention behind the proposal was highly controversial and sectarian. Both Haughey and FitzGerald had agreed to it during a well-organised and well-funded campaign by groups who wanted to make the constitution conform with Roman Catholic teaching; even the exceptions they were prepared to allow (in cases of cervical cancer and ectopic pregnancy) were those allowed by the Church. FitzGerald's support for the amendment sorted ill with his declared purpose of altering the constitution, and society in the Republic, to make them more liberal and less sectarian; Fianna Fáil saw the issue, more simply, as one which might win them some votes.

Their attempt to exploit the issue electorally failed — at any rate from their own viewpoint. A Fine Gael candidate who they had claimed was in favour of abortion denied it, and increased her vote. Two deputies did indeed lose their seats at least partly on this issue, but without any gain for Fianna Fáil. Michael D. Higgins, chairman of the Labour Party and leader of the left wing, lost his seat in West Galway to Fine Gael; Labour took Jim Kemmy's seat in East Limerick. Kemmy (who was undoubtedly the subject of a smear campaign) contested this election not as an independent but as leader of the new and tiny Democratic Socialist Party; he put up six other candidates, all of whom lost their deposits.

Fianna Fáil's other diversionary measure was the attempted playing of the "green card", and in this they were helped by a strange blunder by FitzGerald in the middle of the campaign, when he proposed the establishment of an all-Ireland court to try terrorist offences, and of a cross-border police force. (Spring, showing an early independence, dissented from the latter proposal; he also called for the re-establishment of consensus in the Dáil on the Northern question). Fianna Fáil opposed both — without much credibility on the all-Ireland court, a proposal which they had supported in the past; with more plausibility but much exaggeration on the seemingly ill-thought-out and possibly unworkable cross-border police idea. They raised the bogeys of RUC border crossings, and even of the re-establishment of the Royal Irish Constabulary, disbanded sixty years earlier. It seems unlikely that many voters were frightened by these spectres, since Fianna Fáil, so far from gaining by the "green card", actually lost two seats, one to Fine Gael and one to Labour, in border constituencies.

Another shadowy and incongruous figure flitted through the campaign: that of the Duke of Norfolk. It emerged that this worthy, some months previously, had given FitzGerald lunch in the House of Lords, and had afterwards made a speech praising the Fine Gael leader's enthusiasm for Prior's Northern Ireland plans. Fianna Fáil claimed that this proved, one, that FitzGerald had consorted with an important cog in the wheel of British intelligence, two, that FitzGerald supported the setting up of the assembly and thus a Northern "internal solution". They were wrong, for the allegation about the Duke's connection with British intelligence appears to have arisen from a misunderstanding, and FitzGerald did not support Prior's proposals; in fact, before leaving office the previous March he had privately warned the British Government against proceeding with them. What it did prove was that the Duke of Norfolk had very little grasp of the Irish question, or FitzGerald's stand (the lunch had been cunningly arranged by a friend of Prior with the object of dissuading the Duke from bolting to the anti-assembly right wing, who were planning a revolt) and that FitzGerald had shown considerable political naivety in allowing himself to be used in this manner.

The rumpus over the Duke added a little colour to an otherwise dull election campaign, but the affair also had a more serious side. Haughey had a point when he told the British not to interfere in Irish elections. Their preference for FitzGerald was the more obvious the more they officially denied it; it could have damaged him, though it does not appear to have done so; and while the election campaign was in progress quite important people at Westminster were saying openly that they hoped he would win the election, and then force the SDLP to take their seats in the assembly. FitzGerald does not have the power to do that, even if he had the will: this is yet another good example of British misunderstanding of Irish affairs.

The election gave Fianna Fáil 75 seats, Fine Gael 70 and Labour 16. Fine Gael and Labour together thus had a majority of 11 over Fianna Fáil, and a Dáil overall majority of 6. Intense secret negotiations took place between FitzGerald and Spring before the new Dáil met on 14 December; the newspapers reported difficulties and disagreements, but there was never any doubt of the result. Agreement was reached on a coalition deal, approved by the Fine Gael parliamentary party with only one dissentient voice, and endorsed by Labour's special delegate conference by a large majority. FitzGerald on his election as Taoiseach announced a curiously composed cabinet which contained a good many apparent square pegs in round holes. The most striking appointment was that of Alan Dukes as Minister for Finance, which prompted Haughey to ask whether the absence of Bruton from that ministry (he became Minister for Industry and Energy instead) signalled an unwarranted "flexibility" to please the Labour Party instead of the rigidity the country needed. He need not have worried; Dukes in office soon showed himself a model of inflexibility, rejoicing in the nickname "the Iron Chancellor", piling on more taxes, infuriating his Labour colleagues, and (with grave social implications) at once alienating the workers and demoralising the middle classes.

While Haughey worried about flexibility, the left fretted over the perennial problem of the danger to Labour's identity in coalition. Although since the election ominous signs of social unrest have appeared, it may be doubted whether the great mass of the people cared much, for the time being, about any such questions. They wanted unemployment curbed, inflation brought down, their living standards protected; but most of all they wanted stability. After three elections in a year and a bit, they wanted the coalition to stay in office for a long time, regardless of who the members of the Government were or what policies they pursued. In this mood they were little disposed to concern themselves with events in Northern

Ireland — except to register shock and dismay at news of the Ballykelly massacre; but Ballykelly apart, two significant events took place towards the end of the year.

In December the Supreme Court in Dublin ordered the extradition to Northern Ireland of a man accused of a terrorist murder. Legal experts said that similar rulings could be expected in future. They believed that the court had reinterpreted the constitution and law to rely on the nature of the alleged crime instead of on the alleged motive. Have we thus seen the end of the great extradition controversy? If so, we may be sure that the Unionists will come up with fresh grievances.

A little earlier the Long Kesh protest finally and formally ended when the Provo and INLA prisoners agreed to do prison work. In reality the protest had ended more than a year earlier, not long after the death of the last hunger striker, Michael Devine, on 21 August 1981. Considerable concessions had been made to the prisoners, for example in the matter of clothing, though Mrs Thatcher denied, and apparently did not believe, that there had been any. However, the legacy of the hunger strike remained: the ghosts of the ten dead men had come back to haunt the North in the shape of the 10 per cent of votes gained by the Provos in the assembly election.

Nagasaki II

The man who talked about going to Belfast instead of Nagasaki didn't mean it. Let us suppose, if only for the sake of charity, that the many English people who have spoken, and written, about gas chambers or "towing the island out to sea and sinking it" have done so likewise in moments of exasperation, and repented when calm.

The British pride themselves on their tolerance, and they have a very good claim to this virtue. Following great atrocities, or some action or inaction by Irish governments, the Irish in England are made to feel a terrible English frost; more rarely, they become the victims of hotly expressed English outrage. In London between 1970 and 1973 I received countless abusive telephone calls: I particularly liked the ones that began with "Let's discuss this reasonably, old man" and ended with "Why don't you all go back to your bogs?" Worse has happened to others who have been assaulted or had their windows broken, and in some right-wing quarters a more generalised anti-Irish feeling prevails, sometimes as part of a wider xenophobia, but these are the exceptions. Hundreds of thousands of Irish people enjoy in England the living their own country has denied them; their children are assimilated; they live at peace and on friendly terms with their neighbours. Few peoples would have shown themselves so tolerant as the English. And they show this tolerance in spite of the rantings of the right-wing lunatic fringe.

But if the differences between the two islands are ever

to be composed, the British will have to remain patient a little longer — and they will have to exert themselves a good deal more. They might remember a saying of Clemenceau when somebody asked him what he thought history would say about the Treaty of Versailles: "History," he replied, "will not say that Belgium invaded Germany." Our troubles have very deep roots in history.

What, then, of the Irish? A British diplomat whose opinion I respect detected what he considered deep and widespread anti-British feeling in Ireland at the time of the Falklands crisis. I do not believe that he was right; I think it possible for passionate opposition to British *policy* to coexist with a liking for British *people*. As Anthony Cronin, cultural adviser to Charles Haughey as Taoiseach, once eloquently pointed out, it is very hard for Irish people, especially educated Irish people, to hate the English. Like them, we are brought up — or were until television and technology ushered in a new age of illiteracy among the educated — on the great English playwrights, poets and novelists (and if Shakespeare and Shelley have enriched *us*, Joyce and Yeats have enriched *them*). As to British policy in Ireland, few fair-minded people could deny that since 1969 it has contained more than its due share of mistakes, fumbling, indifference and downright deceit. Yet I imagine that, like myself, most Irish people would attribute the great bulk of its faults to fate and time and chance and human frailty, rather than to outright ill-will.

Lord Cornwallis, viceroy and commander-in-chief in Ireland, suppressed the 1798 rising with great bloodshed, but he was essentially a humane and witty man. When he was defeated in America he ordered the band to play "The World Turned Upside Down". Of the Union of 1801 he wrote: "I wish England could make a union with the Irish nation instead of making it with a party in Ireland." A union on the model of that of 1801 is off the agenda now, but the task still remains for Britain to come to an arrangement with Ireland and not with "a party in Ireland".

In this book I have tried to explain how certain events

came to pass, and to dispel certain myths — for example, the myth that the Provos brought down the old Stormont, and the myth that the UWC strike brought down the power-sharing executive. This task has been made the easier by my often-close acquaintance with the chief participants, most of them neither towering statesmen nor evil plotters, but fallible men and women. I have also attempted the harder task of linking these events with the complicated strands of Irish nationalism. It falls to me, in conclusion, to try to suggest what may be the future course of events, and to outline how the two countries, and the different elements within them, might seek to reach forward for a solution which could accommodate all: Britain, the Republic, Northern Protestants, Northern Catholics. I am a reporter, not a prophet, and if I have learnt anything in thirty years in journalism, it is that few questions exist on which everybody agrees — and on the rare occasions when this happens, everybody is very likely to be wrong. I walk here on unsteady ground.

First let me say that, amid all the horrors, there has never been a time altogether without hope, for hope always arises and is one of the finer manifestations of the human spirit. The more spectacular "peace movements" in Northern Ireland have run into the sands, the plea for an end to violence by Pope John Paul II at Drogheda in 1979 went unheeded, but some have never ceased to hold the candle. So far from condemning the Irish nation for her husband's murder, Lady Ewart-Biggs — sometimes naive and volatile, but always heroic — has raised her voice tirelessly in support of peace and understanding between the two countries. A recent anniversary recalled a similar magnanimity on the part of Lady Frederick Cavendish after the murder of her husband in Dublin in 1882. But far more impressive are the voices of humbler victims of violence, so many of whom have cried out for forgiveness, not revenge. Such people justify and celebrate humanity.

Good example however, is not enough. Too many in power or influence in Britain, the Republic and Northern Ireland, finding the problem over-taxing, ignore it or fall back on simplistic "solutions" such as extradition or internal reform in the North. Such attitudes are not merely unhelpful, but positively harmful. We must go to the roots, some of them centuries deep.

We Irish must ask ourselves, what makes a nation, and how far we have succeeded in creating and maintaining our nationhood?

There is a dusty answer to that question. Measured against the unfulfilled ideals of the 1790s, we have not succeeded at all well in creating a liberal and pluralist society in our Republic; we have failed to do what de Valera advocated (though he had very curious notions on this subject) and make our society so attractive that Northern Protestants would wish to join it; and without the Northern Protestants we are incomplete. Our main political parties manifest elements of the various strands of Irish nationalism: constitutional, republican/separatist, agrarian, Catholic. If Fine Gael seem to descend somewhat more from the constitutional element, and Fianna Fáil from the agrarian agitators, these are details: more significantly, Labour has failed to build on the synthesis of socialism and nationalism propounded by James Connolly; and Irish nationalism, so closely in touch with the great progressive movements of thought from the late eighteenth to the early twentieth century, seems after independence to have lost touch, drawn in upon itself, drunk at the wrong fountains.

It is not enough to blame partition. It is not partition alone that has divided and confused our opinion-formers, and caused us to abandon our once sturdy (if exaggerated and puritanical) self-respect. We need to regain that self-respect, something we can do only by the practice of some old-fashioned virtues. Politically, above all we need consensus. The earlier consensus, though often feeble and ignorant, was better than nothing. It was mortally wounded by the 1973-77 coalition government, and buried after Haughey's accession to power in 1979. The attempt to create a new consensus has lately begun, but in the face of dreadful difficulties and setbacks.

The British, too, need a consensus. It existed, at least between the main parties, in the early seventies. As in Ireland, it needs to be restored, but on a sounder basis. Ideally it should form part of an honest and searching re-appraisal of Britain's defence and foreign policy, and of Britain's general role in Europe and the world. Obviously the present great differences between and within the British political parties constitute a huge obstacle in the way of this. The British need to become more honest with themselves, and more united among themselves, before they can be more honest with the Irish and others.

The British and Irish alike need to re-examine the reality of the strategic question. There is certainly not much reality in Irish professions of neutrality. Talk of bilateral defence pacts or of Irish entry into NATO or some similar multilateral defence arrangement has little meaning when British defence experts say that in the event of conflict in Europe, or even of a seriously threatening increase in tension, NATO would simply require Ireland, by main force, to fulfil any role considered desirable — in com-munications, for example, or in providing bases. But it is surely rash to assume that the present British defence policy will remain fixed for a generation. Mrs Thatcher will not be Prime Minister for ever; in the meantime, how long will public opinion tolerate the proposal to site cruise missiles in Britain, under American control and with no British say as to if and when they are to be used?

In Ireland, it is time for us to come to grips with the fraudulence of our position. It will no longer serve for us to deny that we are part of the Western alliance in all its material respects save membership of NATO, or that when our ministers discuss "security" as part of the process of EEC political co-operation, that question is somehow sep-arable from that of "defence". According to official estimates, 90 per cent of our foreign policy is now conduc-ted through the EEC. Since that proportion is unlikely to be substantially diminished, it would be better for us to abandon the pretence that we remain outside alliances, and to use our position in the Community to argue, along with other small Western European countries, for saner foreign, defence and security policies.

Why does Britain stay in Northern Ireland: for fear of civil war and chaos in the event of withdrawal, because of the commitment to a million Unionists, for age-old strategic reasons, or a combination of all three? Haughey is not alone among Irish politicians in believing the defence question to be by far the most cogent, and in doubting British honesty on the guarantee. His view is borne out at least in part by senior British politicians who say privately that they consider independence for Northern Ireland the easiest option for themselves, but that for other reasons independence is "not on". Where Haughey has been unquestionably right is in grasping the point that British withdrawal cannot come without Irish guarantees on defence; and when the time comes we may (the above comments notwithstanding) have to go a very long way to satisfy the British in the matter of guarantees.

There has always been confusion about the standing of the Unionists. Do they have the rights of a community (as they claimed when they opted out of the Anglo-Irish Treaty settlement) or the rights of a majority (which they claimed when they abused their power within Northern Ireland)? Do they (as the "two nations" theorists argue) constitute a nation, with the right of self-determination? That right, by the way, has always been limited by the British, who offer them only two options, remaining in the United Kingdom or joining the Republic. Are they Irish, or British, or a bit of both?

All these questions have to be taken into account in any worthwhile settlement. The last is possibly the easiest to come to terms with, since proposals have been made over many years that the people of Northern Ireland should be offered dual nationality. These proposals should be implemented. On both sides we need redefinitions of sovereignty and jurisdiction (and I assume that Garret FitzGerald and his colleagues will redefine them in terms of a proposed new Irish constitution). "Pure" republicanism and separatism are as out of date as British imperialism

— though the best elements of republicanism could still make a bridge between North and South and between Catholics and Protestants.

To seek a British declaration of intent to withdraw from Northern Ireland, with a time-scale, may perhaps be to ask too much. What the British can, however, do — as they did to a considerable extent in the Sunningdale Agreement — is to make Jack Lynch's "declaration of interest in Irish unity", giving assurance that they will do nothing to stand in the way of unity, and acting accordingly.

We need both Anglo-Irish institutions and, more to the point, cross-border institutions. The latter should include some sort of rudimentary inter-parliamentary body. The British and Irish Governments should press ahead with the formation of such institutions regardless of Unionist opposition, employing if necessary the "empty seat" tactic. One form of co-operation that might appeal to the Unionists will be discussed below, but first the question must be answered: what has Dublin to offer in return?

What Dublin can offer, in short, is to replace the British guarantee with an Irish guarantee: to acknowledge a Northern right to self-determination, retaining the aspiration to a united Ireland but accepting that it cannot come about without a vote in its favour by a majority in the North. Could a freely made offer from Dublin have the effect of making a beginning to the end of the "siege mentality", counterbalancing the fears of British "betrayal" which are bound to arise from a perceived British push in the direction of Dublin, and replacing Britain by an Irish consensus as the arbiter of Irish destinies?

It hardly needs saying that Catholic rights within the North must be protected, at the very minimum by a bill of rights. A greater task is to bring the Protestants out from behind their earthworks. For generations they have suffered terribly from a deplorable lack of leadership. A *cri de coeur* from one of them, John Robb (a surgeon, campaigner for a new Irish settlement based on understanding and reconciliation, later appointed a senator by Haughey) appeared in an article in the Belfast *Sunday*

> As far as the Northern Protestant is concerned I believe that we have remained dependent on a fickle England for too long and that is one reason why we feel so vulnerable. As far as Catholic Ireland is concerned it seems at times unable or unwilling to acknowledge how the tables have turned — the British empire has gone, the Union is breaking, you have gained new self-respect with independence, the momentum of history is with you and yet you still want to perceive the Protestant Ulsterman as an imperial oppressor when in fact he belongs to one of the most cornered ethnic groups in Europe ...
>
> It seems increasingly clear that the people of Great Britain will sooner or later withdraw Westminster control from Northern Ireland. For ten years now I have contended that rather than wait to be spurned by Great Britain or outvoted into an extension of a twenty-six county Republic a Protestant leader worthy of his people would serve them far better if he were to make it plain (and the sooner the better) that we are as sick to death with the uncertainty of London as we have been with the ambivalence of Dublin and that we will unite Ireland on terms first agreed with our fellow Northern Irish Catholics, terms which I believe no Dublin government could refuse and yet retain its self-respect before the community of nations.

Here is a most attractive idea, put forward by a man who vindicates the archaic republican ideal; but the "Protestant leader worthy of his people" has not yet emerged. Haughey once thought he might have found him in Paisley: that seems unlikely now. Robb exaggerates both British indifference (in the Thatcher era) and Irish Catholic self-respect, but his underlying thesis is sound.

A precondition for the agreement between Catholics and Protestants in the North, for which Robb pleads, is the setting up of an institution to bring them together in debate and in the disposition of power. This is not at all an argument for an "internal settlement", which on its own would certainly be foredoomed. In the first place the Catholics — through the SDLP and possibly through parties yet unborn — would bring to an assembly and to a share in power the "Irish dimension" in their own persons and in an acknowledged aspiration to Irish unity. Secondly, the "Irish dimension" would have concrete form in the cross-border parliamentary body proposed above. Thirdly, the Irish and British Governments would have a crucial say in the course of events.

Some such formula may emerge from the deliberations of the "forum for a new Ireland", comprising representatives of the three main parties in the Republic and the SDLP. The agreement in early 1983 to set up this body represented in itself a small triumph for good sense and a step towards the creation of the new nationalist consensus. It was not reached without difficulty, and it began with disagreement on its composition and aims: FitzGerald wanted to invite the Unionists to participate, though they were certain to refuse to attend: Haughey's reluctance to spell out a position has been mentioned earlier. Very obviously the move owed almost everything to the insistence of Hume.

Critics at once complained that its true purpose derived from Northern party politics: that it was devised as a "lifeline" for the SDLP, threatened with yet another Provo challenge in the approaching Westminster election. That would be no bad thing in itself; the real objections to the forum lie elsewhere.

In the first place, the forum runs the risk of being bedevilled by *Southern* party politics. If the Southern parties use it to score points off one another, they could bring it to a rapid and calamitous end. But that risk has to be run.

The temptation to play politics with the forum, and with the Northern question more generally, must be particularly strong in the case of Fianna Fáil. At the beginning of 1983 Haughey survived yet another attempted *Putsch* in the parliamentary party. This followed the disclosure of yet more scandals which had occurred in the course of his last, brief, unfortunate administration, this time centring on the tapping of journalists' telephones and the "bugging" of a conversation between two former ministers, MacSharry and O'Donoghue. Among the consequences it brought were the premature retirements of the commissioner and deputy commissioner of the Garda Siochana. Haughey, however, remained leader of the party, narrowly winning a vote which had appeared certain to go in the other direction. His survival was attributable less to confidence in him within the parliamentary party than to the absence of a credible, much less an agreed, alternative leader. In the wake of this latest crisis Fianna Fáil employed, as one of their methods to restore a semblance of internal unity, a fierce opposition to FitzGerald's government on almost every issue. To put the case at its mildest, they will find it hard to restrain themselves from carrying that opposition into the field of Northern policy.

A much more serious threat to the credibility of the forum is posed by the preposterous decision to insert in the constitution a clause forbidding abortion — something already stringently forbidden by law, and unlikely in the highest degree to be made legal either by legislation or by a ruling of the Supreme Court.

This issue has been seized upon by Fianna Fáil in a seeming attempt to supplant Fine Gael as the "clericalist" party. FitzGerald, having in the first instance unwisely accepted an amendment wording which stated the equal rights of the foetus and the mother, had second thoughts and introduced in the Dáil a watered-down version. The campaign by the "pro-life" organisations, now openly supported by the Catholic bishops, intensified. On the wilder shores of the campaign, extraordinary things happened. The more fervent spirits disclosed their intention not merely of reinforcing the ban on abortion as normally understood, but their desire to ban the use of intra-uterine contraceptives and the "morning after pill" and to seek

242

court injunctions to prevent women from travelling to England for abortions. In the Dáil, a combined front by Fianna Fáil, and a number of defections from the Fine Gael right wing, ensured the passage of the original wording.

At first sight, these developments looked altogether disastrous. It seemed that Irish parliamentary representatives had accepted tamely the dictates of the bishops and of the powerful pressure groups. FitzGerald had been shown weak and indecisive. What had become of his "constitutional crusade" when the Republic was about to become more, not less sectarian? Did not these proceedings make a mockery of the forum? Liberals, especially the Northern Protestant liberals to whom he had so often appealed, despaired.

I take a somewhat more optimistic view. In spite of the divisiveness of the issue and the intensity of the campaign, the public remained calm. In the Dáil, thirteen deputies had the courage to vote against any constitutional amendment on abortion. Many others publicly deplored the bullying tactics of the "pro-life" campaigners, and the way in which they smeared their opponents as "abortionists". In the opposition to the amendment, the hopeful could discern a healthy alliance between suburban liberals and those concerned with working-class issues (a new Workers' Party deputy made an eloquent speech on contraception and working-class women). The controversy increased the internal strains in both Fianna Fáil and Fine Gael; there is as yet no clear sign of the long-overdue realignment in Irish party politics, but it may have been forwarded just a little. I do not believe that the affair has made Irish society more sectarian or clerically dominated; rather that it has been one more symptom of the terribly prolonged growing-pains of our slow evolution.

For the time being, this affair may have strengthened the hand of those who claim that the Republic should ignore the North, and tolerate direct rule *faute de mieux*. But apart from the argument against direct rule (or integration with Britain) from history, discussed above, there is one strong present and practical argument against direct rule, namely that under it there is clearly no hope of a satisfactory answer to the security problem.

In my opinion a solution to the security question necessitates the withdrawal — at first to barracks, later to Britain — of the British Army, and the devolution of security powers to a local administration. But such devolution would have to be subject to the following conditions: first, hugely increased recruitment and promotion of Catholics in the RUC; secondly, the disbandment of the Ulster Defence Regiment and the recruitment of a militia which would contain appropriate numbers of Catholic officers and other ranks; thirdly, control of those forces to be vested in a quasi-independent authority answerable to a power-sharing administration; fourthly, an all-Ireland institution to oversee the whole process. (It was envisaged in 1973 that the stillborn Council of Ireland should have such an oversight). Possibly, FitzGerald's ideas of an all-Ireland court and, more doubtfully, a cross-border police force, might harmonise with these proposals.

The advantage to the Unionists would lie in a more fundamental tackling of the security problem than anything hitherto undertaken, as well as, for the first time, a means of ensuring Catholic community support for the security forces. The disadvantage, from the Unionist viewpoint, would be insistence both on power-sharing and an all-Ireland element. But would the prospect of peace not be worth that price?

Terrorism, of course, may by now have become an endemic or semi-endemic plague, in Ireland as in many other countries. It certainly cannot be eradicated by security measures alone. Northern Catholics must have the opportunity to play their full part in society, and the young people of the ghettos must be offered the chance of a better life in place of their present state of hopelessness.

I derive little comfort from the emergence and electoral successes of the bright young "officer class" in Provisional Sinn Féin and the Provisional IRA. I do not believe that the apparent politicisation of all the Gerry Adamses and

Danny Morrisons weakens my contention (see Chapter Six), that the Provos are basically apolitical. They cannot really engage in "normal" politics, since it would contravene their insistence that all institutions, North and South, are illegitimate, and their desire to seize power in all of Ireland; this desire seems unattainable in the foreseeable future, since they were dismissed in the Republic's general election of February 1982, and did not contest the November election that year. Moreover, if the Adamses and Morrisons did try to tread a purely constitutional path (on the lines, say, of the SDLP in the North or the Workers' Party in the Republic) there are more than enough of the old-fashioned "godfathers" still about to ensure that the old ways would still, to some extent, be maintained.

There are, I believe, three ways in which terrorism can be, if not eradicated, at least reduced to relative insignificance. The first is the security proposal outlined above. The second is a renewed effort to stop the flow of arms and money from the United States; this requires not only the collaboration of the American authorities but a demonstration to Irish-Americans of all-party Irish support for the proposition that such activities do nothing but harm to Ireland. The third is highly controversial, but needs stating.

Sooner or later attention must be given to the question of an amnesty. The very mention of the word annoys many Unionists and their Tory allies; but to hold out the prospect of amnesty makes sense. It could be partial, and it would obviously have to be linked with a substantial reduction in the level of violence. There are precedents of a sort: "conforming" prisoners in Northern Ireland are granted 50 per cent of their sentences, and a number of prisoners of both stripes have been released on compassionate grounds after serving a proportion of their sentences. If amnesty were a serious prospect, it could bring pressure on the Provo and INLA (and some Loyalist) leadership both from within the prisons and from the families of prisoners. It is worth recalling that one of the factors which ended the Long Kesh hunger strike in 1981 was the persuasive force brought to bear on the hunger strikers by their families, acting in concert with FitzGerald and his officials, and with priests.

A rigid approach to security, the administration of justice, or other areas of contention, will never solve the problems — internal and interlocking — that beset Britain, the Republic and Northern Ireland.

Ian Paisley once said: "We have learnt from history. History is repeating itself." This was a sad and frightening remark, for it is an old truism that those who fail to learn from history are condemned to repeat it.

Unless we learn from history, and shape a different sort of future, Ireland — and possibly Britain too — could sink into a bog of despair and inanition over the North. It is up to the present generation to seize its own destiny, to find new ways of living together. The task is immensely hard, yet it has to be undertaken. Failure to act could threaten what cohesion or self-confidence we already possess; but a courageous and successful push towards a worthy settlement could enable Irish people to go forward together to design a better role for the country in the world. History has mauled Ireland, but if we can prove ourselves able to learn from it, we may once again find ourselves in a position to teach.

INDEX

Intent' 129, 165, 239;
Sunningdale (Assembly) 124
passim, 131, 137, 141, 155,
158, 163, 165-6, 193, 239
see also Conservative Party,
Labour Party
British Army 41-2, 47, 76, 101;
in Northern Ireland 55, 56
passim, 62, 70, 74, 77-8, 81,
86, 117, 122, 135-6, 139;
in Belfast 71, 115-16, 118;
Bloody Sunday 87 *passim:*
internment 82-5: Operation
Motorman 114 *passim;* SAS
116-17
British Embassy, burning of 88
British Intelligence 139, 208,
209
Brookeborough, Lord 16, 48
Bruton, John 202, 203, 210,
231
B Specials 17, 47, 52, 55, 56,
71, 76, 79
Burke, Richard 156
Burntollet Bridge 52, 53

Callaghan, James: Home Secre-
tary 56-8, 62, 77, 111;
Prime Minister 132, 142,
145, 148-9, 176
Carey, Governor Hugh 168
Carrington, Lord 81, 185, 186,
221
Carron, Owen 196
Carson, Sir Edward 41, 42
Carter, President James 168
Castle, Barbara 111
Castlereagh, Lord 28, 30
Castlereagh police station 146,
149
Catholic Emancipation 28, 31,
32, 33, 39
Catholics *see* Roman Catholics

Cavendish, Lady Frederick 235
cease-fires (IRA) 86, 113, 114,
147
censorship 92
Central Bank 107
Central Intelligence Agency
(CIA) 139
Chamberlain, Joseph 37
Channon, Paul 113
Chesterton, G.K. (quoted) 67
Chichester-Clark, James 53-4
56, 57, 73, 79, 80, 97
Chichester-Clark, Robin 54
Childers, Erskine 156
Childers, Mrs Rita 157
Church of Ireland 51
Churchill, Lord Randolph 41
'citizens' defence committees'
63, 64
civil liberties 33, 105-6, 161,
165, 194
Civil Liberties, Irish Council for
161
Civil Rights movement 15, 49-
50, 52-3, 55, 73, 82, 104,
151; demonstrations 52-3,
55, 87 *passim*, 100
Civil War (England) 23-4
Civil War (Irish Free State) 12-
13, 35, 46, 98, 150
Clemenceau, Georges (quoted)
234
Cluskey, Frank 156, 171, 178,
202, 227, 228
coalition governments *1948* 44;
1954-7 93; *1973-7* 106, 125,
155 *passim; 1981* 201 *passim;*
1982 231; and Northern
Ireland 155-6, 166-70, 180
see also Fine Gael party,
Labour party
Colley, George 171, 176, 177-
8, 181, 217

elections: *1977* 170 *passim,*
1981 200, *1982* 211-12;
1982 (2) 228-31; in government 64-5, 98 *passim,* 155,
216 *passim,* 227; and Northern
Ireland 63-5, 104-5, 140,
163 *passim,* 190, 236, 241;
republicanism 97-8, 183,
213, 236; *see also* de Valera,
Eamon; Lemass, Sean;
Lynch, Jack; Haughey,
Charles
Fine Gael party 46, 92, 101,
104, 106; and abortion
referendum 229, 242-3;
economic policies 200, 212,
228; elections: *1977* 170-1,
1981 199-200, *1982* 210-11,
214, 215, *1982 (2)* 227, 230;
in government 44-5, 106,
125, 155-6, 165, 170-1, 199,
201 *passim,* 210, 231; and
Northern Ireland 63, 190,
241-2; and Presidency 156-9
see also Cosgrave, Liam;
FitzGerald, Garret
Fitt, Gerry 48, 52, 115, 126,
128, 153-4, 207, 208
FitzGerald, Alexis 203
Fitzgerald, Lord Edward 27
FitzGerald, Garret 93, 125,
134, 140, 161-2, 171, 178,
180-2, 190-1, 199, 202, 206,
210-11, 213, 227, 230; 'constitutional crusade' 204-5,
238; and EEC 108,
155, 192; and Northern
Ireland 86, 179, 206-7, 22,
241
Fitzsimmons. William 14
Foot, Michael 148, 223
Foreign Affairs, Dept. of 101
foreign investment 107

Foreign Office (Britain) 56,
101
Forum for a New Ireland 241-2
France 24, 28, 33, 34, 44, 49,
104, 111, 191; French
Revolution 27, 30, 35, 97
Free Presbyterian Church 51,
207

Gaelic Athletic Association
(GAA) 34
Garda Siochana 174-5, 217,
242; 'heavy gang' 160, 161
George III 26
George V 12, 150
Germany 41, 42, 43, 46, 81,
173, 191, 222
gerrymandering 16, 49
Gibbons, James 65, 178
Gilbert, Dr John 9, 10
Gilmour, Sir Ian 185
Girdwood Barracks 82
Gladstone, W.E. 36 *passim*
Godley, Wynn (quoted) 148
Gonne, Maud 44
Government of Ireland Act
(1920) 11
Gowrie, Lord 205
Gregory, Tony 212-13, 215
Griffith, Arthur 30
Guardian 9

Haig, Alexander 222
Hailsham, Lord 202
Harland & Wolff shipyard 17
Haughey, Charles 164-6, 176
passim, 180-2, 186 *passim,*
190, 206 211-12, 215 *passim,*
226-7, 239-40, 242; Arms
Trial 65, 166, 178, and
Falklands war 218
passim; and Northern Ireland
179-80, 186 *passim,* 193

178, 204, 217, 242
Official IRA *see* Irish Republican Army: Official
Official Unionists *see* Unionists
O'Hagan, Des 84
O'Kennedy, Michael 165, 170
O'Leary, Michael 156, 171, 202, 212, 213, 227-8
O'Malley, Desmond 101, 177, 181, 217
O'Malley, Ernest 67-8
O'Neill, Hugh, Earl of Tyrone 22
O'Neill, T.P. 168
O'Neill, Terence 58, 74, 79, 80, 97, 144, 151; and civil rights 48-9, 51, 52-3, 99-100
'Operation Motorman' 114-15, 118
Opus Dei 96
Orange Order 29, 35, 39, 41, 54, 78, 80, 208, 209
Osmond, Andrew 14
O'Sullivan, Dr Donal 88
O Tuathail, Seamus 84

Paisley, Rev. Ian 39, 51-2, 72, 80, 87, 89, 126, 142-5, 193, 207, 208-9, 240, 246; and Britain 125, 144-5, 190, 205, 207 *see also* Democratic Unionist Party
paramilitary groups 74-5, 102, 118 *passim*, 158, 196, 209 *see also* Irish Republican Army; Ulster Defence Association
Parnell, Charles Stewart 36, 37, 41, 95
partition 11 *passim*, 42, 44, 45, 65, 66, 140, 236
peace movements 235
Peel, Robert 31

penal laws 25
People's Democracy 50, 52
Pitt, William 28, 30
Plantation of Ulster 23
police *see* Garda Siochana; Royal Ulster Constabulary
'political status' *see* special category prisoners
Pompidou, Georges 167
population 22, 31, 32, 40, 121, 172
Powell, Enoch 111, 112, 133, 144, 148, 176, 224
Power, Paddy 220
power-sharing 137, 138, 144, 145, 244
Presbyterians 23, 25, 27, 39, 51
press, freedom of 106, 161, 162, 166
Prince, The (Machiavelli) 57
prisons 82, 84, 113
prisoners, treatment of 84-5 161; 'special category' 113, 146, 147, 197
Prior, James 185, 205-9, 216, 224-6, 230
protectionism 94, 98-9, 107
Protestant Unionist Party (PUP) 51
Protestants 16, 25, 40, 95-6; in Northern Ireland 11, 13, 23, 40, 74-5, 121-3, 141, 207, 236; in Republic 16, 40, 95-6, 'siege mentality' 18, 194, 239 *see also* Orange Order; Unionists
Provisional IRA *see* Irish Republican Army: Provisional
Pym, Francis 185

Queen's University, Belfast 50

Index compiled by Helen Litton